# Long-Range
# Environmental Outlook

# Long-Range Environmental Outlook

*Proceedings of a Workshop*
November 14–16, 1979

ENVIRONMENTAL STUDIES BOARD
Commission on Natural Resources
National Research Council

NATIONAL ACADEMY OF SCIENCES
Washington, D.C.   1980

NOTICE: The workshop that is the subject of this report was a special project of the Environmental Studies Board and was approved by the Governing Board of the National Research Council.

This report has been reviewed by a group other than the participants of the workshop according to the procedures approved by a Report Review Committee consisting of members of the National Academy of Sciences, the National Academy of Engineering, and the Institute of Medicine.

This workshop was supported by the Office of Research and Development, U.S. Environmental Protection Agency, Contract No. 68-01-2430.

Library of Congress Cataloging in Publication Data
Main entry under title:

Long-range environmental outlook.

  Proceedings of a workshop held Nov. 14-16, 1979 in Washington, D. C.
  1. Environmental protection—United States—Congresses.    2.   Environmental poli-
cy—United States—Congresses.    I.   National Research Council. Environmental Studies
Board.
TD169.L66        304.2'8        80-16190
ISBN 0-309-03038-2

Available from:

Office of Publications
National Academy of Sciences
2101 Constitution Avenue, N.W.
Washington, D.C. 20418

Printed in the United States of America

iii

# Contents

v

# List of Figures

# List of Tables

# Preface

Responding to an often repeated Academy recommendation suggesting development of anticipatory research programs by the U.S. Environmental Protection Agency (EPA), the Office of Research and Development requested that the Environmental Studies Board conduct a workshop to address a long-range environmental outlook.

In July 1979, the board held a meeting to develop a focus and format for the workshop, drawing upon the expert advice of board members as well as the following non-board members:

R. Engelbrecht, University of Illinois,
S. Friess, Naval Medical Research Institute,
J. Neuhold, Utah State University, and
R. Ridker, Resources for the Future, Inc.

It was recognized at the outset that a more narrow focus would be needed in order to plan a useful meeting. Thus, four general areas were chosen from among a wide range of potential topics. Task groups were established to discuss future trends in energy, agriculture, toxic substances, and hazards of facility siting and the potential environmental problems that may develop. The charge for each group was to identify specific future problems, establish the priority of importance and recommend research that would assist EPA and other agencies in resolving these problems.

Participants in each group were carefully chosen to represent diverse expertise and viewpoints. The aim of the workshop was not to reach a consensus on the future environmental outlook, but rather to identify a wide range of problems within the four categories.

On behalf of the board, I would like to thank Janis Horwitz, Adele King Malone, and Suellen Pirages for their contributions in organizing the workshop and preparing the proceedings. Other staff members providing assistance included Judith Cummings, Maggie Elliott, Raphael Kasper, Estelle Miller, John Richardson, and Robert Rooney.

Finally, I wish to express my gratitude to all participants for their effort toward a successful workshop.

JOHN CANTLON, *Chairman*
Environmental Studies Board

# 1 Summary of the Workshop

J. CANTLON
*Michigan State University*

Strategic planning for ensuring an environment of high quality in the future presents a difficult challenge. The environment of the future will be determined by the technological, economic, social, and political actions taken by the individuals, families, industries, agriculture, communities, states, and nations that make up the modern world, and history confirms that such actions remain difficult to predict. Scientific breakthroughs may permit the use of technologies totally unforeseen now, remove constraints from potentially useful technologies, or spell the end of already deployed technologies. Resource scarcity or substitution and various economic shifts can also impose changes. People's fears, desires, knowledge, and ignorance, when focused either politically or economically, can advance a new technology or kill an existing one. The mission of the U.S. Environmental Protection Agency (EPA) is to nurture research programs that will, over time, accumulate the information base with which to address the essential environmental protection decisions of the future while recognizing these uncertainties.

The workshop devoted its efforts to problem identification and attempted to rank environmental problems in terms of their probable prominence in the next 25 to 50 years. The participants also attempted to identify opportunities that would permit avoidance or alleviation of environmental problems in the future.

In several areas, substantial federal and industrial efforts are under way to assess the probable environmental and economic impacts of potential new technologies. The U.S. Department of Energy (DOE) and the Office of Technology Assessment (OTA), for example, are providing assessments of each of the potential new energy technologies. Participants in this workshop are aware of the extent of these other assessment activities. The EPA might do well to encourage similar efforts in transportation, agriculture, communications, defense, and natural resource management.

The participants recognized that EPA's regulatory authority is essential to its mission of protecting the environment. In several different contexts, however, they suggested that other approaches—especially those that rely on market mechanisms—may be more likely to catalyze both incremental technological change and major technological breakthroughs.

The advantage of addressing environmental problems by better consolidation of, and articulation between, technologies also came up in several different contexts during the small group discussions. Clearly, governmental regulations that discourage such articulation will interfere with opportunities to convert the waste streams from present industrial processing plants into the resource streams for plants of articulated industries. In particular, exploration of ways to allow various industries to explore such questions without jeopardizing themselves under anti-trust law is needed.

A common theme in several of the workshop sessions was the need to improve our understanding of complex ecosystems. We need to be able to discriminate between environmentally or technologically imposed changes in ecosystems and irreparable damage to them, and we need a far better understanding of the capacity of various types of ecosystems to dissipate and assimilate potentially hazardous substances. It seems likely that more effective use can be made of both natural and man-made ecosystems, such as forests, rangeland, and crop agriculture to process residual materials.

Another subject that came up in two or more of the workshops is the fact that a wider range of materials will be required for emerging technologies. Such metals as titanium, gallium, vanadium, niobium, and chromium, as well as coal and oil shale liquids and biologically generated chemical feedstocks, are likely to become much more common. Anticipatory research should address the entire range of questions raised by new materials, from identification and gathering to processing, use, recycling, and, where necessary, disposal.

Over the next 25 to 50 years, a number of trends will emerge that are likely to have opposite impacts on environmental problems. Further, these trends could be quite different for the United States and other technologically advanced nations as compared with the rest of the world. Some examples of U.S. trends that will probably tend to alleviate environmental problems over the next five decades include:

1. A gradual reduction in the large backlog of chemical compounds for which adequate risk information is now lacking. This backlog will diminish both as research chisels away at the problems and as "problem" compounds are withdrawn from U.S. markets. In addition, fewer new chemicals lacking adequate assessment of their potential impacts on health and the environment will reach the market each year. The growing cost of producing acceptable risk assessment data, plus the liability costs that ensue from deploying chemicals without adequate risk assessment, will reduce the number of small chemical companies marketing new compounds. For similar reasons the larger companies will also develop fewer new chemicals for the U.S. market.

2. Inflation and the price of energy will continue to push costs upward, with the result that wasteful or marginally productive uses of costly chemicals and materials will decline.

3. Next-generation technologies will avoid some environmental problems by altered processes or by articulating the industrial components able to use present waste streams as feedstocks.

4. Improved containment and clean-up procedures will substantially alleviate the hazards of existing dump sites, and next-generation regulations will lead to more recycling, destruction, and safer containment.

5. Growing scientific understanding of the impact of mixtures of toxic substances—their co-factors, inhibitors, synergisms, and interferences—will provide the public with better knowledge of the risks from toxic materials.

6. The data base, research models, training and data processing in human epidemiology will provide a firmer base for decision makers, researchers, and public understanding.

7. Industry will pay far more attention to end-use risk assessment, and will design products, instructions to users, and disposal requirements accordingly.

8. Wider and more sophisticated use of the "bubble concept" in determining the trade-offs related to environmental improvement will bring market forces actively to bear on improving the environment.

In the view of the workshop chairman, there may be several other trends that could help alleviate environmental problems over the next 20 to 50 years. The following items are examples.

9. Priorities in the expenditure of public and private funds will begin to reflect the rate of real risk abatement per unit of investment.

10. Growing public concern about improving U.S. productivity to allow this country to compete more effectively in world trade will tend to bring important environmental and occupational safety issues into sharper focus.

11. Growing public sophistication will ameliorate demands for zero risk technologies.

12. Experience will build better articulation among federal, state, local, and industry risk abatement and environmental protection efforts, thus making for more cost-effective use of scarce resources.

13. Improved siting assessments, as well as decision-making processes that are perceived to be equitable to most of the people affected, would speed up plant siting decisions, reduce the amount of nuisance litigation, and provide more cost-effective environmental protection efforts.

14. The public's post-Watergate, post-Vietnam sag in confidence about national institutions will change, and decisions will be more widely accepted only if the decision-making process is strengthened by using scientifically sound information.

Trends were also recognized that may complicate environmental problem solving as well as advance our efforts for resolution, especially in the developing countries, over the next 25 to 50 years. Among others, these include the following:

1. The growing pressure of the world's population on the earth's resources of energy, raw materials, water, and food will lead to increased use of polluting technologies without waiting for more benign next-generation replacements. In particular increased atmospheric pollution from $NO_x$ and $SO_x$ are likely to continue throughout the 20- to 50-year period. From an overall risk abatement point of view this may appear quite correct in developing countries, because poverty, hunger, poor public health, poor communication, and poor transportation all lead to more mortality and morbidity than polluting technologies.

2. Improved scientific understanding of the effects of toxic materials on human health and behavior will undoubtedly lower the threshold for many materials. (Improved understanding can also help alleviate many problems.)

3. Improving instrumentation and data handling will provide a clearer picture of the extent of risk areas and times, and add to the list of materials having subtle effects upon humans, animals, and plants.

4. Increasing experimental demonstrations of synergism and other types of interaction among toxic materials and their promoters will make risk assessment more complex, but also more accurate.

5. Improvements in the quality of epidemiological research, the data base, and its accessibility will give environmental, labor, and other groups a broader basis for pressing for safer environments.

6. Improvements in our knowledge about ecosystems will turn up more sensitive species, such as the sensitivity of lichens to $SO_x$, leading to arguments for tighter constraints on air and water pollution.

7. Better data on the atmospheric and marine transport of pollutants will confirm that disposal of unwanted materials can create difficultieis beyond the national boundaries, making resolution of the problem more difficult.

8. Better information on the unsafe use of hazardous materials by the general public will illuminate a larger risk than is currently acknowledged.

9. Further improvement in the biochemical procedures for analyzing blood, serum, and cell tissue, combined with decreasing costs, are likely to show a wider population of human beings and animals with some degree of chemical contamination.

10. Growing public concern in the United States about such things as the nation's defense capability, its trade deficit, and global economic recession will continue to influence Congress, the courts, and the general public, making it more difficult to pursue environmental improvements without very strong data validating serious effects from environmental hazards.

## RECOMMENDATIONS

Some general recommendations emerged that cut across those of the small groups.

1. EPA should support long-term research on instrumentation and data handling systems for improving the cost effectiveness of environmental monitoring.

2. EPA should fund long-term research on multi-species system responses to toxic and other pollutant materials.

3. EPA should support research on the impact of common mixtures of pollutants on plants, animals, microcosms, and ecosystems, as well as continue research on single pollutants.

4. EPA should fund research on natural processes that detoxify or retoxify materials released into the environment.

5. EPA should continue to encourage research into technological developments that would avoid common environmental problems.

6. EPA should seek to strengthen our understanding of the complex social and political processes that influence the public's perceptions about environmental safety and environmental quality,

especially as those perceptions affect site selection and agency decisions approving or disapproving the use of chemical materials.

7. EPA, working with the National Institute of Environmental and Health Sciences (NIEHS), should improve the research base on environmental health beyond the areas of cancer and birth defects. Epidemiological understanding of learning impairment, behavioral changes, and cardiovascular and pulmonary responses to environmental pollutants, to name only a few important areas, needs to be improved.

8. EPA needs to improve its articulation with the scientific communities in both the United States and foreign countries. It would be especially prudent to help fund epidemiological studies of technologies deployed overseas that have yet to be deployed in the United States. Global dispersal mechanisms and global contamination processes, such as marine pollution, $CO_2$ build-up, and ozone layer problems need enhanced international attention.

9. EPA needs to support research that focuses on regional environmental problems, such as hazardous waste disposal, acid precipitation in the northeast, smog in southern California, and the deterioration of air transparency in the western mountain states. Long-term interdisciplinary studies are apt to be most productive in this area.

Although this workshop was planned and convened on relatively short notice, it seemed in retrospect to be effective in identifying the number of issues likely to emerge, to become important, or to decline in the next 25 to 50 years, issues for which EPA should have research under way. The usefulness of the effort would probably be enhanced if this report were to be distributed broadly to the agency's advisory panels with the request that individual scientists make additions to or take issue with specific statements. The effort should be viewed as one element in an ongoing process rather than an end in itself.

# 2 Overview of a Long-Range Environmental Outlook

G. SPETH
*Council on Environmental Quality*

I want first to thank Dr. Cantlon and the others who planned this National Academy conference for asking me to be here today to address such a simple and straightforward matter. Since the President asked me to become Chairman of the Council on Environmental Quality, I have noticed that most speaking requests are to address unanswerable questions. Whereas as a mere member of the Council I would be asked to speak on issues such as nuclear power or $CO_2$, now I'm asked to answer questions such as what is the world environment going to look like in the year 2025?

I hope my humility is showing here before you today. You have the technical expertise, the experience, and the backgrounds to provide answers for some of these problems. Therefore I will defer to you, and look forward to your conclusions.

I can best help, I believe, by calling your attention to four or five decisions that will be key determinants of environmental quality in the future—areas where this country and other countries face major choices in the years, indeed in the months, ahead. How those decisions are made will be basic factors in deciding the future of the environment.

The first area in which it seems to me that we face a major decision, and a major turning point, is the energy area. It's not difficult to sketch out alternative energy futures. It is difficult to sketch them out accurately. Thanks to a number of important studies that have been done, we now have a series of possible energy futures. They suggest that energy decisions will be very critical determinants of the future environment, and of the types of problems we will have to face.

7

We are now consuming about 58 quadrillion Btus (quads), in 1977 or 1978 numbers, of oil and gas; about 14 quads of coal, about 3 quads of nuclear energy, and about 4 quads in renewable resources, almost entirely hydro. This amounts to 78 quads; today's value may be as high as 80 quads.

I would like to focus particularly on two possible futures, one given in the report of the Council on Environmental Quality (CEQ), *The Good News About Energy* (1979), and the other developed by the U.S. Department of Energy (DOE) in the *National Energy Plan II* (1979).

The CEQ future calls for about a 90-quad energy demand for the year 2000, suggesting a relatively low energy growth over the next 20 years, one averaging half a quad per year. The base case developed by the DOE estimated the demand in the year 2000 at about 120 quads, or 30 quads more than the CEQ estimate. This represents a difference between a manageable energy future with some significant environmental impacts and an energy future that will impose very serious, and perhaps unacceptable, environmental impacts on the country.

A look at oil and gas use in the low-growth, CEQ future indicates that consumption of these diminishing resources can drop from 58 quads today down to 43 quads. In the high-growth, DOE future, oil and gas consumption remains the same over this 20-year period, nearly 59 quads. Coal use would rise from 14 to 19 quads in the CEQ future. That additional coal use is roughly the coal development we have in the construction pipeline today. In the high-growth future, coal consumption doubles to 36 quads. Nuclear power use in the low-growth future increases to 9 quads in 2000. Like coal, this is roughly the nuclear use to which we are already committed. In the high-growth future, nuclear would rise to 16 quads. Demand for renewable resources in the CEQ future is 19 quads, but only 10 quads in the DOE future. This 19-quad energy demand in renewable resources is consistent with the President's goal to achieve 10 percent of our future energy needs from solar and other renewable sources by the turn of the century. The Interagency Solar Domestic Policy Review concluded that this level of solar penetration (19 quads) could be achieved by the turn of the century with a maximum practical effort.

The environmental differences between a 90-quad future and a 119-quad future are rather profound. In the high-growth future, there is no real reduction in our dependence on oil and gas, and we will need nearly 300 additional coal-fired or nuclear power generating plants more than in the low-growth future.

The impact of the extra 25 or 30 quads is very significant when demands for water, land use, air pollution, and increased atmospheric $CO_2$ are considered. A rough calculation indicates that year 2000 $CO_2$ production in the high-growth future is perhaps 50 to 60 percent higher than the $CO_2$ production in the low-growth future. This is due primarily to the difference in overall consumption, but it is also due to the different mix of the technologies contributing to energy growth. Risks associated with reactor accidents, radioactive wastes accumulation, nuclear proliferation, and safeguard problems would be significantly more serious in the high-growth future.

So we do have a very definite choice. One factor to be considered in that choice is the economic impact resulting from low energy growth. There have been a number of studies investigating these impacts. One (Hudson and Jorgenson 1978) concludes that a significant but small reduction in GNP will result from adopting policies aimed at reducing energy consumption in the year 2000 from 116 quads to only 90 quads. This reduction of 26 quads would require a 4 percent reduction in GNP by the turn of the century. This would be a significant decrease, but not a major one.

Is the price worth paying? In my judgment, considering the environmental effects that are not considered in the GNP figures, considering the national security implications, and considering the other strains that would accompany growth from a 90- to a 116-quad future, the cost is well worth paying. Thus, a basic decision faces us, and our choice will affect a wide range of environmental and social issues over the coming decades.

Another important future need is the ability to develop an effective means to determine land-use priorities while protecting our land resources. We are currently losing 2 to 3 million acres per year of productive cropland because of soil erosion. Another 3 million acres per year is lost because of the conversion of agricultural lands to other uses. It is estimated that probably a half a million acres per year of wetlands are destroyed. There has been little planning associated with urban sprawl or transportation system design. Adverse effects have occurred as a result of these actions. Landscapes and communities that are part of our priceless heritage have been lost; we are faced with over-development on the barrier islands and coastal areas.

The current strategy is to attack these problems on a case-by-case basis. They are addressed through single or limited purpose regulatory programs and planning requirements. That's an important way to proceed. It may be the only way to proceed now. But I raise the question of whether that is the best way to proceed over the long run. My view is that it isn't. We are going to have to develop a more effective and more comprehensive approach to land-use management in the United States. Again the choice is there: Will we develop it or will we continue with current patterns?

A third choice affecting our future is the accommodation we seek between economic and environmental issues. There are many dimensions to this problem. We could sketch out, for example, four critical points in a continuum, from all-out, unrestrained, unregulated economic growth on the one hand to a steady-state economy on the other. One mid-point is an economy that gives attention to identifying deleterious environmental effects requiring regulation, indicating important social decisions, and determining the trade-offs that must be made. This is the current course of action. It assumes that growth itself is no problem, but that regulations are needed to channel growth in socially beneficial directions. There are, however, some shortcomings to this approach. For example, even the best regulatory program is only partially effective. Regulation is being fought tooth and nail today, and what actually gets enforced against polluters is sometimes a far cry from the swift and sharp pollution reductions envisioned in our air and water laws. Also, unanticipated impacts always arise, and often we realize too late that regulatory efforts were not effective. Other shortcomings exist as well.

Another point on the continuum—one that recognizes the limits of this "regulated growth"—is what I would refer to as the "conserver society." This conserver society would provide mechanisms to better channel economic growth and would reflect a greatly diminished societal importance attached to aggregate economic expansion. Measures supplemental to traditional environmental regulation—such as incentives to control population and encourage recycling, programs to ensure the public assessment of new technologies, and constituency participation in the governing of large corporations—would be implemented. GNP per capita would increase in this future as technology progressed and population grew, but there would no social premium put on increasing GNP *per se*. Greater income equality through redistribution and other means would tend to replace steady economic expansion as a force for social stability, and full employment would be approached through programs aimed directly at providing private and, as necessary, public sector employment and not by aggregate economic stimulation.

A second dimension of this question of how to accommodate environmental and economic issues is the resolution of our current debate over regulation. Are we going to resolve successfully the current dispute over government intervention in favor of more regulation, or will strict limits be imposed on regulatory power? Frankly, my own view is that regulation is here. Perhaps it can be economically more sensitive in places but it is here to stay. Indeed it is essential to preventing cancer, to protecting our resources, and to protecting the economy from itself in the long run.

A controversy exists on these issues at present. One factor that will affect the outcome is the type of data on health effects generated over the next 5 or so years on the effects of toxic chemicals. Certain information now raises our concern. If these concerns are verified by additional studies, that will strengthen the hand of the regulators.

The final dimension, and it is probably the most important, is the global context in which our own domestic environmental problems will be addressed. We are now engaged in a study at CEQ, one we refer to as the "Global 2000 Study," which is trying to make projections about the world's environment, resources, and population at the turn of the century. We have come to the conclusion that we will experience two basic and profoundly important tendencies. One will be the strong tendency in the decades ahead for per capita incomes to diverge in rich countries and poor countries. Even if percentage growth in rich and poor countries tends to be equal, the absolute dollar gap between the rich and the poor will grow. Unless countervailing factors intervene, most of the world, and most of its people, could see their lot falling relative to the lot of those of us who are much better off.

A second tendency involves the basic question of the world's resource and planetary carrying capacity: resource limits will begin to bind in the decades ahead in a way that has not yet occurred, except perhaps in the oil area. We are going to be facing more serious global water problems, deforestation problems, desertification problems, and biological impoverishment problems, to mention a few. Several of our renewable resources will become more inaccessible and expensive.

I am inclined to agree with the conclusion of Lester Brown (1978) in his book, *The Twenty-Ninth Day*:

> The social changes that must be compressed into the next two decades promise to be profound. . . . Each of us will be affected. Arresting the deterioration between ourselves and the earth's natural systems and resources will affect what we eat, how much we pay for housing, how many children we have. Some will view this with alarm, others, including the author, believe that the problems are manageable, but that managing them will require an exceptional exercise of political will and human ingenuity.

Addressing these two world problems—income disparities and global resource limits—will take every effort we can give in the years ahead. If we do not cope successfully with them, the world will surely become less livable, less enchanting, less secure, more desperate, and fraught with risks, including the risks of nuclear weapons proliferation and war.

If these global problems demand our every effort, the question is: Are we suited and prepared for the demands of the coming decades? I think that we are, but it is going to require that we put our own house in order, getting more of our domestic divisions behind us. In particular, I think we are going to have to learn to share the plenty at home in order that we can appreciate the needs abroad. And we cannot expect other countries to live within global resource limits if we do not do a better job of living within our limits.

At least three factors will be important in deciding how we make the choices before us: the attitudes and aspirations of our people, the imperatives of our economic system, and the resource constraints that we all will be operating within, including the technological resources. The growth imperatives of our economy will by and large push us in a certain direction. Resource constraints will tend to act as a brake and as an incentive to more efficient use of natural resources in the productive process. The decisive factor is likely to be the public's desires and aspirations as we face these fundamental choices.

## REFERENCES

Brown, L.R. (1978) The Twenty-Ninth Day. New York, N.Y.: Norton Publishers.
Council on Environmental Quality (1979) The Good News About Energy. GPO Stock No. 04101100441. Washington, D.C.: U.S. Government Printing Office.
Hudson, E.A. and D.W. Jorgenson (1978) Energy Policy and U.S. Economic Growth. Am. Econ. Rev. 62(2).
U.S. Department of Energy (1979) The National Energy Plan II. Washington, D.C.: Department of Energy.

# 3 Energy

## FUTURE DEVELOPMENTS IN FOSSIL ENERGY RESOURCES AND TECHNOLOGY—1980-2000

R. AYRES, C. BLOYD, *and* J. MOLBURG
*Carnegie-Mellon University*

### INTRODUCTION

Since the overall purpose of this workshop is to explore the long-range environmental outlook, and since future energy resources and technology cover an enormous amount of territory, we have deliberately put most of our emphasis on energy technologies that are likely to have a major environmental impact. Moreover, we have tried to focus, principally, on impacts that are "new" in the sense that they have not yet attracted significant regulatory attention. To further limit the scope of our discussion, we have elected not to consider technologies whose impact seems likely to be primarily nonenvironmental in nature.

Nuclear energy technologies do have very severe occupational safety, accident, and/or international weapons proliferation risks attached, but these are not "environmental" problems in the usual sense. Radiological health problems associated with conventional nuclear power do arise in connection with uranium-mining waste disposal, spent-fuel-rod reprocessing waste disposal, and possible leakage of certain radioisotopes in small quantities. These latter problems are not "new" in the above sense. They are also primarily responsibilities of the Nuclear Regulatory Agency (NRC) and the National Institutes of Health (NIH), rather than of the EPA. The breeder reactor does introduce a new factor (plutonium recycle) that deserves continued attention as long as the breeder remains an active candidate. The breeder also would have beneficial environmental impacts, insofar as the need for uranium mining and the associated occupational health risks would be reduced. The same is true of fusion power, although there appears to be no prospect of fusion power becoming commercially viable within the next 3 decades. Solar power satellites (SPS) offer a "new" environmental problem, microwave radiation, but can be disregarded because the earliest possible practical implementation of SPS almost certainly lies beyond the year 2000 and major environmental impacts would be further delayed. The same holds true for ocean thermal energy conversion (OTEC). Terrestrial solar collectors, active or passive, have few major environmental problems except to the extent that land requirements become very large. One caveat deserves note: many of these energy technologies, as now conceived, might require fairly large increases in the use and hence the production and mining of certain "exotic" materials. Examples include chromium, titanium, zirconium, gallium, arsenic, and niobium.

Petroleum extraction *per se* has only one major environmental impact, spills, that may increase in frequency as more offshore drilling is carried out and more oil is shipped by tanker. But oil spills are not really a new problem. The shipment of liquid natural gas (LNG) by tanker also has significant risks attached, although they would probably not be classed as "environmental" in nature. For all these reasons we restrict our attention in the remainder of this discussion primarily to coal (and lignite), tar sands, and oil shale, together with mining, cleaning, and conversion of these fuels. Again, occupational health problems (e.g., associated with coal mining) will not be our main concern.

We conclude with a brief discussion of two common problems associated with combustion of most carbon fuels, such as oxides of sulfur and nitrogen leading to acid rain among other problems and carbon dioxide ($CO_2$) build-up in the atmosphere and possible climatological impacts. While significant impacts would not occur for many decades, at the earliest, the problem is so fundamental and potential solutions affect all energy planning in so profound a way that serious attention must be given to it. This problem has already received international attention among scientists, but not, as yet, among regulatory agencies.

## THINKING ABOUT THE FUTURE

At first sight the range of future possibilities seems so great, and the uncertainties so overwhelming, that a long-range forecast of environmental problems is of questionable value. However, on closer scrutiny, the major uncertainties appear to lie in three areas, which can be considered individually.

First, there is a high degree of uncertainty about the future demand for energy. A few short years ago a major government-industry study of future energy supply-demand (National Petroleum Council 1972) placed the 1980 U.S. demand between 95.7 and 105.3 quadrillion Btus (quads). It pegged 1985 estimates at 112.5 to 130 quads. Only 2 years later, the Ford Foundation Energy Policy Project (EPP) Report (1974) presented several scenarios (historical growth, "technical fix," and zero growth by the year 2000) that yielded 1985 projections between 91 quads for the lowest case and 112 quads for the highest. For the year 2000, these trends resulted in projections of 100 quads for a zero energy growth case to more than 180 quads for the historical growth case. EPP projected 125 quads for their central case, a projection that was severely criticized by some reviewers as far too low. A recent study by Resources For the Future, Inc. (RFF), sets the base case at 114 quads, with scenarios ranging up to 166 quads (Ridker and Watson, in press). A more recent MITRE study (1979) for DOE, however, places the base case for 2000 at only 95 quads. Conservationists have even suggested that energy consumption in the year 2000 by the United States will be below current levels, *viz.* 75 to 80 quads (e.g., Lovins 1979). A number of these comparisons, "normalized" to the year 1975, are presented in Figures 1 and 2, as well as Table 1.

Clearly, most of this variation is due to a major change that has taken place in the world since 1972. The Yom Kippur War (1973) triggered the Arab oil boycott of winter 1973 to 1974 and set in motion a series of dramatic oil price increases, from $2.11/bbl for light Arabian crude in 1970 to $18 to 23.50/bbl as of June 1979, and up to $40.00/bbl on the Rotterdam Spot Market. These figures are in current (inflation-prone) dollars. Even in constant dollars, the price increase has been dramatic. This has created both recession and inflation in the industrialized world and a major transfer of wealth to the OPEC countries. The effects did not stop there. Iran tried to use its new wealth—export earnings rose from $4.8 billion in 1972 to $22 billion in 1974—to carry out an ambitious program of industrialization and social transformation in a single generation. The effort failed, for various reasons, and the new revolutionary regime has cut back production by one half. Libya and Kuwait also

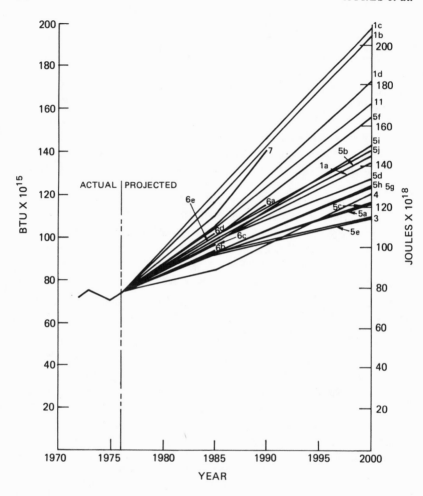

SOURCE: Planning Research Corp. (1978)

FIGURE 1  Total energy projections: U.S. Government.

have cut production well below their capacity, and other producers seem ready to do likewise. The Iranian experience (among other things) has convinced other countries, including Mexico, of the need to funnel oil revenues into a restricted number of carefully planned capital projects to avoid an explosive and inflationary expansion of consumer spending.

After the 1973 to 1974 embargo and price rise, most energy economists assumed that oil prices were, if anything, too high and that market

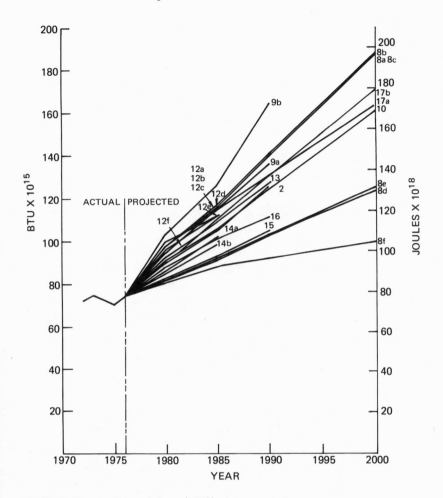

SOURCE: Planning Research Corp. (1978)

FIGURE 2   Total energy projections: Nongovernment sector.

adjustments would bring forth new supplies, creating a "glut" by the early 1980s. Virtually all long-range studies carried out during this period assumed prices would decline or at worst remain at 1974 levels (in real terms). Indeed, real prices did not increase significantly during the period 1974 to 1978, appearing to confirm the hypothesis that natural market forces would tend to reestablish a price equilibrium. Curiously though, long-range oil and gas supply estimates made since 1973 to 1974 have *not*

TABLE 1 Comparison of U.S. Energy Demand Estimates

| Identifier | Source of Forecast and Date | 1980 Joules | 1980 BTU | 1985 Joules | 1985 BTU | 1990 Joules | 1990 BTU | 2000 Joules | 2000 BTU |
|---|---|---|---|---|---|---|---|---|---|
| 1a | Atomic Energy Commission, 1974, Case A | — | — | 101.5 | 96.2 | — | — | 142.7 | 135.3 |
| 1b | Atomic Energy Commission, 1974, Case B | — | — | 123.0 | 116.6 | — | — | 205.7 | 195.0 |
| 1c | Atomic Energy Commission, 1974, Case C | — | — | 125.9 | 119.4 | — | — | 210.5 | 199.6 |
| 1d | Atomic Energy Commission, 1974, Case D | — | — | 110.5 | 104.8 | — | — | 183.8 | 174.3 |
| 2 | Banker's Trust, 1976 | 94.6 | 89.7 | 110.7 | 104.9 | 132.6 | 125.7 | — | — |
| 3 | Department of Commerce, 1977 | | | 91.9 | 87.2 | — | — | 120.2 | 114.0 |
| 4 | Council on Environmental Quality, 1974 | | | 88.2 | 83.5 | — | — | 127.6 | 121.0 |
| 5a | ERDA, 1977, Scenario SF1 | | | 98.5 | 93.4 | 104.9 | 99.4 | 123.2 | 116.9 |
| 5b | ERDA, 1977, Scenario SF2 | | | 103.7 | 98.0 | 116.1 | 110.1 | 146.7 | 139.1 |
| 5c | ERDA, 1977, Scenario SF4 | | | 97.5 | 92.5 | 106.1 | 100.5 | 123.4 | 117.1 |
| 5d | ERDA, 1977, Scenario SF5 | | | 103.8 | 98.4 | 113.0 | 107.1 | 134.3 | 127.3 |
| 5e | ERDA, 1977, Scenario SF6 | | | 96.2 | 91.5 | 102.0 | 96.7 | 114.4 | 108.5 |
| 5f | ERDA, 1977, Scenario SF7 | | | 103.7 | 98.4 | 122.6 | 116.2 | 164.8 | 156.2 |
| 5g | ERDA, 1977, Case 3A | | | 97.9 | 92.8 | 106.3 | 100.7 | 130.3 | 123.5 |
| 5h | ERDA, 1977, Case 3B | | | 97.2 | 92.2 | 106.0 | 100.4 | 130.8 | 124.1 |
| 5i | ERDA, 1977, Case 3C | | | 101.8 | 96.6 | 115.3 | 109.1 | 150.7 | 142.9 |
| 5j | ERDA, 1977, Case 3D | | | 105.7 | 100.3 | 113.9 | 107.9 | 148.3 | 140.5 |
| 6a | FEA, 1976, Reference Case | 86.1 | 81.6 | 104.3 | 98.9 | 120.2 | 114.0 | — | — |
| 6b | FEA, 1976, Conservation Case | | | 98.3 | 93.1 | — | — | — | — |
| 6c | FEA, 1976, Accelerated Case | | | 101.4 | 96.2 | — | — | — | — |
| 6d | FEA, 1976, Electrification Case | | | 107.1 | 101.5 | — | — | — | — |
| 6e | FEA, 1976, Regional Limitation Case | | | 103.5 | 98.1 | — | — | — | — |
| 7 | Federal Power Commission, 1975 | 100.5 | 95.3 | 121.7 | 115.3 | 148.2 | 140.5 | — | — |
| 8a | Ford Foundation, 1974, Historical Growth Scenario, Domestic Oil and Gas Case | | | 122.4 | 116.0 | — | — | 197.3 | 187.0 |
| 8b | Ford Foundation, 1974, Historical Growth Scenario, High Nuclear Case | | | 122.4 | 116.0 | — | — | 198.3 | 188.0 |
| 8c | Ford Foundation, 1974, Historical Growth Scenario, High Imports Case | | | 121.3 | 115.0 | — | — | 197.3 | 187.0 |

| ID | Source | | | | | | | | |
|---|---|---|---|---|---|---|---|---|---|
| 8d | Ford Foundation, 1974, Technical Fix Scenario, Self-Sufficiency Case | — | — | 97.1 | 92.0 | — | — | 130.8 | 124.0 |
| 8e | Ford Foundation, 1974, Technical Fix Scenario, Environmental Protection Case | — | — | 96.0 | 91.0 | — | — | 131.9 | 125.0 |
| 8f | Ford Foundation, 1974, Zero Energy Growth Scenario | — | — | 92.8 | 88.0 | — | — | 105.5 | 100.0 |
| 9a | Hittman/Army, 1975, Optimistic Case | 103.8 | 98.2 | 121.1 | 114.8 | 143.9 | 136.3 | — | — |
| 9b | Hittman/Army, 1975, Pessimistic Case | 108.6 | 102.9 | 132.8 | 125.9 | 173.3 | 164.3 | — | — |
| 10 | Hudson & Jorgensen, 1976 | 95.5 | 90.5 | 111.1 | 105.2 | — | — | 170.1 | 161.2 |
| 11 | Department of the Interior, 1975 | 91.9 | 87.2 | 109.2 | 103.6 | — | — | 172.4 | 163.5 |
| 12a | Lawrence Livermore Laboratory, 1974, Option A | 103.5 | 98.1 | 121.6 | 115.3 | — | — | — | — |
| 12b | Lawrence Livermore Laboratory, 1974, Option B and E | 103.3 | 98.0 | 121.6 | 115.3 | — | — | — | — |
| 12c | Lawrence Livermore Laboratory, 1974, Option C | 103.5 | 98.2 | 121.6 | 115.3 | — | — | — | — |
| 12d | Lawrence Livermore Laboratory, 1974, Option D | 103.8 | 98.5 | 122.8 | 116.6 | — | — | — | — |
| 12e | Lawrence Livermore Laboratory, 1974, Option F | 104.7 | 99.4 | 117.8 | 111.7 | — | — | — | — |
| 12f | Lawrence Livermore Laboratory, 1974, Option G | 100.9 | 95.8 | 117.8 | 111.7 | — | — | — | — |
| 13 | National Petroleum Council, 1974 | 98.0 | 92.8 | 114.7 | 108.8 | 134.3 | 127.2 | — | — |
| 14a | Organization for Economic Cooperation and Development, 1977, Reference Case | 90.7 | 86.0 | 107.7 | 102.2 | — | — | — | — |
| 14b | Organization for Economic Cooperation and Development, 1977, Accelerated Policy Case | — | — | 104.2 | 98.9 | — | — | — | — |
| 15 | Petroleum Industry Research Foundation, Inc., 1977 | 86.9 | 82.4 | 98.1 | 92.9 | 108.8 | 103.1 | — | — |
| 16 | Shell Oil Company, 1976 | 93.0 | 88.1 | 107.4 | 101.8 | 123.2 | 116.8 | — | — |
| 17a | Tetra Tech/Maritime Administration, 1975, Base Case | 100.3 | 95.0 | 121.3 | 115.0 | — | — | 173.0 | 164.0 |
| 17b | Tetra Tech/Maritime Administration, 1975, Low Oil/High Electricity Case | — | — | — | — | — | — | 180.3 | 171.0 |

Note: Metric Units, Joules × 10$^{18}$; English Units, BTUs × 10$^{15}$.
SOURCE: Planning Research Corp. (1978).

risen in comparison with earlier estimates, as neoclassical economic theory implies they should. Though energy demand has softened and recent long-range projections are far lower than earlier ones, projections of indigenous energy supply have fallen even more, resulting in a series of upward revisions of projected net oil imports (Bodman and Hamilton 1979).

Cutbacks in oil production, even below output levels permitted by production equipment now in place, have led to sharp reassessments of world oil supply levels over the next 20 years. As he left his post in mid-summer 1979, Secretary of Energy James Schlesinger stated that Mid-East production is unlikely to expand much, if at all, and is unlikely to drop below current levels (Wall Street Journal 1979). Both the International Energy Agency (Lantze 1979) and the U.S. Geological Survey (Root and Attainasi 1979) estimate that world oil production will peak before 1995. The CIA also has suggested that peak world output may already have been reached (U.S. CIA 1979). A few years ago the oil industry was notably impatient with such gloomy predictions. Today, Schlesinger's final pronouncement can probably be regarded as the best-available intelligence on the subject. Implications for the United States include continued inflationary pressures, reduced rates of economic growth, accounting for much of the difference between earlier and later energy consumption projections, and fairly strong incentives to develop alternative domestic resources.

This leads us to the second of our three major imponderables. The question is: How much energy can be "saved" in the medium to longer term through conservation or the use of "soft paths" such as (passive) solar hot water, firewood, etc.? Most people confuse conservation with austerity, but this should not be a problem for the present audience. It is more accurate to suggest that in the very short run (e.g., on a scale of days or weeks), austerity is the only viable mode of conservation for most energy users. People can heat their houses a little less, drive a little less, drive slower, turn out lights, etc. Much of this kind of thing is probably beneficial, but there are limits, and the short-run limits are probably already quite close for most Americans.

In the longer run, though, many other options exist. Weather-stripping, insulation, storm windows, and so forth exemplify the next set of alternatives available to homeowners. Owners of large cars can trade for smaller, more fuel-efficient ones, or they can use bicycles or buses for some trips. In the still longer run they can also choose residential locations closer to their jobs, or vice versa. Industrial and commercial enterprises, too, can insulate, introduce heat exchangers to use waste heat, monitor energy use more carefully, rationalize processes, and so on. In the still longer run they can develop and introduce new and more energy-efficient processes. In some cases more human labor can be substituted for energy-intensive capital. More commonly, in the industrial world, additional capital investment is the effective substitute for energy. The availability of capital, therefore, becomes the factor that limits the *rate* at which energy-conserving changes can take place.

Economists and others have engaged in a long controversy over the extent to which higher prices, alone, will be effective in inducing such substitutions. The problem is that historical experience prior to 1974 offers little useful long-run guidance, because prices moved very slowly, and mostly down. The period 1974 to 1977 is still pretty much "short run," confused by changes in several other political and economic factors. Despite the numerous strong opinions that have been expressed, it is not clear that meaningful price elasticities can be specified by econometric techniques. This may be an area where engineering knowledge has more intrinsic relevance than statistical analysis of historical time series data. This is particularly true with regard to use of fuel for industry and automotive transportation. Moreover, to a reasonable first approximation, one can link automobile fuel economy to oil import requirements. If cars are as efficient as is technically possible by 2000, the United States will not have to import very much petroleum. Liquid synthetic fuels from coal will, at most, be a minor factor by 2000.

Between now and the year 2000 it is reasonable to expect, and we do expect, that most nonautomotive uses of petroleum (except petrochemicals) will have been largely eliminated in the United States. This, despite the fact that other uses, such as home heating, have higher short-term (political) priority. Conservation measures also will have been implemented to the extent that these are driven by energy prices. Passive solar collectors will be quite widely used in residential applications, mainly for hot water. Windmills can provide a small amount of electricity in certain areas. Process-heating and space-heating applications in the year 2000 will, however, be based on natural gas to the extent it is available (i.e., to the limits of supply). Beyond that limit, the alternatives for space and process heat will be:

- syngas (from coal) to supplement natural gas,
- coal combustion for boilers, and
- electric heat (mainly via heat pumps) derived from coal-based or nuclear-power generating plants.

This leads to the third imponderable, which has to do with the technical feasibility *and cost* of large-scale coal gasification as compared to the technical feasibility *and cost* of an acceptable nuclear-electric power system (with or without breeders). Unfortunately, pipeline gas and electric power are not simple substitutes for each other from the point of view of industrial/commercial uses. A major capital commitment must be made to one form of usable energy or the other. The problem is acute because even the United States probably cannot afford all-out parallel development of both sources of energy. The choice is, more or less, between two paths. The first is to undertake high-Btu coal gasification on a large scale, with its uncertain but probably high costs, and continue to utilize the present investment in gas pipelines, gas-fired industrial and residential furnaces, kitchen appliances, etc. The second alternative is to reemphasize centralized nuclear-electric power generation and to force many consumers (both industrial and residential) to substitute electric furnaces, stoves, heat pumps, etc., for their present gas/oil-fired equipment. It is reasonably clear that a high degree of electrification (that is a further substitution of electric power for gas in marginal or competing uses such as space heating) should not be coal based; but beyond this it is not clear what will or should be the correct choice.

In the summer of 1979, President Carter proposed an ambitious program to produce 500,000 bbl/day of synthetic fuels by 1985, rising to 2,000,000 bbl/day by 1990 (Office of White House Press Secretary 1979). This would allegedly cost $88 billion (1979 dollars), to be paid for out of a yet-to-be approved "windfall profits" tax on decontrolled domestic oil. Except for the tax, this was exactly what the non-nuclear energy industry had said it wanted. Already, however, the efficacy of this program is being seriously questioned and its ultimate fate is now somewhat in doubt.

One reason for caution about the future of the program is that analysis since the initiative suggests that some of the underlying assumptions are weak. For example, the MITRE (1979) study suggested that the President had underestimated the costs of achieving 2.5 mmb/day synfuel capacity by 1990 by at least $36 billion, while overestimating the revenues from the proposed windfall profits tax by at least $20 billion. Moreover, MITRE projects that oil imports would not exceed 8.5 mmb/day in any case, dropping to 4 mmb/day by 1990, although the President's initiative would accelerate the decline. Finally, MITRE projects that particulate emissions, in particular, would be 40 percent higher with the President's initiatives than without them. The two cases are compared in Figures 3, 4, 5, and 6.

Forecasts of future energy supply (by fuel) are certainly as numerous and diverse as forecasts of demand. A few years ago most of the forecasts emphasized electricity production and gave nuclear power the leading role. A sharp rise in costs, an even sharper cutback in new orders, and a spate of cancellations have changed the outlook dramatically. Of course, this may change again, but at the present juncture, despite doubts about the realism

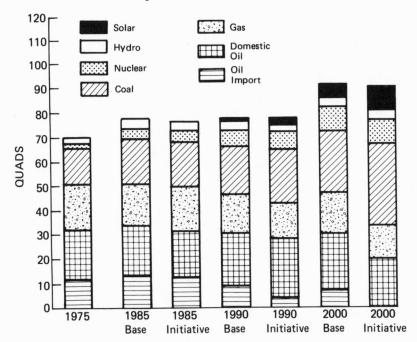

SOURCE: MITRE Corp. (1979)

FIGURE 3   Energy resource forecast.

of the President's initiative, coal seems likely to account for the bulk of whatever growth does occur in domestic energy supply over the next 20 years (and beyond).

Obviously, coal is not a new fuel. Actually, from the 1890s until recently it has been in a long decline. Once it was used to make gas for domestic use, as a fuel for industrial boilers and railroad locomotives, and as a fuel to heat most homes, as well as for generating electricity and making coke for smelting iron and other ores. Not long ago nuclear power was widely expected to displace coal from the next to last of its markets (electric utilities) and possibly even from its longest established use in smelting. Today, it seems much more plausible to suggest that coal may regain some of its other former markets in competition with fuel oil and natural gas. It may even become a feedstock for manufacturing synthetic liquid fuels.

Gasification and liquefaction of coal are, as yet, economically unjustified, but environmental controls on utilization of "unconverted" coal will probably help narrow the economic gap. Flue gas desulfurization (FGD) is now a requirement for new utility boilers and it may turn out to be more

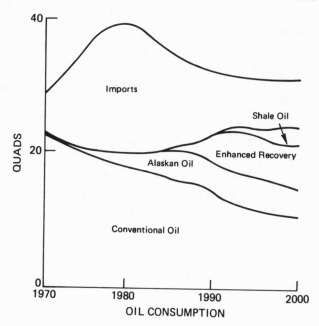

SOURCE: MITRE Corp. (1979)

FIGURE 4   Projected trends in energy imports, base case.

attractive to gasify the coal before combustion (removing the sulfur in the process) and use the resulting clean gaseous fuel in the power plant. This option is now called the "combined cycle." By similar logic, FGD and other air pollution control requirements may provide an incentive to cascade a high-temperature conversion process (such as MHD) and a lower temperature conversion process (such as a Rankine Cycle turbine using an organic or halocarbon working fluid). A given amount of "clean" fuel, once having paid its environmental tax, so to speak, can yield more useful output energy in this manner.

In this connection, by-product sulfur or sulfur oxide recovery from coal or heavy oil represents a significant potential energy resource. For example, sulfur dioxide can be used to manufacture chlorine as was done during World War II, thereby reducing the need for energy-intensive electrolysis. Thus, while some environmental controls, especially electrostatic precipitators and filters, are parasitic energy consumers, there are often some compensating economic benefits. Overall efficiency of energy conversion might eventually even be improved in consequence of the imposition of environmental standards relating to air pollution. Unconventional problems will arise also, however, as a result of a major shift back to coal and other fossil fuels. A more detailed discussion of the relevant technologies follows. (Amy and Thomas 1977, Lang 1977, White 1979, Jones 1977, University of Oklahoma 1975, Parker and Dykstra 1978, Ghassemi et al. 1978, Cavanaugh 1977, Koppenaal and Manahan 1976, Tennessee Valley Authority 1977, Leo and Rossoff 1978, Keeling and Bacastow 1977, Manabe amd Wetherald 1975.)

## COAL EXTRACTION

### UNDERGROUND MINING

Conventional room-and-pillar, continuous room-and-pillar, and longwall are the three most common methods of underground mining. The conventional room-and-pillar method utilizes blasting to fracture the coal, which is then loaded and removed by machine. Continuous room-and-pillar employs an electric scraper or continuous miner, which removes and

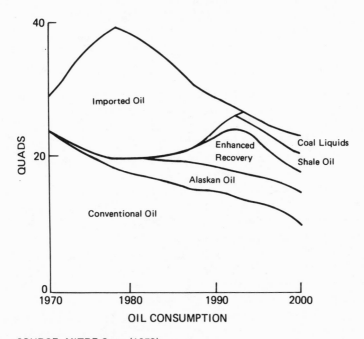

SOURCE: MITRE Corp. (1979)

FIGURE 5   Projected trends in energy imports, initiative case.

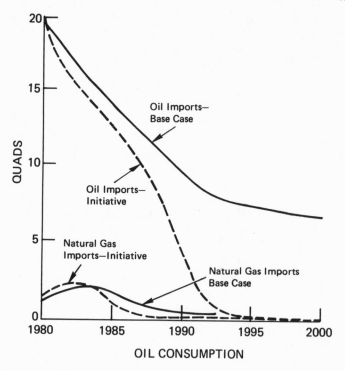

SOURCE: MITRE Corp. (1979)

FIGURE 6   Projected trends in energy imports, comparison of base and initiative case.

loads coal directly from the seam. In both room-and-pillar methods, about 50 percent of the mining area is left as "pillars" to provide the ceiling support. On some occasions the coal in the pillars themselves is mined. This is done as the mining equipment is moved back toward the mine entrance. Mining the pillars and allowing the roof to collapse permits extraction of up to 80 percent of coal seams. This "retreat" mining is not possible if subsidence is unacceptable.

Conventional room-and-pillar mining allows greater selectivity than continuous room-and-pillar, which produces more waste. This waste must be removed by mechanical cleaning.

Longwall mining involves the use of mechanical scrapers along the entire length of a mine wall. The coal is moved to the end of the wall by a conveyor linked to a continuous transport system that carries it to the mine entrance. Hydraulic roof supports that advance as the mine wall advances prevent the ceiling from falling on the scraper. The roof collapses as these supports are removed, however, causing substantial land subsidence. Longwall mining permits recovery of about 85 percent of the coal.

Although continuous room-and-pillar mining appears to be more economical than conventional room-and-pillar, the coarser coal from the latter has several advantages, including less methane diffusion due to smaller surface areas, a smaller amount of respirable dust, and lower energy consumption.

## Environmental Effects

The most serious adverse environmental impact of underground coal mining is acid drainage. Another problem, runoff from refuse piles, results in siltation as well as acid drainage. In addition, groundwater pollution can result from leakage through fissures created by blasting.

Air emissions can result from coal refuse piles that spontaneously combust, releasing particulates, sulfur oxides, and other combustion products. This is a more significant problem in existing and abandoned coal fields in the East, where refuse has been often carelessly maintained. Air emissions that result directly from mining include methane gas and the coal dust removed by mine ventilation systems. The ventilated dust ordinarily meets the effluent air quality standard ($2.0$ mg/m$^3$). In addition, some fugitive emissions can be expected from handling materials.

Acid mine drainage results from the contamination of mine water by iron pyrite ($FeS_2$) oxidation products, including sulfuric acid and soluble iron sulfates. The resulting acidic water dissolves heavy metals more easily than water of normal acidity and will not support aquatic life, with the exception of certain molds and algae. The water also corrodes metal structures and is useless for recreation.

## Control of Acid Mine Drainage

Careful choice of mining locations and proper design of mine drainage systems are the first line of defense against acid mine drainage. The second line of defense is the use of appropriate land reclamation techniques, such as covering the overburden from surface mines and the refuse from deep mines with vegetation to inhibit contact of the pyrites with rainwater. Contaminated water must be treated. The basic processes are neutralization with lime and precipitation of solids using settling basins. This creates a sludge disposal problem. Other disadvantages of this treatment technique include a possible increase in water hardness, an increase in total dissolved solids, and inadequate reduction of sulfate and iron concentrations.

Surface mining is used where removal of the overburden is practical or where the coal seam has been exposed by erosion or previous mining. If it is necessary to remove overburden, either area or contour strip mining is used. Area strip mining is appropriate in fairly flat areas. Overburden in this process is continuously removed, stored, and reclaimed after removal of the coal. In hilly regions contour strip mining is employed. Starting at an outcropping, overburden is removed and deposited on the hillside below the seam. The exposed coal is mined and the process continued until overburden removal becomes impractical. At this point auger mining may be used where coal is removed by boring horizontally into the seam.

### Environmental Effects

Aside from the considerable disturbance, the most serious adverse environmental effects of surface mining result from mine drainage. Silt, sulfuric acid, arsenic, copper, lead, manganese, and zinc are potentially significant components of such drainage.

Solid wastes resulting from surface mining can be dealt with through proper land reclamation. However, disturbance of the land, especially underlying aquifers, can result in alteration and pollution of groundwater systems. Careless handling of overburden prior to reclamation also can result in sedimentation problems. In addition to damage of the land receiving such sediment, flooding and degradation of water quality may result.

Air emissions from surface mining result principally from the use of diesel engines for the transport and handling of overburden and coal.

## COAL PREPARATION

### PHYSICAL CLEANING

Physical cleaning of coal is accomplished through some combination of crushing, separation by size, separation by specific gravity, and dewatering. The essential operation is specific gravity separation, which removes denser, impurity-laden coal from relatively clean coal. Though this may be done with simple hydraulic or pneumatic jigs, dense-media washing or froth flotation may be used, especially for fine particles of coal.

The most critical operating characteristic of the coal cleaning operation is the overall yield. As yield is reduced the quality of the coal is increased, but so are production costs and generation of refuse.

*Environmental Effects*

Generation of coal refuse is the primary effect of physical cleaning of coal. This refuse offers the same hazards as mining refuse. In some instances the wastes from cleaning are more hazardous, however, because pyrite and ash are more concentrated in the cleaning refuse than in mine refuse. Additionally, coal cleaning involves intimate association of process water with the coal. Therefore, water treatment and ponding are necessary, although water pollution can be limited if a closed-circuit water system is used.

Aside from fugitive emissions during handling of materials and possible refuse-pile combustion, air emissions from coal cleaning are limited to largely controllable emissions caused by combustion in the thermal dryer. These include $NO_x$, $SO_2$, CO, and TSP.

## CHEMICAL CLEANING

Chemical cleaning methods have been developed for the purpose of removing sulfur from coal. In general, these involve treating coal with a reagent to form soluble or volatile sulfur compounds. Although such processes are not yet used on a commercial scale, increased demands for coal and enforcement of federal emission standards are encouraging greater interest in them.

The Meyers process converts pyritic sulfur to soluble sulfur products, removing 90 to 95 percent of the pyritic sulfur with a coal loss of less than 5 percent. Some ash is simultaneously removed by this process, which employs ferric sulfate as the reagent.

The Battelle hydrothermal process uses aqueous sodium hydroxide to convert pyritic and organic sulfur, as well as some ash, to soluble compounds. The sulfur removal efficiency is nearly 1.0 for pyritic sulfur and 0.7 for organic sulfur. Coal loss is about 5 percent.

Both processes need energy for heating the coal-reagent slurries to encourage chemical reaction.

*Environmental Effects*

Potential sources of pollution from the Meyers process include spent leachate solution from the leaching circuit, by-product iron sulfate from the backing circuit, elemental sulfur from the sulfur recovery circuit, and solvent-vapor loss from the sulfur recovery circuit.

For the Battelle hydrothermal process the potential sources of pollution are spent solution (purged), fugitive emissions of $H_2S$ and $SO_2$ from the sulfur recovery circuit, particulate emissions from grinding, and by-product sulfur.

## COAL TRANSPORT

### COAL SLURRY PIPELINE

Although coal slurry pipelines are not currently economically competitive with the shipment of coal by barge or train, the technology is proven and available. The slurry is a mix of water and coal (14 mesh XO). Typically, between 45 and 55 percent of the slurry is composed of solids. Pumping pressure in slurry pipelines is maintained by intermediate pumping stations. Upon arrival at the point of use, the slurry is dewatered and dried as needed. Because of its fine size, slurry coal requires less pulverizing for use in conventional boilers than normal bulk coal. However, some processes, notably Lurgi gasification, cannot utilize feed coal of such size.

*Environmental Effects*

Coal slurry pipeline construction poses the same environmental problems—mainly land disturbance, dust, and fugitive emissions—as construction of other types of pipelines. These problems have been well-publicized. Possible environmental effects that are unique to the slurry pipeline include excessive water consumption (12 gal/$10^6$ Btu transported), fugitive dust from slurry preparation, slurry leakage, and leakage or improper treatment of process water.

## FLUE GAS DESULFURIZATION (FGD) OF COAL

All current scrubbing systems for removing sulfur oxides from flue gas have in common the use of an alkaline reagent to consume the sulfur species as it is absorbed by the scrubbing solution. In the case of regenerable systems, the resulting compounds are processed in a chemical plant to produce sulfuric acid and elemental sulfur. In the only common nonregenerable systems, those utilizing lime and limestone scrubbing, gypsum ($CaSO_4 \cdot 2H_2O$), and calcium sulfite hemihydrate ($CaSO_3 \cdot 1/2H_2O$) must be removed from the solution and discarded along with the flyash. Thus, at least for the nonregenerable process, a solid-waste disposal problem is substituted for an air pollution problem. Solid waste is not produced by regenerable systems, but these systems cannot be used to remove flyash from flue gas. Therefore, separate removal and disposal of flyash is required with associated solid waste problems.

The dewatering characteristics of the sulfur residues are important, because they seriously affect the problem of disposing of the residues. Of the two major residue components, gypsum and calcium sulfite, the former is the more desirable. This is due largely to its better dewatering characteristics, but also to the possibility that it may have some commercial value as a building material, namely plaster of paris. The oxidation of calcium sulfite to gypsum (calcium sulfate) can be controlled to some extent.

Minor flue residue components include chlorides and other trace elements present in the coal. Most of these are probably derived from the ash, but it has been shown that separate flyash removal prior to wet scrubbing does not substantially or consistently reduce trace element concentration in the residue. Apparently the first flyash particles, which are not removed by dry collection and which have the largest surface area for leaching, are most effective in contaminating the residue with trace elements.

ENVIRONMENTAL EFFECTS

FGD residues can have adverse environmental effects on air, land, and water. The possibility of water contamination depends on the disposal method, but, in general, pollution of surface waters results from runoff or leaching. Runoff occurs when rainwater displaces the residue or leaches chemicals and erosion particulates from the residue surface and carries these contaminants away from the disposal site. Percolation of rainwater through untreated residue results in leaching of contaminants that may subsequently enter groundwater.

Runoff from the disposal site can be controlled by diverting the drainage to a treatment facility, or the site may be covered with topsoil and revegetated. This reduces or eliminates contact of rainwater with the residue.

Leaching can be reduced by residue treatment or fixation. Residue that has been solidified by one of the available treatment techniques is approximately one order of magnitude less permeable than untreated FGD residue.

Treatment also has implications for land-use problems, because the greater stability of treated residue allows more possible uses of reclaimed land. Exact characterization of treated and untreated residue in terms of strength and long-range stability has not been accomplished. Similarly, the long-term effects of weathering and freeze-thaw cycles on residue permeability have not been established. Although revegetation is cited as a useful runoff and erosion control, little is known of the effects of subsurface FGD residue on vegetation.

Several alternatives to chemical treatment and landfill show promise as means of residue disposal while protecting the environment. The conventional method of flyash disposal, ponding, has been applied to flue residues and residue-flyash combinations. Success of such ponds is contingent on their integrity. Elastomeric material or impermeable clay can be used as lining to prevent seepage into groundwater. After a pond is filled to capacity it must be retired, either by being dried and covered or by being maintained as a lake. It is possible that restrictions should be placed on use of the resulting lake or land site. Another ponding method uses deliberate underdrainage. The continuous removal of residue liquor from the pond helps to prevent its seepage into groundwater. It also allows the use of liquid transfer of residue to the pond, because used water can be returned to the plant site by the drainage system.

Mine disposal of flue residues has been considered. Area surface mines and active eastern room-and-pillar mines seem to be the most promising types of mines. For surface mines the residue must be dewatered to make it compatible w.th other landfill. Residue could be used to compensate for some of the mined coal, thus bringing the reclaimed surface closer to its original elevation. Such disposal, however, might result in an increase in total dissolved solids in area water. This effect can be mitigated by placing overburden on the stripped area before depositing the flue residue sludge. The disposal of sludge in underground mines should be studied to determine appropriate characteristics for transportation to and storage in such mines. The possibility of using fixed sludge to reduce subsidence and perhaps even to increase the yield of room-and-pillar mines by providing roof support should be investigated.

Disposal of fixed residue in concentrated and dispersed dumps in the ocean also has been considered, but the environmental consequences of this method are simply not known.

Finally, several disposal systems have been demonstrated that utilize flue residue. Regenerable systems that produce sulfur or sulfuric acid have already been mentioned. Another system forces oxidation of the residue into gypsum, which is used for wallboard. This process has been used in Japan with residue from oil-fired boilers, and the same technology is likely to be possible with coal-fired boilers as well. Another building material, synthetic aggregate, has been produced from residue and used for road base material, dikes, and lining for disposal sites.

It should be also mentioned that coal cleaning can be used to reduce the solid waste impact by removing sulfur before combustion. In some cases, the total solid waste, including coal refuse produced by a system using coal cleaning and FGD, may be less than that for a system using FGD only. Even if this is not the case, it may be advantageous to produce coal refuse at a coal-cleaning site rather than FGD residue at a power-generating plant site.

## COAL UTILIZATION

### FLUIDIZED BED COMBUSTION (FBC)

A fluidized bed is a suspension of solids created by vertical air motion. The mixture exhibits some fluid-like properties and mixing reactions, and heat transfer among the bed constituents is very efficient. Boiler tubes can be placed in close contact with the fluidized bed, an arrangement that results in quite efficient heat transfer. This is possible because the relatively low combustion-chamber temperature in a fluidized bed boiler does not damage the tubes, unlike the higher temperatures of a conventional boiler. Other advantages of FBC over conventional combustion are the relatively small size of boilers, the possibility of burning a wide range of coals, and less coal preparation because larger coal particles can be burned.

Two variations of the basic fluidized bed boiler are being developed: pressurized and atmospheric pressure. Pressurization reduces the needed volume and simplifies construction of the combustion chamber, but the combustion gases must be passed through a turbine to recover the energy efficiently. To protect the turbine, efficient removal of particulates is required. Atmospheric pressure FBC is expected to be commercial by 1985, while pressurized FBC will probably not be commercially available before 1990.

### Environmental Effects

The primary environmental benefit of FBC is the removal of $SO_2$ from the flue gas by dolomite or limestone that is entrained with the coal in the bed. Spent limestone is discharged continuously as fresh limestone is injected. From current evidence it appears likely that fluidized bed boilers can be designed that are capable of meeting the New Source Performance Standard (NSPS) for $SO_2$ for virtually any coal without other controls. An additional benefit is reduced $NO_x$ emission compared to that of conventional boilers, due to lower combustion temperatures. The NSPS for $NO_x$ also is considered attainable. In addition, the expected efficiency of a pressurized fluidized bed-gas turbine system is higher than that of a conventional combustion system with scrubber. This reduces resource consumption and the production of pollutants.

FBC also has a negative side, the production of spent sorbent (about 1,000 tons/day from a 500 MWe plant). Disposal of this material poses problems similar to those in the disposal of FGD residue. Leaching of trace elements and solids threatens water resources in the same manner. More dry waste is likely to be produced by FBC than by FGD, but FBC waste is almost entirely calcium sulfate ($CaSO_4$) that does not form a residue similar to the calcium sulfite-sulfate combination common in FGD wastes. This simplifies dewatering and landfill operations, but the greater solubility of $CaSO_4$ increases the likelihood of groundwater contamination by FBC waste.

As is the case with FGD wastes, an alternative to FBC waste disposal is utilization. Some promising possibilities are using it to correct soil acidity levels or as a plant nutrient. Successful application to peanut crops already has been demonstrated. Potential structural uses include turning the waste into wallboard, aggregate blocks, and using it as a soil stabilizer. Other possible uses include the production of mineral wool, treatment of acid wastes, and sulfur or sulfuric acid production. Finally, several processes for sorbent regeneration have been demonstrated.

Another negative effect of FBC is that the use of solids in the bed and the low-combustion temperature (too low for slagging of ash) are likely to result in the production of more particulates than conventional systems. This will increase the load on particulate removal systems.

## TAR SANDS

### EXTRACTION

Tar sands are among the most promising of unconventional fossil fuel resources. Estimated reserves equivalent to 900, 200, and 30 billion barrels of oil are located in Canada, Venezuela, and the United States, respectively. Tar sands are a mixture of sand, porous rock, and mineral-rich clays impregnated with heavy hydrocarbon oils (about 83 percent carbon). Recovery of this material is currently hampered by the large fraction (about 85 percent) of solids associated with the oils, the high oil viscosity, and in some cases the depth of the deposits.

There are three basic processes for recovery: mining of oil-laden sands, in situ separation of oil from the sands, and in situ conversion. Mining technologies for tar sands have been borrowed from coal and oil shale mining, including underground and surface mining methods modified to accommodate the physical characteristics of the sands. Recovery or separation of the oil from the sand is accomplished by heating the deposits with steam or water to reduce the oil viscosity and enables the oil to be pumped. Other proposed methods include extraction with solvents and pyrolysis, the latter being a form of in situ conversion.

### Environmental Effects

From an environmental viewpoint, the main difference between oil sand and coal mining is the tremendous amount of granular solid material necessarily removed to recover significant amounts of oil. In the case of surface mining this means serious degradation of the landscape or difficult reclamation problems as well as possible water pollution, soil erosion, and watershed modification.

### PROCESSING

Separation of oil or bitumen from the tar sands is accomplished by mixing the sands with steam, hot water, or solvents, resulting in a bitumen-rich froth and wastewater laden with sand, clay, solvent, and process water. An alternative is to dissolve bitumen in a solvent such as naphtha, which is later separated from the extracted bitumen and reused. Pyrolysis involves partial combustion, thus reducing the bitumen to lighter fractions. This method is similar to those used in coking processes. All of these methods have been used commercially except pyrolysis, which is in the pilot-plant stage. The recovered bitumen or pyrolysis products must be hydrogenated to form synthetic crude oil that can be transported and processed much as natural crude oil is. If pyrolysis is not used for extraction it may be needed prior to hydrogenation anyway, although a direct hydrogenation process at high temperatures and pressures has been proposed.

### Environmental Effects

The use of hot water extraction of oil from tar sands in Canada has been a source of concern, because the suspended solids and the waste water form a sludge that must be controlled in settling ponds. It is anticipated that decades may pass before such a sludge pond can be successfully reclaimed. The Canadian experience suggests the recommendation that methods be developed to minimize or eliminate the sludge production or to accelerate the settling and treatment process.

A less pernicious but more massive problem is the disposal of solid waste from tar sand processing. Control is basically by mine disposal and, in the case of surface mining, reclamation. As in the case of oil shale solids, the main difference between this and proven coal mine reclamation is the magnitude of the wastes involved. Furthermore, the waste generated by shale and tar sand mining is more likely to cause permanent degradation or modification of the environment.

Air pollution from tar sand production results mainly from pyrolysis and includes the usual fossil fuel combustion products, including $SO_2$. The sulfur content of tar sands varies roughly over the same range as that of bituminous coal. Control of these pollutants is accomplished by conventional means. A coke desulfurization process for bitumen-based petroleum cokes has been investigated. Treatment with sodium carbonate followed by calcination and ponding has been shown to be capable of removing 90 percent of the sulfur in certain cokes derived from Canadian tar sands.

## OIL SHALE MINING

Oil shale extraction is accomplished by the same techniques as those used for coal extraction, namely, underground and surface mining. There are differences, however. About three times more material must be extracted per unit of energy recovered for oil shale than for coal; the shale deposits are much thicker than coal seams (30 to 100 ft), and shale is harder than coal. Room-and-pillar methods are the most promising for underground mining of oil shale. It is expected that 65 percent of the resource can be recovered in a typical room-and-pillar mine. Surface mining resembles quarrying because of the thickness of shale deposits. The availability of surface mining sites is limited, however, because most of the oil shale is deeply buried.

### ENVIRONMENTAL EFFECTS

Saline water deposits are likely to be encountered in oil shale. Inadequate control or careless disposal of this water could result in damage to ground and surface water. Commercial-scale control methods have not yet been demonstrated.

The environmental effects of solid waste from oil shale are due to the large amount of material that must be handled because of the relatively low specific energy content of oil shale. This increases the fixed land requirement for mine operation.

Air emissions due to oil shale extraction are expected from blasting, crushing, and vehicle operations. These may be controlled by wetting to reduce dust and the use of vehicle emission control systems. Mine residuals will be exhausted by the mine ventilation system.

## COAL CONVERSION

### GASIFICATION

The process of producing clean synthetic gas from coal is divided into four basic operations: pretreatment of the coal, gasification of the coal, cleaning of the gas, and gas upgrading. The extent to which pretreatment is necessary depends on the quality of the coal utilized as well as the gasifier type. Pretreatment ranges from simple crushing to the partial devolatilization necessary to prevent caking of coal in the gasifier. The principal component of a coal gasification facility is the gasifier, where coal is combined with oxygen, hydrogen, and heat to produce combustible gases (primarily $CO$, $CH_4$, and $H_2$). To date, there are about 70 gasifiers at various stages of development. The gasifiers vary by method of heat introduction (direct or indirect), oxidant used (air or $H_2$ gas), operating temperature and pressure, and coal-bed type (fixed, fluidized, or entrained). Along with the feed coal characteristics, the above characteristics determine the composition of the coal gas that is termed product gas. Product gas is generally classified as low Btu (100 to 200 Btu/scf) or medium Btu (201 to 500 Btu/scf) gas.

Product gas cleaning generally consists of sequential particulate removal, water quenching, and acid gas removal. The purpose of the water quenching is to cool the product gas to the temperature of the acid gas removal outlet and to remove condensible fractions (e.g., tars, oils, phenols) as well as ammonia. High-temperature acid gas cleaning units are currently under development for which cooling is not required.

Low-Btu product gas may be used on-site as an industrial boiler fuel or to power a combined-cycle electric-power generation unit. Medium-Btu product gas may be used off-site as a combustion fuel, a synthesis gas (chemical feedstock), or it may be upgraded to synthetic natural gas. Upgrading consists of a catalytic water shift conversion to adjust the ratio of hydrogen to carbon monoxide, followed by transfer to a catalytic methanation unit that converts the hydrogen and carbon monoxide to methane.

### Environmental Effects

Coal gasification facilities can emit a wide range of solid, liquid, and gaseous pollutants. It is difficult to generalize about the emissions, however, because both the type and quantity are a function of coal type and facility components (i.e., type of pretreatment, gasifier, gas cleaning, and gas upgrading). For example, the amount of condensate from the water quenching of a Lurgi fixed-bed gasifier is directly related to the coal moisture content, which can range from 2 to 35 percent. The condensate will contain tars and oils whose composition is a function of coal type and gasifier pressure and temperatures. The amount of condensate from the Foster Wheeler entrained-bed gasifier, however, is relatively independent of the coal moisture content. In addition, very few tars and oils are produced because the Foster Wheeler gasifier has a higher operating temperature that tends to crack heavy hydrocarbons. Although emissions vary with coal and facility type, a majority of them can be anticipated and controlled using available emission control technology. A summary of the available information has been provided by Radian Corporation as part of EPA's Synthetic Fuels Assessment Program (Ghassemi et al. 1978, Cavanaugh et al. 1977, Koppenaal and Manahan 1977).

The hazardous organic chemicals and heavy metals that stem from coal conversion facilities are drawing increased concern, however. These chemicals can be divided into three classes: polycyclic aromatic hydrocarbons (PAHs), heavy metals and organometallic compounds, and low molecular weight aromatic compounds. Most of the available information on these materials and their control comes from the petroleum refining and coking industries.

Seven classes of PAH compounds that are either known or suspected carcinogens have been associated with coal conversion wastes (Cavanaugh et al. 1977). The most discussed of these are probably the benzopyrenes. PAHs are created in the gasifier and are absorbed on particulate matter leaving the gasifier and found in the gasifier tars and oils. Thus, PAHs may be found in most of the gaseous, liquid, and solid wastes from coal conversion facilities.

Like PAHs, many of the heavy metals associated with coal gasification emissions are either known or suspected carcinogens. The heavy metals enter the facilities in the coal and in the catalysts used in methanation. They are absorbed onto particulates that leave the facility in gaseous and liquid streams and are present in the coal/char fines, ash, and process sludges. Less is known about the formation and toxicity of the organometallic compounds that may be formed in coal conversion facilities. However, several have been identified in refinery wastes, and the chemical nature of coal in combination with conversion conditions are conducive to the formation of organometallic compounds (Tennessee Valley Authority 1977).

The low molecular weight aromatics are present primarily in the liquid and gaseous waste streams. Of those identified in coal conversion wastes, benzene, the aminobenzenes, and the napthylamines are known or suspected carcinogens.

Technologies to control these substances include activated carbon for the removal of many of the PAHs and low molecular weight aromatics from liquid streams. Various standard particulate removal devices (e.g., electrostatic precipitators and fabric filters) may be applied to the gaseous streams. However, these cannot be applied to the expected fugitive emissions, and the problem of how to dispose of the wastes captured by the control technologies remains unsolved. Although some organic chemicals in petroleum refinery sludges have been shown to be degradable when mixed with soil, the highly aromatic nature of coal conversion sludges may make them less degradable (Cavanaugh et al. 1977). In addition, the sheer volume of the solid wastes associated with coal conversion facilities that could be contaminated with hazardous substances makes disposal an important problem.

LIQUEFACTION

Four steps are involved in the production of synthetic oil from coal: pretreatment of coal, liquefaction of coal, purification of the oil, and upgrading of the oil. Pretreatment, purification, and upgrading depend on the specific liquefaction technology utilized. During pretreatment the coal is sized and then either dried or slurried with a process-derived solvent. The liquefaction processes include direct hydogenation, pyrolysis, and synthesis, with hydrogenation processes the most advanced of the three. Here, the coal is hydrogenated using a hydrogen-rich solvent or by reacting it catalytically with hydrogen gas. In pyrolytic processes the coal is heated in the absence of an oxidant until it decomposes to liquid hydrocarbon, gas, and char. Synthesis processes first utilize the coal to produce a medium-Btu gas, which is then cleaned and reacted over a catalyst to produce liquid fuel.

In all three methods, the resultant liquid fuel must be purified and upgraded before it can be refined. The mixture of liquid and gaseous fuel produced is significantly affected by the technologies utilized. In a detailed analysis of three conversion processes (synthoil, H-coal, and Exxon Donor Solvent), it was found that the gaseous fraction varied from 2 to 1,096, light oil from 10 to 25 percent, middle oil from 5 to 50 percent, and heavy oil from 1 to 45 percent (Ghassemi et al. 1978).

*Environmental Effects*

As with coal gasification facilities, emissions from a coal liquefaction facility will vary significantly with coal type and facility design. The emissions, however, are influenced more by the auxiliary processes (pretreatment, purification, and upgrading) than they are by the coal conversion reactor, as is also the case in gasification. It is expected that a majority of the high-volume wastes from liquefaction, such as $SO_2$, $H_2O$, and $NH_3$, can be handled using presently available control equipment. One exception is the solid residue from the phase separation of the purification system. About 5,000 T/day of waste containing ash, tars, heavy metals, and other hazardous organic and inorganic compounds will be produced by a typical 50,000 b/day (about 25,000 T/day coal input) coal liquefaction facility. Because this waste contains a high percentage of carbon, it has been suggested that it be pyrolyzed to recover oil and then incinerated to recover additional energy (Ghassemi et al. 1978). The feasibility of either process, however, has yet to be demonstrated.

The previous discussion of the smaller volume hazardous emissions from gasification applies equally as well to liquefaction. In addition, the liquid fuel itself contains appreciable quantities of PAHs. This results from the high aromatic content (about 70 percent) of the product, as compared to 30 percent for petroleum crude. Also, because the principal product has a high organic and PAH content, these chemicals will be formed in most of the other process streams. Possible sources of air emissions of volatile organic and inorganic compounds include flue gas emissions, fugitive emissions, and evaporation from wastewater storage and evaporation ponds. As with gasification, the production of substances known or suspected to be carcinogens varies with the conversion process chosen. It has been found that the percentage of carcinogenic compounds in the tar fractions increases rapidly with reactor temperature (Ghassemi et al. 1978).

## OIL SHALE PROCESSING

### SURFACE METHODS

Once oil shale is mined, it must be crushed, retorted, and then upgraded before it can be utilized. Because of the hardness of the shale it is usually crushed in several stages, and the final size may vary from less than 0.5 to 3.1 inches in diameter, depending on the specific retort being used. Retorting is the term used to describe the pyrolytic reaction through which the kerogen (the organic material in oil shale) is released as both a gas and as the heavy oil called shale oil.

Most of the differences in oil shale processing are related to the retort procedure. The principal difference concerns the method in which the heat needed for pyrolysis is supplied. The shale can be heated indirectly, using hot gases or hot solids, or directly, by injecting into the retort a limited amount of air permitting partial combustion of the process gas. An additional process has been developed by Superior Oil Company, which not only produces shale oil but also recovers nahcolite, alumina, and soda ash (sodium carbonate) from the shale. As a result of this mineral recovery, the spent shale (the solid waste from the retort) retains only 90 percent of its original volume. Other processes cause the volume of spent shale to increase by about 12 percent over the amount of shale mined.

The major difference in the energy products of the various processes is in the heating value of the gas produced. Because of its dilution with air, the gas produced by directly heated retorts contains about 100 Btu/scf, while indirectly heated systems produce a gas with about 800 Btu/scf. In the first case, about 20 percent of the energy leaving the retort is contained in the gas, while in the latter case, the gas contains about 10 percent of the energy. Shale oil must be upgraded because of its high nitrogen, sulfur, and paraffin wax content before it can be processed in a conventional refinery. Conventional refinery technology is used in the upgrading.

## Environmental Effects

The principal large-volume emission that must be dealt with is spent shale. A typical proposed facility producing 50,000 b/day of upgraded shale oil (using oil shale containing 30 gallon/ton of shale) would require the disposal of over 53,000 T/day of spent shale. Spent shale has a high salt content as well as toxic elements, such as arsenic, heavy metals, and organics (including PAHs), all of which may leach from the shale. Proposals for the disposal of spent shale include reclamation and containment. Reclamation involves the application of 6 or more inches of top soil to piles of spent shale so that the pile can support vegetation, but revegetation may require large amounts of water for up to 12 years. The success of revegetation on a large-scale basis has not been demonstrated.

Containment would involve building a large basin using compressed spent shale as a building material. Because compressed shale is impermeable to water, the basin would trap water that would not leach the shale. Water from the basin would then be treated periodically to remove contaminants and released to the environment. Another alternative is to return spent shale to the mine for disposal. An underground mine, however, can only accomodate about 60 percent of the spent shale generated. In addition, underground mines must operate for 5 to 10 years, and surface mines up to 30 years, before backfilling can begin. An advantage of the Superior Oil Company process mentioned earlier is that the volume of shale is reduced to the extent that all of the spent shale can be returned to the mine. However, the hazardous substances in the spent shale may leach into underground water.

Low-volume wastes that are potential problems include toxic inorganic chemicals, heavy metals, and PAHs. These substances have been identified in particulate and wastewater streams as well as in the spent shale. A number of PAHs that are known or suspected carcinogens have also been identified in shale oil. The concentration of PAHs in shale oil varies with retort design. It has also been found that the organic content of the spent shale varies inversely with the retort temperature. Thus, the spent shale from directly heated retorting processes (which generally operate at much higher temperatures than do indirect ones) contains smaller amounts of organic compounds.

IN SITU METHODS

In situ processing refers to in-place or underground retorting of oil shale. This mode of processing has received increased attention lately because it reduces some major environmental and handling problems. Environmentally, it greatly reduces or eliminates the spent shale disposal problem and reduces the requirement for water disposal. In situ processing can be classified as either true in situ or modified in situ. The latter requires underground mining of a portion of the oil shale in the seam that is to be processed. Both processes require the same upgrading stage required in surface retorting processes.

In true in situ processes, parallel rows of wells are drilled along two sides of an oil shale deposit. The shale is retorted by injecting a fluid (hot gas or steam) into one side of the deposit. The fluid advances as a temperature or flame front across the shale deposit, thus providing the heat necessary to retort the shale and forcing the retorted oil and gas into the wells on the other side of the deposit. Because most shale is fairly impermeable to liquids and gases, the shale bed must be fractured so that the temperature or flame front can pass through it. This fracturing may be accomplished hydraulically or with explosives. The problems associated with this process have been in achieving consistent fracturing and in maintaining an even flame front. In some cases the problem of fracturing has been bypassed by utilizing certain types of deep shale beds that have some natural permeability, making fracturing unnecessary.

In modified in situ processes, about 20 percent of the shale is removed from the mine using conventional mining techniques. This shale can then be processed using surface retorting technologies. The remaining 80 percent is fractured with explosives. After sealing the shale-filled chamber, air and steam are injected through wells drilled into the top of the chamber and the wells are ignited. As the flame front advances through the fractured shale, the retorted oil flows to a sump chamber and is pumped to the surface. Variations in this process involve the design of the shale chamber, the fracturing technique, and whether or not the chamber is pressurized. Modified in situ processes are generally thought to be much closer to commercialization than true in situ processes.

## Environmental Effects

The true in situ techniques avoid the major environmental problem of surface disposal of spent shale. The modified in situ techniques reduce the problem but do not eliminate it. A combined modified in situ/surface retorting plant producing 50,000 b/day of upgraded oil would produce about 22,000 T/day of spent shale. Some proposals eliminate the spent shale disposal problem by not retorting the excavated shale. In these cases, about 36,000 T/day of raw shale require disposal. However, because raw shale contains inorganic salts, toxic metals, and some toxic organics, its disposal presents a problem. The leaching of hazardous substances into groundwater from in situ retorts may result from fluids injected during the retorting process or from natural water seepage.

## OXIDES OF SULFUR AND NITROGEN

As noted earlier, sulfur is intimately associated with coal (and petroleum) and a substantial degree of its removal, either prior to use, or at the point of use, is now mandatory. As already noted, this may result in a severe solid waste disposal problem. Alternatively, it may result in a significant by-product resource. However, sulfur removal will never be 100 percent efficient, and some sulfur oxides ($SO_x$) will continue to reach the atmosphere as a result of combustion processes. Combustion at very high temperatures with excess oxygen also inevitably results in the creation of some oxides of nitrogen ($NO_x$) that also reach the atmosphere.

Both sulfur and nitrogen oxides tend to be further oxidized in the atmosphere by various spontaneous processes (e.g., reaction with ozone), and these oxides are soluble in water. The end result of these complex atmospheric processes is the creation of sulfurous and sulfuric acids, and nitrous and nitric acids, respectively. The acids may or may not react with ammonia, creating a form of fertilizer capable of inducing eutrophication when it is washed out of the atmosphere with precipitation. If the acids are not absorbed by particles and brought to earth near the point of origin, they are eventually scavenged from the atmosphere by raindrops. The result is "acid rain." This latter problem is mainly attributable to $SO_x$, and occurs in a "plume" up to several hundred miles downwind of a major source, such as a large coal-fired electric-generating plant.

A similar but more localized problem arises in connection with old coal mines and dumps of materials from coal-cleaning operations. The sulfur oxidizes on contact with air and may find its way into surface or groundwaters, and eventually into rivers. In some cases, the level of acidity seriously interferes with natural living systems and processes.

Much scientific knowledge remains to be gathered in regard to the long-term ecological effects of acid rain and acid mine drainage. These are not "new" problems, of course, but their full impact may not yet have been felt and effective countermeasures have yet to be devised.

## THE BUILD-UP OF CARBON DIOXIDE IN THE ATMOSPHERE

The combustion of all carbon-containing fuels creates carbon dioxide ($CO_2$). Fossil fuels in their natural state contain upwards of 80 percent carbon and downwards from 20 percent hydrogen, after allowance for inert elements. Combustion of natural gas yields the minimum amount of $CO_2$ per unit of useful energy output; oil products generate more $CO_2$, and coal yields more still. Synthetic liquids or gas derived from coal generate at least twice as much $CO_2$ per unit of "finished" fuel as natural gas. Thus, the rate of $CO_2$ output in the future will grow faster than the rate of fossil energy consumed.

The build-up of $CO_2$ in the atmosphere has already been measured. In fact, $CO_2$ has increased about 1 ppm/year for the last 20 years, to a level of 330 ppm in 1976. The level was probably about 290 ppm before industrialization began in earnest, say 1850. The climatic impact of an increase in $CO_2$ is known as the "greenhouse effect." On the basis of current mathematical models, it appears that a doubling of the pre-industrial $CO_2$ level (from about 300 to 600 ppm) would result in a higher equilibrium temperature for the lower atmosphere (Manabe and Wetherald 1975). The average worldwide temperature increase would be 2.5°C (4.5°F), but the effect on the poles would be amplified severalfold, perhaps resulting in major changes in weather patterns and areas of precipitation. The consequences for the world's wheat-growing regions, for instance, might be catastrophic.

The dynamic relationship between $CO_2$ emissions and $CO_2$ build-up, however, has not been fully determined. It is known that some of the $CO_2$ added to the atmosphere, perhaps up to 75 percent, is quickly taken up by the surface waters of the oceans. The controlling elements in this process are thought to be temperature itself and $CO_3^-$ ions in solution. The contributions of biological processes to modifying the long-run equilibrium are not known at present, but appear to be minimal.

It would, therefore, appear that the world cannot remain totally dependent on fossil fuels for another century without grave risk. Only the timing and the severity of the climatic impact are really in doubt. This problem quite possibly should be regarded as the most important of all those noted in this discussion.

## CONCLUSIONS

It is difficult to draw reasonable and balanced conclusions about the relative importance of future environmental problems arising from fossil fuel use when so many of the relevant factors are speculative. A number of points do emerge clearly, however.

1. Toxic and hazardous wastes can, for the most part, be eliminated by appropriate process design. The hasty introduction of new coal conversion technology before the "bugs" have been worked out may result in unnecessary environmental impacts.
2. Bulky solid wastes, sludges, and residues will be increasingly produced by the fossil fuels industry. These wastes can be contained and rendered environmentally harmless by appropriate means, but at some cost. Markets for these wastes, particularly as building or paving materials, should be actively developed with help from EPA.
3. Sulfur represents a significant by-product resource, and ways should be sought to recover it in marketable form, e.g., as elemental sulfur or sulfuric acid. The value of this resource will increase as underground deposits of pure sulfur are gradually exhausted.
4. Land disturbance will be an increasingly important problem associated with the extraction and processing of fossil fuels. Land-use planning to reconcile competing demands for water, for instance, will become a practical necessity before the end of the century. New approaches for speeding up the land reclamation process should be actively sought.
5. The $CO_2$ problem is potentially so important that, despite the very long time-horizon involved, efforts to gather needed data and formulate responses should be intensified.

## REFERENCES

Amy, G. and J. Thomas (1979) Factors that Influence the Leaching of Organic Material from In-Situ Spent Shale. Symposium Proceedings, Second Pacific Chemical Engineering Congress, Denver, Colorado.

Bodman, J.R. and R.E. Hamilton (1979) A Comparison of Energy Projections to 1985. Monograph 1. Vienna: International Energy Agency.

Cavanaugh, W.E.C. et al. (1977) Environmental Assessment Data Base for Low/Medium-Btu Gasification Technology: Volumes I and II. EPA-600/7-77-125 a and b. Washington, D.C.: Government Printing Office.

Ford Foundation Energy Policy Project (1974) A Time to Choose. Cambridge, Mass.: Ballinger.

Ghassemi, M. et al. (1978) Applicability of Petroleum Refinery Control Technologies to Coal Conversion. EPA-600/7-78-190. Washington, D.C.: Government Printing Office.

Jones, D.C. et al. (1977) Monitoring Environmental Impacts of the Coal and Oil Shale Industries. EPA-600/7-77-015. Washington, D.C.: Government Printing Office.

Keeling, C.D. and R.B. Bacastou (1977) Impact of Industrial Gases on Cilmate. In: Energy and Climate, Panel on Energy and Climate. Washington, D.C.: National Academy of Sciences.

Koppenaal, D.W. and S.E. Manahan (1977) Hazardous chemicals from coal conversion processes? Environmental Science & Technology 6:1104-1107.

Lang, D.D. (1977) The Environmental Impact of Oil Sands Processing on Land Reclamation. Symposium Proceedings, Second Pacific Chemical Engineering Congress, Denver, Colorado.

Lantze, U. (1979) Welcome and opening remarks. Workshop on Energy Data of Developing Countries. International Energy Agency, Organization for Economic Cooperation and Development, Paris.

Leo, P.P. and J. Rossoff (1978) Controlling $SO_2$ Emissions from Coal-Fired Steam-Electric Generators: Solid Waste Impact, Volume II, Technical Discussion. EPA-600/7-78-044b. Washington, D.C.: Government Printing Office.

Lovins, A. (1979) Address to the International Conference on Energy Use Management, Los Angeles, California, Oct. 25, 1979.

Manabe, S. and R. Wetherald (1975) The effects of doubling the $CO_2$ concentration on the climate of a general circulation model. J. Atmos. Sci. 32:3-15.

MITRE Corp. (1979) Energy, economic and environmental impacts of a national energy initiative, TAC Briefing paper. McLean, Va.: MITRE Corp.

National Petroleum Council (1972) Page 37, U.S. Energy Outlook. Washington, D.C.

Office of the White House Press Secretary (1979) Fact Sheet on the President's Import Reduction Program. Washington, D.C.

Parker, C.L. and D.I. Dykstra, eds. (1978) Environmental Assessment Data Base for Coal Liquefaction Technology: Volume II, Synthoil, H-Coal, and Exxon Donor Solvent Processes. EPA-600/7-78-184b. Washington, D.C.: Government Printing Office.

Planning Research Corp. (1978) Energy Demands, 1972-2000, PRC Energy Analysis Company, prepared for the Environmental and Resource Assessment Branch, Division of Solar Technology, U.S. Department of Energy. Washington, D.C.: Planning Research Corp.

Ridker, R.V. and W.D. Watson (In Press) To Choose a Future: Resource and Environmental Problems of the U.S., Long Term Global Outlook. Washington, D.C.: Resources for the Future, Inc.

Root, D.H. and E.D. Attainasi (1979) World Petroleum Availability. 37th Annual Technical Conference, Society of Plastics Engineers, New Orleans, Louisiana.

Tennessee Valley Authority (1977) Utility Boiler Design/Cost Comparison: Fluidized-Bed Combustion Versus Flue Gas Desulfurization. EPA-600/7-77-126. Washington, D.C.: Government Printing Office.

University of Oklahoma, Science and Public Policy Program (1975) Energy Alternatives: A Comparative Analysis. GPO No. 041-011-00025-4. Washington, D.C.: Government Printing Office.

U.S. Central Intelligence Agency (1979) The World Oil Market in the Years Ahead. Washington, D.C.: Government Printing Office.

*Wall Street Journal*, August 17, 1979.

White, I.L. et al. (1979) Energy from the West: Energy Resource Development Systems Report, Volumes II and III, EPA-600/7-79-060 b and c. Washington, D.C.: Government Printing Office.

# DISCUSSANT'S REMARKS ON THE PAPER BY R. AYRES ET AL.

H. E. KOENIG
*Michigan State University*

The following additional points need to be made in reference to the future energy costs, supplies, demands, and delivery systems for the deployment of fossil based energy.

## ENERGY COSTS

One effective measure of the real cost of energy is the ratio of the consumer cost in dollars per unit of energy to the average industrial wage rate in dollars per hour. Data from the U.S. statistical abstracts show that this ratio, which represents the average hours of labor required to deliver a unit of energy to final consumption, decreased by more than 5 percent per year from 1940 to 1973 as indicated in Figure 7. From 1973 through at least 1977, the real cost as determined by this ratio, increased at a rate of 4.8 percent for electricity and 14.7 percent for natural gas. Similar changes pertain to petroleum-based fuels. Much of this increase in real cost is

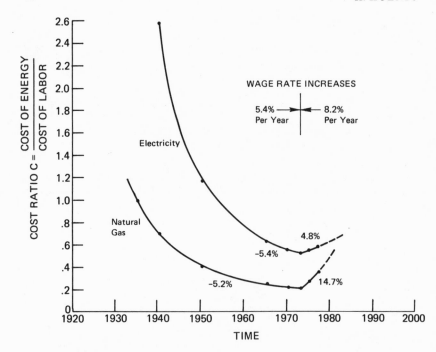

FIGURE 7   Changing cost of energy relative to wage rates.

directly attributed to the growing engineering difficulties of deploying our energy resources, including both recovery and environmental protection.

One measure of the technological and engineering difficulties involved in deploying resources is the *energy gain, G,* defined as the ratio of the gross energy delivered by an energy deployment system over its useful lifetime to the energy invested in building, operating, and maintaining the system.

The theoretical real cost of producing energy from any given system is given by $C = G/(G\text{-}1)$ (Michigan Transportation Research Program 1978). The theoretical cost, $C$, which represents the ratio of money cost of the energy delivered to the pecuniary costs of conversion (all nonenergy costs, including labor) is essentially unity for high-gain systems but increases without bound as the gain approaches unity.

Although there are computational difficulties in assessing the energy gain of alternative systems, the following general perspectives can be provided:

1. When oil and gas were first tapped in Oklahoma and Texas, the energy gain of the recovery and distribution systems was on the order of

hundreds, whereas gains from present domestic wells are on the order of 35 to 45.

2. The gain of synthetic fuels from coal is in the vicinity of 15 ± 5.

3. The gain from light water reactors is in the vicinity of 10 ± 5. (Preliminary assessments suggest that the gain of the breeder reactor may be as high as 35 or 40; if this proves to be the case, then its potential significance extends beyond simply that of being another source of energy.)

4. The gain from most renewable resources (except for high-head hydro and high-velocity wind regimes) are generally less than 10.

Although the gain of the energy conversion systems can be improved to a degree by technological innovation, there apparently will be a long-term irreversible decline in the aggregate gain of our resources as we move from natural oil and gas to alternatives. Therefore, on physical and engineering grounds it can be inferred that the real cost of energy will increase in the foreseeable future, even though it is not possible as yet to estimate the rate.

## POTENTIAL ENERGY SUPPLIES

Growth in energy consumption in the United States by fuel types since 1920 is shown in Figure 7, along with future gross supplies that from a technical and engineering perspective (without regard for cost) potentially could be made available through the year 2000 (Hayes 1979, Duane 1977).

Limitations on our energy supplies are determined not simply by the quantities of energy present in our environment or the gross production capacity of the energy industry, but by the fraction of gross production that can be made available for consumer end-use at any given point in time. This may be substantially less than the gross projections indicated in Figure 8.

The net energy, $N$, available for consumer end-use from alternative sources and technologies can also be quantified in terms of the energy gain, $G$, defined in the above section. It is given by $N = 1 - 1/G$. A comparison of the range of energy gains attainable from alternative energy sources shows a decline in net energy returns as we move from natural oil and gas to alternatives. These very basic and apparently irreversible changes in the technical characteristics of our energy resources assuredly will or should have long-term implications to comprehensive environmental protection policies and programs.

The net energy delivered to end-use *at any given point in time* by an expanding energy industry depends both on the rate, $R$, of industrial growth *and* on the energy gain, $G$, of energy conversion processes used by the industry. Of particular concern is the time delay after the initial

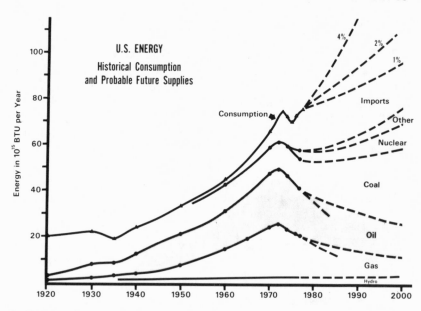

FIGURE 8   U.S. gross energy supplies.

development of a new conversion system when the industry becomes a net producer, rather than a consumer of energy—the *break-even point*. This time delay is shown in Figure 9 as a function of the system gain, *G*, and industrial development rates, *R* (Duane and Dumas, work in progress).

Because of the declining gain of the aggregate resources *and* the time delay in net-energy returns from developing energy industries, the fraction of the gross energy in the year 2000 that might be available for end-use is significantly less than it was in 1978. Hayes (1979), for example, estimates that 95 quads of gross energy in 2000 is roughly equivalent to 90 quads in 1978, and that per capita energy growth must come to a halt in the 1990s. This estimate is most likely overly optimistic because it apparently does not take into consideration the delayed break-even points associated with high growth rates of low-gain alternatives, adaptations in end-use equipment, and many other structural changes involved in switching from universally applicable liquid and gas fuels to less versatile alternatives.

If the above assessments are correct, then declining aggregate gains and rising real costs of energy provide a somewhat new context for environmental regulation:

1. The demands for energy in the United States may stabilize or

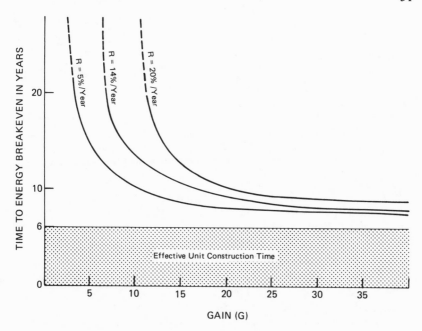

FIGURE 9  Time to positive energy returns (breakeven point) in relationship to energy gains, G, and industrial growth rate, R.

actually decline somewhat in the face of inevitable increases in the real cost of energy. Conservation (broadly defined) is now an imperative to maintaining our standard of living, and there is ample opportunity for reducing energy requirements through technological improvements, increased product life, and adjustments in land-use patterns to reduce the need for travel and to pave the way for more efficient modes of transportation and district heating systems. Per capita energy consumption in the United States in 1950 was approximately half the 1973 levels.

2. The systems for the deployment of energy will almost surely become more decentralized in the future. During the era of declining real energy costs, the real cost of most consumer products, on the average, decreased from year to year. These reductions were the result of well documented benefits of energy and capital-intensive technologies and large-scale centralized and specialized operations. However, these benefits, achieved at the expense of longer food chains and open material and energy loops, are generally available only in an era of declining real energy costs.

In an era of rising real energy costs, sustained reductions in the real cost of basic commodities may not be possible under any conditions. The hope is to reduce the *rate of increase* in the real cost of energy, food, and other consumer products. In the long term, such reductions can be realized through the selective integration of unit operations and regional and community economic diversifications rather than continued differentiations of operations and regional specialization.

Rising real costs of energy and increased dependence on biologically derived resources, for example, will eventually have a significant impact on human settlements. Rural and urban communities will become increasingly dependent upon the *integrated* use of forests and other ecological and physical resources (e.g., wind, hydro, solar-thermal) as supplements or partial replacements for nonrenewable materials and energy resources. Of particular import is the economic feasibility of promoting the evolution of the existing urban/suburban structures toward multinucleated cities. This requires an increase in the intensity and economic diversity of land use around existing malls and community centers so as to support both public transportation and district heating systems and to reduce the need for travel. Areas in between that are currently dominated by 5- to 80-acre plots could remain low density, preserving the option for high-intensity garden farming and recreation at some point in the future.

Direct burning of coal in medium or small cogeneration facilities in the context of such land-use patterns has the potential for reducing local emission levels because of the reduced scale of each plant. It has the potential for reducing the regional and national levels by virtue of the increased thermo-efficiency of the integrated community energy system. It has the potential for greatly reducing social problems involved in power plant siting because the perceived environmental risks are closely identified with the benefits.

Likewise, grid-connected wind electric systems may find their early application as an integral part of integrated energy farms where the marginal labor costs for maintenance are low and the basic maintenance skills are readily available on the farm. Risks are directly associated with the benefits, and marginal environmental impacts are small.

## RECOMMENDATION

The potential for reducing environmental risks and pollution control costs by the deployment of integrated community energy systems appears to be very great and consistent with economic conditions of the future. However, to avail ourselves of these opportunities, EPA (perhaps in conjunction with other agencies) must take a lead role in evaluating the environmental risks and economic benefits of such alternatives in relationship to the present highly centralized and nonintegrated system. Such assessments are necessary *now* to accommodate the long lead times (decades) required to make the necessary adjustments in land-use and other structural changes in the economy.

## REFERENCES

Duane, J.W. (1977) World and national oil and gas demand and supply. Aware Magazine, October.
Duane, J.W. and R.M. Dumas (In press) Net Energy Analysis: Analysis of Gain, Rate of Development and Breakeven Time. Jackson, Mich.: Consumers Power Co.
Hayes, E.T. (1979) Energy resources available to the United States, 1985 to 2000. Science 203:233-239.
Michigan Transportation Research Program (1978) Coping with Energy Limitations in Transportation: Proposals for Michigan. Ann Arbor, Mich.

# SUMMARY OF THE TASK GROUP

P. McCARTY, *Stanford University*
J. RICHARDSON, *National Research Council*

## INTRODUCTION

The United States will be striving to achieve a satisfactory balance between environmental protection and the provision of its overall energy needs over the next 20 to 50 years. The purpose of this Task Group on Energy was to recommend research that will underlie this task.

The actual mixture of energy sources that is put into place will be affected by three interrelated factors: level of demand; costs of different sources of supply, including costs of environmental protection; and public acceptability of the risks of particular technologies. Some appreciation of these factors guided the direction and scope of the research recommendations of the Task Group.

Projections of demand are important because environmental impact is probably sensitively dependent on the level of energy production, especially as we approach permissible environmental loading. This relationship must be understood through research, wherever the incremental impact might be disproportionate to the incremental production. On the one hand, demand will increase because of growing populations and growing energy use per capita in the United States and other nations. On the other hand, demand is modified by opportunities for conservation, which become increasingly attractive as the price of energy rises. Some members of the Task Group felt strongly that conservation will become more and more significant—even to the point of stabilizing the level of demand—as the real cost of energy inevitably grows. At any rate, the magnitude of the environmental research problem is closely related to the magnitude of demand.

The second factor—costs of different sources of supply—would be especially sensitive to research yielding improved processes of production and environmental protection. New technologies are being actively devised and will almost surely come on line in both the near and long-term future in response to the decline in domestic oil and gas supplies and the uncertainty and global competition for foreign liquid and gaseous fuels. Each of these technologies will have its own environmental impacts. As the cost of controlling the impacts of one technology rises or falls, the competitiveness of an alternative technology rises or falls. Research that provides reliable information on the nature and magnitude of such impacts and their associated costs is important to policy choices that will enable the achievement of an optimum mix of supply.

The third factor—public acceptability of environmental risk—must certainly be approached, at least, from the soundest factual and analytical information about risk that can be assembled. Research on environmental risks and their variation with different control measures is important to sound industrial and governmental decisions and the presentation to the public of the facts that underlie these decisions.

Although we can perceive these broad factors in the energy-environment balance, our ability to make highly specific research recommendations is blunted by the uncertainties at lower levels of detail. For example, the total U.S. energy demand has been projected only to lie within a broad range: 90 to 120 quads/year by the year 2000. The dependence of quantity on price is not well known. As to supply, we certainly do not have a comprehensive picture of the specific technologies that will become available within the next 50 years. Nor do we know the rate of development and deployment of those technologies that we can identify. Nevertheless, the identification and recommendations of the Task Group were guided, at least in part, by the rationale described here and, in part, by the need for research to narrow some of the very uncertainties just mentioned.

## IDENTIFICATION OF FUTURE PROBLEM AREAS

This Task Group considered that future problem areas could best be approached by examining the specific newer technologies that are candidates for significant energy production. Study of the extraction, conversion, distribution, and use characteristics of these technologies would reveal a number of environmental problems specific to each. Generic problems, common to many technologies, would also be recognized. These specific technologies are listed and briefly discussed below.

### COAL TECHNOLOGY

Energy in recoverable coal resources is large compared to the projected U.S. energy consumption between now and 2030. Hence, coal will probably remain a significant and growing source of energy over the next 25- to 50-year period. However, the environmental problems in its extraction, cleaning, transportation, conversion to gaseous and liquid fuels, distribution, and management of gaseous, liquid, and solid waste streams will produce both environmental disturbances and the generation of a wide range of toxic materials. Atmospheric and downwind effects of increased $CO_2$, $SO_x$, $NO_x$ and various particulate are common to coal and other fossil fuel technologies.

### NUCLEAR BREEDER REACTOR

The breeder reactor is the only nuclear technology that has the potential to become a large energy resource when compared to energy demand over the next 20 to 50 years. Consequently, the environmental aspects of the breeder reactor figure importantly in its technological evaluation. Radiobiology and radiation health, use of "waste" heat, and long-term storage of wastes will be major environmental problems.

### OIL SHALE AND TAR SANDS TECHNOLOGY

These technologies have in common the disruption of large portions of the topography and the production of large amounts of solid waste materials. The substantially larger $CO_2$ release in preparing fuels from oil shale is an especially difficult problem.

GEOPRESSURE

In places where geopressure becomes an important local source of energy, the possibility of toxic or polluting emissions—such as oxides and salts of sulfur—must be examined.

SOLAR ENERGY

Photovoltaic solar energy conversion may involve environmental problems arising from the large-scale manufacture of specialized solid-state devices such as those using gallium and arsenic. In addition, the typically large areas necessary for photovoltaic and other solar energy systems could present land-use problems.

WIND POWER

Wind power is technically attractive because the ratio of energy produced to energy invested during the life cycle of wind power equipment is rather large, typically 25 to 30. Wind power installations may have an impact upon the local ecology, in particular, upon bird species.

BIOMASS

This Task Group noted that biomass production interacts closely with the subject matter that was considered by the Task Group on Agriculture. The latter is best equipped to discuss the trade-offs between food production and biomass production on agriculturally marginal land.

THERMAL AQUIFER STORAGE AND UNDERGROUND PUMP STORAGE

Utilization of these storage methods would have an impact on the ecology of a region because of the thermal exchange and the modification of normal geologic conditions that would be occasioned by their use.

OCEAN THERMAL ENERGY CONVERSION (OTEC)

Environmental effects are not well known but are not presumed to be negligible. OTEC systems must pump large volumes of deep ocean water to the surface. Surface temperature may change over a large area, and the nutrient material brought to the surface may cause algal blooming. Increased amounts of carbon dioxide may be released to the atmosphere.

FUEL CELL AND MAGNETOHYDRODYNAMICS

These technologies will be of environmental concern largely because of the specialized materials that must be employed in their manufacture and utilization. The impacts resulting from release of these materials must be carefully considered.

SOLAR POWER SATELLITE

The solar power satellite concept involves using very large geosynchronous orbiting photovoltaic surfaces and beaming high-power microwave radiation to the earth's surface from space; the biological and atmospheric effects of microwave radiation are not well known. Furthermore, launching of the satellites will deposit large amounts of rocket exhaust at all elevations of the atmosphere. A major study of the environmental, economic, social, and political impact of this technology is currently under way in several quarters.

FUSION

The Task Group on Energy was no more able to address the specific environmental consequences of fusion than any other group has been. The ultimate configuration of fusion energy production is simply not known, because the requisite scientific advances have not yet been made. However, should fusion come into use within the next 50 years, it is almost certain that it, too, will bring environmental problems. One of these will be associated with the control of tritium; another will be associated with a large-scale use of the "exotic" materials and processes necessary to the operation of fusion processes.

## PROBLEM PRIORITIES

The Task Group recognizes that over the next 50 years, major changes in demand, available production technologies, and available techniques for environmental protection will evolve. Because the long-term future is so difficult to predict, the Task Group quite naturally gives priority to shorter-term research issues.

Coal received priority over other forms of energy production simply because it appears today to be the most abundant fuel and, arguably, a relatively manageable one from an environmental point of view. Expansion in the use of nuclear technology while considered probable was not developed in great detail, because its use involves greater uncertainties, and this technology falls more within the mission of the U.S. Nuclear Regulatory Commission (NRC) than within that of the EPA. However, EPA should remain alert to its special mandate to protect the environment, and if the NRC fails to address this issue, EPA will have to do so.

By and large, domestic issues took priority over international ones. Nevertheless, it was recognized that there are important connections between the international and domestic energy scenes, such as ocean spills of fossil liquid fuels, radiation contamination, and global production of $CO_2$, $SO_x$, $NO_x$, and particulates. Continued research on the international environmental aspects of energy technologies will certainly be necessary. To this end, EPA should continue developing interaction with foreign scientific experts.

In order to discuss priorities in further detail, an ideal analysis of the impact of energy production on the environment would be useful. Such an analysis would consist of a table of environmental consequences for each technology at several assumed levels of production. These consequences would include:

1. the identification of the magnitude and geographic locations of the environmentally significant emission streams for alternative technologies in relationship to levels of energy produced,

2. assessment of the environmental risks associated with each stream in relationship to the ecological and physical characteristics of local and regional environments, and

3. assessment of the real and economic costs of reducing the emission streams to acceptable risk levels.

Such a task would provide a comparative assessment of alternative technologies. It would identify the economies and diseconomies of scale that could be expected and it would form a basis for choosing an environmentally optimum supply mix. However, because of the uncertainties mentioned in the introduction, the Task Group hesitated to recommend such a comprehensive research task. Instead, a less structured approach to research based on the following assumptions was finally suggested.

Environmental assessments for many technologies have already been carried out by the Assistant Secretary for Environment of the U.S. Department of Energy (DOE). The assessments are embodied in their Environmental Developmental Plans (EDPs). At the preliminary developmental stage of many of these technologies, it is assumed that EDPs would provide satisfactory interim information on research issues. The technology of greatest importance in meeting long-term energy needs is assumed to be coal, followed by the recovery of fossil fuel from oil shale and tar sands.

It is assumed that the production of energy will have a much larger impact on the environment than occurred heretofore. Therefore, it will be important to analyze energy-environment interactions in a more comprehensive and holistic way. It will no longer be adequate, for example, simply to specify permissible concentrations of individual contaminants. We must rather strive to understand the total effect of many burdens on the entire ecosystem. As one participant said: "By undertaking the recovery of coal and other fossil fuels so intensively we are proposing to unlock things that have been locked away for millenia in our geological structures."

As a part of the process of seeking public acceptance for the commitment to various technologies, it is assumed that risks must be adequately assessed and communicated. Accordingly, we need improved knowledge of exposure levels and their health and environmental consequences. To this end, improved methods for epidemiological surveys and risk assessment will be important topics for research.

## RECOMMENDATIONS

Broad cross-cutting long-range environmental research topics concerning these next-generation technologies include understanding the toxic properties and biogeochemistry of exotic materials, the use of which is likely to increase dramatically if several of these technologies expand. Tritium will be a problem both in fusion and breeder technologies, and more research on its environmental and health effects is warranted.

The research that the Task Group on Energy deems necessary to achieving a satisfactory balance between environmental protection and energy needs is outlined in the recommendations that follow. When properly compiled, the results of such research would provide a useable and accessible data base that would serve at least three purposes. It would support the decision makers who must choose which alternative technologies are to be emphasized; guide the developers of the technologies in minimizing environmental impacts; and educate those who will be responsible for the continuing regulation of the resulting industries.

Although the recommendations are arranged in rough order of priority, the ranking should not be viewed too literally.

1. Improved methods of assessing risk incurred vs. benefit expected, together with the cost of controlling risks at acceptable levels, are basic to judgments on the deployment of future energy technology.

Research on improving the assessment of these risks should be process-oriented; that is, it should deal with the various operations in the energy production-consumption-residual management chain from extraction through transportation, distribution, and deposition of waste products. The risks may variously affect occupational groups, different sectors of the public, vegetation, particular ecosystems, materials used in commerce, and so forth. This research should range broadly from theoretical modeling and simulation to specific site assessments to retrospective case studies. More effort needs to be expended in getting scientists, economists, and public administration specialists working in sustained team efforts.

2. Statistical studies to determine health effects on human populations from various environmental aspects of energy technologies can constitute valuable quantitative input to risk assessment. Such studies must be started early because of the long lead time required for the acquisition of significant data. They should involve both prospective and retrospective analyses designed around programs at the scale of pilot demonstrations. They should focus on the occupational work force, which is likely to receive greater exposure than the general population and will thus serve as a preview of the more general impact of a technology.

3. More research is needed on the environmental effects of present and projected future loadings of $SO_x$, $NO_x$, trace heavy metals, and trace organic compounds. The trend for emission streams of such pollutants is inevitably upward. Consequently, full scientific understanding of their effects is necessary for adequate control. Research aimed at improving removal of sulfur oxides, nitrogen oxides, and toxic substances from emissions streams at reduced costs should be undertaken.

4. Methods for the deposition and storage of solid wastes in an environmentally sound and aesthetically acceptable manner must be devised. These wastes promise to grow because of increased levels of production and the lower grade of remaining fuel ores. New techniques of landscape restoration will be required that will ensure the replacement of suitable vegetation cover and will not result in contamination of water, land, and air resources.

5. Comparative assessments on both a technical and socioeconomic basis should be developed for the environmental problems associated with those alternative energy technologies available for present choice. These assessments will put the risks, environmental benefits, and control costs in perspective to permit comparison of the choices between coal, oil shale, nuclear, and solar energy. The technical and

socioeconomic comparisons should include assessments on the basis of both a system-wide average and a "best plant" marginal examination.

6. The build-up of atmospheric carbon dioxide could result in potential global impacts, and thus requires continuing research emphasis. If coal and oil shale energy are exploited to a substantial degree, carbon dioxide build-up could occur on a scale far greater than it ever has before. Its global consequences must be fully appreciated before any irrevocable commitment to rely primarily on these technologies is made.

7. The recovery of resources from the waste by-products of energy technology could conceivably reduce the disposal problem and help in energy conservation. Accordingly, research should be undertaken to facilitate the recovery in useable form of substances like sulfur and nitrogen, as well as the manufacture of building materials such as gypsum and cement from flyash, sludges, and tailing.

8. The research of the EPA on residuals must be made consistent; data should be collected in a systematic fashion that reflects the basic differences among ecosystem abilities to handle different residuals. This research should address the capability of an ecosystem to receive a continuing input of residuals (for example, sulfur and nitrogen). The ecological carrying capacity of different ecosystems must be determined.

9. Research on ecosystems must be intensified to provide rigorous scientific definition and understanding of concepts such as resiliency, ecological recovery, and so forth. The result of such research would provide a sounder scientific basis for judging and defining the ecological impact of energy technologies.

10. Once assessments of existing or soon-to-be-developed technologies have been scheduled, the technical and socioeconomic assessment of the environmental problems associated with long-range energy technologies must be undertaken. Technologies such as magnetohydrodynamics, solar power satellites, and nuclear fusion may become candidates for investment in the total mix of energy supply. At such a time, knowledge of the environmental consequences must be at hand, which means research must begin now.

11. Solar energy will bring new materials and new patterns of land use into play. Therefore, we may expect new environmental consequences. These consequences should be explored to help ensure that the most environmentally sound choices are made as solar energy develops to supply a greater proportion of total energy.

12. Continuing research efforts are needed to assess the primary

and secondary environmental impacts that might result from the large-scale use of exotic materials—such as chromium, gallium, niobium, titanium, and vanadium—required by the advanced energy technologies that will become candidates in the long-range future.

The above recommendations are certainly not well enough detailed to constitute a program plan. Nevertheless, the Task Group on Energy believes that these recommendations represent a fair identification of the salient problems that will result from energy production in the short-range and possibly the long-range future. The importance of these research recommendations flows from the fact that the satisfaction of national and global energy demands in the face of declining quantity and quality of mineral resources will constitute one of the greatest burdens that man will place on his environment.

# TASK GROUP ON ENERGY

PERRY McCARTY (*Group Chairman*), Stanford University
STANLEY AUERBACH, Oak Ridge National Laboratory
ROBERT AYRES (*Paper Author*), Carnegie-Mellon University
JOEL DARMSTADTER, Resources for the Future
HARRY ETTINGER, Los Alamos Scientific Laboratory
DAN GOLOMB, U.S. Environmental Protection Agency
HERMAN KOENIG (*Discussant*), Michigan State University
JAY KOPELMAN, Electric Power Research Institute
DON LEWIS, U.S. Environmental Protection Agency
KENT REED, Argonne National Laboratories
PAOLO RICCI, Electric Power Research Institute
JOHN RICHARDSON (*Rapporteur*), National Research Council
LOWELL SMITH, U.S. Environmental Protection Agency

63

# $4$ Agriculture

## FUTURE TRENDS IN AGRICULTURE TECHNOLOGY AND MANAGEMENT

S. H. WITTWER
*Michigan State University*

### INTRODUCTION

The world, including the United States, is in the midst of the greatest food production program ever known. This agricultural revolution is of recent origin.[1] Historical statistics show that until the early 1940s any increases in yields per hectare of the major food crops in the United States were trivial. The connection between yields per unit of land area and World War II was direct (Harlan 1977). It was in the course of manufacturing explosives for the war that the industrialized nations acquired the technology to chemically fix nitrogen on a large scale. After the war, this technology was directed toward the production of nitrogen fertilizer. Organochemical pesticides (insecticides, fungicides, antibiotics, and chemical growth regulants) had a parallel origin, many having been developed to control the insect-transmitted diseases that afflicted armed forces in the tropics. These resource inputs now play a key role in agricultural productivity.

## AGRICULTURAL DEVELOPMENT IN THE UNITED STATES

Scientific development of agriculture in the United States was initiated on July 2, 1862, when President Lincoln signed the Morrill Act. This act created the land grant institutions and served as the cornerstone for the establishment of colleges of agriculture. Twenty-five years later, in 1887, President Cleveland signed into law the Hatch Act, under whose provisions agricultural experiment stations were established at each land grant institution and a federal-state partnership for funding agricultural research was established.

It took a long time for laboratory research studies and experimental field trials to be translated into increased crop yields per hectare. According to Mayer and Mayer (1974), there were no measurable effects from the establishment of the agricultural experiment stations until the mid-1920s. But results since the 1940s have been phenomenal (see Figure 10), and

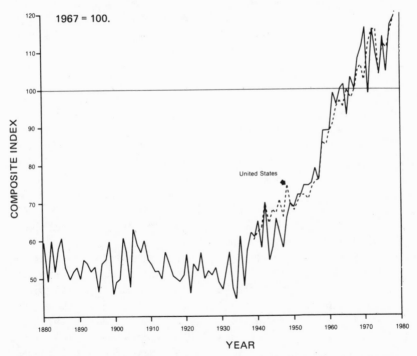

The author is grateful for the assistance of Karl T. Wright, Professor Emeritus of Agricultural Economics, Michigan State University.

FIGURE 10   Composite index of crop yields, Michigan, 1880-1978.

estimated annual returns for investments in agricultural research are now on the order of 50 percent (Evenson et al. 1979). The 1950s and 1960s could be referred to as the "golden age" of American agricultural productivity. After a century of level outputs, the composite index of crop yields doubled within 25 years (see Figure 10). The ingredients of the system consisted of labor-saving technologies, progressively larger-scale operations, and massive inputs of capital, management, and resources. The focus has been more and more on single crop and single livestock systems.

American food production technology has had an important impact abroad as well as at home. During 1978, agricultural exports approximated $29 billion, and they could be as high as $40 billion for 1979. World food supplies heretofore have kept ahead of population. During the 1965 to 1975 decade, the developing countries increased their food production by 38 percent. There is now more food per person, on a global scale, than at any time in recent history. It is well-recognized, however, that food production alone is not enough. Equally important are delivering the food to the people who need it and providing them with the money to buy it. Only poor people go hungry. The primary cause of world hunger now is not a shortage of food. It is poverty.

CURRENT OUTLOOK

A reassessment of our technologies for agricultural production is now called for. No longer is it sufficient simply to "produce two ears of corn or two blades of grass where only one grew before." The United States must irreversibly change its reliance on nonrenewable resources to a reliance on renewable resources. This may not be true of many agriculturally developing countries that may find it necessary to skip, at least in part, the fossil fuel era (Brown and Howe 1978). But as nutritionist Jean Mayer pointed out in 1975, world population growth means that "we have to find in the next 25 years food for as many people again as we have been able to develop in the whole history of man 'til now."[2]

Over 70 percent of the world population is located in the less developed countries, where several hundreds of millions of people are already suffering from malnutrition. Yet projections show a growth of 85 percent in the populations of those countries in the forthcoming decades. The National Research Council's *World Food and Nutrition Study* (1977) says it will be necessary to increase food production by at least 3 to 4 percent per year between now and the start of the next century if significant nutritional improvement is to occur.

During the last 20 years, the outlook for food production has shifted back and forth. In the mid-1960s, the 2-year drought in India and Pakistan cast a cloud of doom. In the late 1960s the "green revolution's" progress aroused a happy euphoria. The poor harvests of 1972 to 1974 brought new predictions of doomsday. More recently, food grain surpluses again abound (see Table 2), the set-aside acreage program again flourishes in the United States, and record harvests for corn, soybeans, and wheat are projected for 1979. But there will be further crises because of the ever-precarious balance between people, climate, and food.

Nonetheless, the contention of the most recent prophets of doom that we have reached the limits of agricultural technology and resources is puzzling. There once was a widespread belief that in the mid- and late-1970s diminishing food production would cause starvation in many areas. But it is local wars that have caused starvation, not agricultural failure. Judgments about the future are too often made on the basis of existing technology. As technology advances, so does the range of natural resources. Far from reaching its scientific or biological limits, the world has only begun to explore the possibilities for increasing food production. Basic and applied research can be the catalysts for stimulating governmental and private sector efforts to increase production stability and expand food supplies.[3] This paper focuses on technological and resource management options to deal effectively with the resolution of agricultural problems.

## EVENTS OF THE 1970s[4]

Many important events related to food production transpired during the 1970s. International agricultural research centers increased in number from 4 to 13, and the current annual budget for these centers now approximates $135 million. A Consultative Group for International Agricultural Research (CGIAR) was created along with its food research priority body, the Technical Advisory Committee. A World Food Conference was convened at Rome in 1974, and an International Conference on Crop Productivity was held in 1975 at Boyne Highlands, Michigan. There was the World Food Conference of 1976 in Ames, Iowa, and the *World Food and Nutrition Study* (NRC 1977) conducted by the National Academy of Sciences. A Famine Prevention and Freedom from Hunger Act was passed by Congress, along with the International Development Cooperation Act of 1978. An Institute for Science and Technological Cooperation has been created this year, whose research and development efforts will be directed primarily at international agricultural problems. It will enhance cooperation between American universities and the U.S. Agency for International Development (AID). Major university-linked programs on small ruminants (California), sorghum and millet

TABLE 2  Major Agricultural and Food Events, United States, 1971-1978*

| Item | 1971 | 1972 | 1973 | 1974 | 1975 | 1976 | 1977 | 1978 | 1979 |
|---|---|---|---|---|---|---|---|---|---|
| Set aside land ($10^6$ acres) | 37 | 62 | 20 | 0 | 0 | 0 | 0 | 14 | |
| Grain stocks ($10^6$ metric tons) | 51 | 69 | 42 | 31 | 27 | 35 | 60 | 74 | |
| Agricultural exports ($10^9$ $) | 8 | 9 | 18 | 22 | 22 | 23 | 24 | 29 | |
| Prices paid by farmers for nitrogen (¢/lb.) | 4.8 | 4.9 | 5.4 | 11.2 | 16.2 | 11.6 | 11.1 | 10.2 | |
| Yields of corn (bu/acre) | 88 | 97 | 91 | 71 | 86 | 86 | 91 | 101 | |
| Milk production per cow ($10^3$ pounds) | 10.0 | 10.2 | 10.1 | 10.3 | 10.4 | 10.9 | 11.2 | 11.2 | |
| Price of corn ($/bu.) | 1.08 | 1.57 | 2.55 | 3.03 | 2.55 | 2.15 | 2.02 | 2.20 | |
| Price of wheat ($/bu.) | 1.34 | 1.76 | 3.95 | 4.09 | 3.55 | 2.73 | 2.33 | 2.94 | |
| Price of soybeans ($/bu.) | 3.03 | 4.37 | 5.68 | 6.64 | 4.92 | 6.81 | 5.88 | 6.75 | |
| Price of sugar, U.S. raw duty paid equivalent, N.Y. (¢/lb.) | 8.5 | 9.1 | 10.3 | 29.5 | 22.5 | 13.3 | 11.0 | | |
| Producer price index of fuels and related products and power (1967 = 100) | 114 | 119 | 134 | 208 | 245 | 266 | 302 | 322 | |
| Income expended for food (%) | 16.4 | 16.3 | 16.3 | 17.0 | 17.1 | 16.8 | 16.6 | 16.5 | |
| Enrollments, colleges of agriculture ($10^3$ students) | 60 | 65 | 73 | 82 | 91 | 98 | 98 | 98 | |
| Gross agricultural income ($10^9$ $) | 61 | 70 | 95 | 100 | 100 | 102 | 108 | 126 | |
| Federal funding of agricultural food and nutrition research | | | | | | | | | |
| Cooperative Research (payments to states) | 60 | 63 | 67 | 68 | 85 | 98 | 125 | 148 | 153 |
| Agricultural Research Service | 179 | 192 | 208 | 205 | 224 | 251 | 287 | 337 | 323 |

*Data provided with the assistance of John N. Ferris, Professor of Agricultural Economics, Michigan State University.

(Nebraska), fisheries and aquaculture (Arkansas, Hawaii, Michigan, Oregon), peanuts (Georgia), field beans and cowpeas (Michigan), and marginal nutritional deficiencies (California) have begun. An International Agricultural Development Service (IADS) has been created to provide information for and strengthen national agricultural research centers.

What of the green revolution? Approximately 44 percent of the wheat and 27 percent of the rice in the developing countries now comes from the new high-yielding varieties. Much of the improvement from new varieties can be ascribed to irrigation, more nitrogen fertilizer, and improved pest control (Dalrymple 1978).

But there also has come a plateauing of yields of the major food crops (see Figure 10). Yields of wheat, sorghum, soybeans, and potatoes in the United States have not increased appreciably since 1970. This is true also of maize, potatoes, wheat, and cassava in Latin America. Yields of rice in India, Bangladesh, Indonesia, Nepal, Pakistan, the Philippines, Sri Lanka, and Thailand were the same in 1976 as in 1970, even with substantial use of high-yielding varieties. Total world grain yields have declined. Prices for farm products have become volatile, while the cost of energy-intensive farm inputs has risen sharply. This has placed the American farmer and American consumer in a uniquely vulnerable position. What are the forces that increasingly impinge on agricultural productivity? There are many contributing factors (Table 3), but the magnitude of each is not known.

ENVIRONMENTAL ISSUES

Degradations of the environment arising from agricultural practices are many, but there are also innumerable farming practices that can improve the environment. Agriculture has a primary responsibility for safeguarding the environment. It is the chief user of our land and water resources. Thus, we should seek agricultural technologies that will result in stable

TABLE 3   Causes of Plateauing in Agricultural Productivity

Soil erosion—Loss of topsoil
Loss of organic matter—Soil compaction
Chemical soil residues—Air pollution
More less-productive land under cultivation
Increased pressures on productive land base
Fewer options for water, fertilizer, pesticide uses
Climate and weather fluctuations
Increased regulatory constraints
Decreased support for agricultural research

production at high levels; be environmentally benign and not subject to ever-increasing regulatory constraints; and be sparing of capital, management, and resources. No new agricultural production technology is likely to meet all the above criteria, but there are those that can meet many of them. We must address ourselves to their development. It has not yet been clarified as to what an environmentally sustainable set of agricultural production technologies might be.

Toxic chemicals in the environment, many of them pesticides and fertilizers used in agricultural production, have been declared environmental threats. Issues of food safety, deleterious effects on fish and wildlife, endangered species, and carcinogenicity are being vigorously debated.

## THE RESOURCE BASE FOR AGRICULTURAL PRODUCTION

### CLIMATE

Climatic conditions must be considered carefully in decisions about agricultural production. That means allocating specific crops to specific locations. Climate, as a resource, should be viewed not so much globally as locally and regionally. In the American Grain Belt, for example, climate makes corn and soybeans the leading crops. In west Texas it is sorghum and cotton; in the Mississippi Delta it is cotton, soybeans, and rice. The climate of the Pacific Northwest, the West Coast, western Michigan, and New York State makes them particularly suitable to the production of fruits and vegetables. There are sites where fruit crops never fail because of good climate.

But there is a challenge for making climate a more useful and less hazardous resource. On a global scale, negative climatic conditions are now exacting an enormous toll, in reduced crop productivity. Desertification, for example, is a menace affecting every continent, with the possible exception of Europe. It annually destroys 12 to 17 million acres, as otherwise arable land is turned into stony wastes or heaps of drifting sand.[5] Prolonged drought often accelerates the destruction. *Climate and Food* (NRC 1976) addresses in detail the effects of fluctuating climate on agricultural productivity.

The impact of climate and weather on agricultural production is most dramatically illustrated by year-to-year fluctuations in grain production in the Soviet Union. The USSR cannot consistently feed itself. Its grain shortfall this year is estimated at 65 million metric tons. Periodic failure of the monsoons in South Asia, the prolonged drought of the early 1970s in the African Sahel, that of the mid-1970s in western Europe, and the drought in the U.S. Corn Belt in 1974 are all recent manifestations of the climatic characteristic that farmers fear most. The latter, for example, resulted in a 22-percent reduction in major food and feed grains, which was more devastating than the climate-induced corn blight of 1970.

But the most serious effects of drought are most manifest in the numerous small nations of the semiarid tropics, where populations are increasing rapidly, resource options are few, and climatic variability is greatest. Yet the magnitude of the impact of climate on agricultural productivity is appreciated by only a small segment of the scientific community and hardly at all among society. As a result, the needed sponsorship of research to alleviate environmental stress is often lacking. For example, the projective document *Agriculture in the New International Development Strategy,* released by the Food and Agriculture Organization of the United Nations, makes no mention of climate.[6]

One climatic issue that has recently gained wide publicity, however, is the climatic change that may be initiated by a rising level of atmospheric carbon dioxide. As a result, there have been dire predictions to the effect that shifts in precipitation patterns will cause serious dislocations in agricultural production. The prospect of climatic change from increasing atmospheric levels of $CO_2$ should not frighten agriculturists, however. Seasonal and interannual variability in climate has always made agriculture uncertain. In fact, a rising level of atmospheric carbon dioxide may have favorable biological effects by increasing photosynthesis and decreasing water requirements of crops. These effects may outweigh any adverse climate-induced agricultural changes. The recent history of agriculture is one of resilience and adaptation to climatic change.

LAND RESOURCES

The United States has a remarkable land resource base for crop production. The Corn Belt constitutes the largest single contiguous area devoted to crop production in the world and its climate makes it relatively immune to major droughts. According to Barlowe (1979) and Vlasin (1975), there are approximately 256 million hectares of land (including 160 million hectares of prime farmland) suitable for cultivation in the United States. About 148 million hectares are now used for cropland. In addition to prime farmland there is the unique farmland used for the production of such specialty crops as citrus fruits, cranberries, olives, blueberries, cherries, and other fruits and vegetables. The area covered by grasslands, pastures, and rangelands in the United States is approximately double that of cultivated cropland. Except for the period 1974 to 1977, significant set-aside acreages have occurred in recent years, and there remain other state and local lands that could be used for agricultural production if it were to become necessary.

This land resource base can also change with time and technology. Land productivity may be improved as well as depleted by cropping. The original croplands of western Europe and Japan were vastly inferior to what they are today. This is currently reflected by wheat yields in western Europe and rice yields in Japan that are double those of the United States. The use of lime, chemical fertilizers, animal manure, green manure, and irrigation has transformed the sandy soils of the eastern American seaboard into some of the most productive vegetable growing soil in the world. Similarly, the acidic, organic-sand soils of the Great Lakes states now produce large amounts of fruits, berries, vegetables, and root crops. Alaska's potential agricultural land is larger than the state of Iowa.

Soil erosion problems persist, however. For 45 years the Soil Conservation Service of the U.S. Department of Agriculture (USDA) has promoted sound conservation practices, but it has not been very effective. No more than 25 percent of our farmlands are currently under approved conservation practices. Meanwhile, we continue to lose 2.8 billion tons of topsoil from our best lands each year (9.0 tons/hectare). The result is continued sedimentation of our lakes, streams, and estuaries. Coupled with massive deforestation, land erosion is even worse in many developing countries (Eckholm 1976).

Land tillage reduction has now become an important land conservation technology. The use of appropriate chemicals for weed control has made it possible to improve crop productivity without plowing the land. In 1978, over 3 million hectares in the United States were planted without tillage, and tillage was reduced from the conventional level on another 22 million hectares. Reduced tillage is the most significant technology yet developed to control soil erosion, maximize ground cover, and conserve energy, labor, water, soil, fertility, and organic matter (Triplett and Van Doren 1977). A higher proportion of the sloping land in hilly areas can be brought into production or planted in more profitable crops, and the no-till system may also greatly increase efficient use of fertilizers and pesticides.

Successful tillage conservation requires, first, an appropriate herbicide, or else mulches, to inhibit weed growth, and second, special seed drills for use on sod or nontilled soil. Herbicides must be registered and approved by regulatory bodies, however, because they may have adverse environmental consequences. They also require fossil fuels for their production. Thus, further development of appropriate chemicals will be necessary to speed the use of zero tillage or conservation tillage in both American and world agriculture. The surface mulches used in conservation tillage may also harbor insects, disease organisms, snakes, or rodents that can destroy both mulch and crops.

Tillage reduction, however, has the potential to reclaim tens of millions of hectares of land heretofore unsuited to agricultural purposes, as well as reducing soil erosion on cultivated land to close to zero. Wherever soils would otherwise erode badly, this method should be adopted. The ultimate opportunity resides in identifying mulches with an allelopathic effect that would eventually eliminate the need to use herbicides. It is already known that mulches from certain grasses and cereal grains have such effects. Their use would greatly reduce or eliminate the present dependence on herbicides.[7]

## WATER RESOURCES[8]

The water resources of the earth are enormous. Seventy percent of the earth's surface is covered with water, most of it salty. Only 1 percent is fresh water, and 99 percent of the fresh water is underground. World food producers must face these water limitations and optimize the management of existing water resources. The next major advance in agricultural production will come about through more efficient soil and water management.

In the 17 western states, irrigation accounts for about 90 percent of the fresh water used, and nationally irrigation accounts for 82 percent of the water consumed. Irrigated agriculture, protected in part from the vagaries of climate, supplies most of our fruits, nuts, and vegetables. Agricultural production, mostly for irrigation, consumes 80 to 85 percent of the total diverted freshwater resources in the United States. The percentage consumption of water for agriculture in the total U.S. water budget far exceeds the percentage consumption of energy (3 percent) by agriculture in the total U.S. energy budget. Currently, 22 million hectares of American farmland are irrigated. Lack of water may become the most serious limitation on further advances in U.S. food production, and not only in the western states. It is now widely believed that the addition of water to achieve optimum moisture levels could be the next major means of increasing crop productivity in the midwestern and eastern parts of the United States. There is never a year when soil moisture is not deficient for optimal growth sometime during the growing season. With corn, for example, the time of silk emergence is particularly critical. This usually occurs during the last half of July when, unfortunately, the probability that the Corn Belt will get at least half an inch of rain a week is the lowest. Groundwater reserves in this country are currently being depleted at the rate of 15 to 20 million acre feet per year. In Texas, for example, irrigation annually consumes 13 million acre feet, of which 7 million are an overdraft on groundwater resources.[9] This overdraft of groundwater is a flagrant misuse of the resource. Water tables are dropping and becoming progressively more salty, and land subsidence is becoming a long-term problem.

The number of kilograms of water needed to produce a kilogram of food is an important variable. Practically no research has been done in this area, although numerous symposia have been held on irrigation and the efficiency of water use. Large differences in transpiration losses exist among species, varying from a scale of 100 for pineapple, to 400 to 500 for cereals and seed legumes, to more than 1,000 for some fruits and vegetables. The water requirement of sugarcane per unit of land area in Hawaii is five times that of pineapple. A report from Israel (Shalhevet et al. 1976) indicates that crops vary widely in efficiency of water use. Sorghum will produce 1.72 kg of grain per millimeter of water, compared with 1.23 kg of wheat, 0.65 kg for peanuts, and only 0.24 kg for cotton. Water limitations can alter the amount of the plant that is harvested for food and, thus, modify the relationship between crop yield and productivity. The adaptations to water limitations found among annual plants under semiarid conditions have yet to be exploited in the United States.

Making more efficient use of available water supplies offers the greatest of agricultural opportunities, and the one least encumbered by regulatory constraints. The efficiency of conventionally applied irrigation water varies from less than 30 percent globally, 20 to 40 percent in the United States, and 80 to 85 percent in Israel. Irrigation efficiency in this country has improved little over the past 30 years.

Drip or trickle irrigation is sometimes referred to as the "blue revolution."[10] First developed for large-scale crop production in Israel, it may reduce by 50 percent the water now used in conventional irrigation systems (flooding, sprinkling, furrow). Worldwide, there are now more than 250,000 hectares of cropland equipped with drip irrigation systems. Almost half of this land is in the United States. There is no leaching, runoff, or drainage water pollution; weed control and distribution of fertilizer can be optimized; crop and soil management and harvest operations can be conducted without interfering with irrigation. Water of higher salinity than would be acceptable with other methods can be utilized, and drip lines can be installed underground, as they are in many sugarcane plantations in Hawaii. This reduces both surface evaporation and growth of weeds. The prospects for high-frequency drip irrigation on some crops hold even greater promise for efficient water use with less capital investment, resource inputs, and management.

The imposition of environmental controls for irrigation must include soil and groundwater. Although the United States lacks an adequate inventory of present saline soils or soils becoming salinized (van Schilfgaarde 1979), restrictions on the discharge of salt from irrigation projects will be forthcoming. One of the challenges for the future will be to increase water use efficiency up to 90 percent without adverse effects on soil salinity. Severe problems have already arisen in the Imperial Valley of California and many other parts of the American West, in the Middle East, and in North Africa.

There are several other serious problems related to irrigated crop production. One is the increasing price of energy for operating irrigation pumps and the growing uncertainty of energy availability. Another is the depletion of groundwater reserves. A third is that the extensive use of pivot irrigation in the West may be increasing the region's vulnerability to drought. Lands previously too hilly or too sandy for surface irrigation are now being used, but much of the soil is highly susceptible to wind erosion, and the installation of center pivots has meant the removal of many shelterbelts (Rosenberg 1979).

One of the promising methods for increasing water resources is augmentation of precipitation through cloud seeding. There is, however, no area of technology so vulnerable to regulatory constraints. Recent precipitation enhancement research in Florida utilizing new cloud seeding technologies suggests very positive results,[11] and many of the types of clouds found in Florida in the summer are similar to those in the Corn Belt. The potential for precipitation enhancement in the Midwest, the major food-producing area of the nation and the breadbasket of the world, has not yet been scientifically determined. Herein may reside the most significant contribution that research can make toward increasing U.S. water resources during the next 10 to 15 years. Any successful technologies for rainfall enhancement, however, will have numerous socio-economic, legal, and environmental impacts.

ENERGY RESOURCES

Agriculture is energy dependent. It is extremely susceptible to both reduced energy supplies and higher energy costs. The most vulnerable input is nitrogen fertilizer, which accounts for about one-third of the total fossil fuel now used in agricultural production in the United States. As much as 20 percent of the energy used in American agriculture goes for irrigation; approximately 5 percent is used to make and spread pesticides. Other energy-vulnerable operations include crop drying, food processing, dairying, transportation, and storage (especially refrigeration).

Thus, energy conservation practices in food production demand attention. Biological nitrogen fixation, as an alternative to chemical fixation, is an example of what can be done. This could become operational at the farm level through more extensive use of legume (green) manure and winter cover crops, and through intercropping legumes with nonlegumes. The no-till or reduced tillage and drip irrigation systems discussed earlier could be adapted to many locations and would conserve not only energy but also soil, water, and organic matter. They would also reduce soil compaction and increase the efficiency of fertilizers and herbicides. New pest-management systems and new technologies for applying pesticides could also reduce energy needs.

Many options exist for the use of alternative energy systems in food production. A major research effort should be directed toward more efficient use of solar energy for crop irrigation, since the greatest water needs are usually positively correlated with solar energy intensities. A new research and development initiative that has emerged involves the feasibility of ethanol production from biomass. While there is renewed interest in the use of biomass, not all biomass is readily available or collectible, and land should not be diverted from food production. Some biomass is also necessary to prevent soil erosion and maintain soil organic matter.[12]

PESTICIDES

Annual field losses from pests (insects, diseases, weeds, nematodes, rodents) are enormous. All major crops suffer losses before harvest that exceed 20 percent, with the greatest losses occurring in developing countries. Losses from insects predominate for most, but not all, crops. Chemical pesticides have played a dominant role in the control of pests and will continue to do so in the foreseeable future. Their use has been one of the most significant reasons for the high yields of American agriculture. Approximately 5 billion pounds of synthetic organic pesticides were produced worldwide in 1976, and annual global expenditures for pesticides range from $6 to $10 billion. Chemical pesticides have accounted for 10 percent of the increase in farm output during the last 3 decades.

Meanwhile, however, regulatory constraints and the costs relating thereto have multiplied exponentially, and yields of the major food crops throughout the world have reached a plateau. Future strategies for pest control will likely result in the use of more pesticides in agriculturally developing nations and less in the more developed. Most of the developing countries are in the tropics, where pest control problems are enormously more complex than in temperate zones. Yet the developing world now uses only 20 percent of all pesticides. The option of greatest promise to the low-income subsistence farmer who cannot afford pesticides is the development of crop varieties with greater built-in resistance.

This will come about as part of the integrated pest-management systems now being conceived.[13] These systems will involve entomologists, plant pathologists, weed scientists, toxicologists, computer programmers, and economists working together within a sympathetic administrative environment. Through these arrangements we will be able to develop plant varieties more resistant to pests, biological pest controls, and better methods of utilizing chemical pesticides, all in concert. This should mean an opportunity to partially replace chemicals with information and to put people with technical information back on the farm.

Integrated pest management is still largely a concept, however. As such, it does nothing to reduce pest losses, save the environment, or reduce health hazards. Chemical pesticides are currently the principal part of all grower- or farmer-supported pest-management programs. It is projected, however, that if integrated pest-management systems become a reality, crop losses can be reduced 50 percent and pesticide use reduced 75 percent.

MECHANIZATION

In the United States the development of agricultural labor-saving technology has been a major goal. One American farm worker today produces enough food for himself and 56 other people, as compared to only 29 people 10 years ago. This is a remarkable achievement that can be attributed in part to better management, more timely operations, and more efficient and productive equipment. Mechanization has enabled farmers to carry out their field work and have time left for farm management activities. It also has been forced by the unavailability, uncertainty, and rising cost of human labor.

The goals of mechanization in agriculturally developing nations must be viewed differently. For most of those nations, the emphasis on increased production and convenience is not applicable. Instead, the need is for more man-hours per cultivated hectare per year, more days worked, more uniformly distributed labor throughout the year, and more food produced per hectare. There is a pressing need for mechanization systems that help to produce more food, protect farm workers from hazardous chemicals, and avoid environmental contamination, while at the same time putting more people to work productively—in other words, to enhance yields, improve efficiency in the use of resources, and minimize crop losses in order to increase the total amount of food available. Seed drills for no-tillage systems are a good example. Agricultural mechanization, of course, must also depend on local manufacturing capabilities. No country except those in the Arabian Gulf area can endure for long the imbalance of payments that results from importing sophisticated agricultural technology.

RESOURCE VERSUS SCIENCE-BASED TECHNOLOGIES

There is now a worldwide shift from a natural resource-based to a science-based agriculture. The goal of this change is to raise output per unit of resource input and thus loosen the constraints imposed by increasingly inelastic supplies of land, water, fertilizer, pesticides, and energy. Ruttan[14] has pointed out that this has already occurred in Japan and certain western European countries. Until recently, agricultural technology in the United States had lagged behind the technology of those countries because of the relative abundance and low cost of resources here. It is now projected, however, that by the end of this century almost all increases in U.S. food production will be a result of increases in yield (output per unit of land area per unit of time) and of growing additional crops on the same land during the year. There are really no other options. New agricultural technologies will not only be those that result in stable production and high yields, but those that are labor-intensive, crop-intensive, and sparing of natural resources. They also must be nonpolluting. Such technologies exist. We have not, heretofore, addressed ourselves seriously to their development.

Agriculture in the developing countries of the world is an agriculture of smallness.[15] Four-fifths of the farms are 5 hectares or less, and nearly half are a single hectare. But outputs per unit of land area and per unit of capital input are often higher on these small farms. They are also labor-intensive. Serious attention needs to be directed toward agricultural production technologies that are small-scale, maximize output, maximize employment, and minimize resource use and capital costs.

Nor should this issue be ignored in the United States. In 1976, 72 percent of all American farms grossed less than $20,000 and were classified as small farms. Yet most U.S. agricultural research efforts are directed to large-scale commercial agriculture.

## RESEARCH IMPERATIVES FOR FOOD PRODUCTION

Directly or indirectly, plants provide up to 95 percent of the world's food supply. Research on biological processes that control or limit crop productivity (photosynthesis, biological $N_2$ fixation, cellular approaches to plant breeding) is therefore crucial. This next generation of agricultural research (see Table 4) should be concerned also with improved efficiency in nutrient and water absorption by plants, greater resistance to competing biological systems, environmental and climatic stresses, and toxic chemicals, genetic improvement through conventional means, and the relation of hormonal mechanisms to plant development. These are the research areas identified in recent National Academy of Sciences/National Research Council reports and elsewhere as grossly underfunded areas where the industrialized nations, including the United States, could make great contributions to the agricultural development of Third World nations. Research efforts directed toward economically important food crops could greatly improve the productivity and stability of agricultural output in the developing countries and would be economically, socially, politically, and ecologically sound. They also could ease the transition from nonrenewable to renewable resources.

INCREASED PHOTOSYNTHETIC EFFICIENCY[16]

Photosynthesis is the most important biochemical process on earth. Improving the efficiency of the process is the key to adequate food supplies in the future. Green plants are the primary "harvesters" of free solar energy—biological "sun traps," one might say. All agricultural practices directed toward increased productivity must ultimately mean an increased "harvesting" of solar energy by plants. Agriculture is basically solar energy processing; solar energy is clean, nonpolluting, noiseless, and renewable. Yet its utilization has been grossly neglected.

Few research efforts on photosynthesis have sought to enhance agricultural productivity. The photosynthetic efficiency of the major food crops averages less than 0.1 percent during the entire year. For most crops the efficiency rate during the growing season does not exceed 1 percent. Even under the best of conditions it is less than 3 percent.

There are many alternatives in research to enhance photosynthesis.

TABLE 4  Next Generation of Agricultural Research

| |
|---|
| Greater photosynthetic efficiency |
| Improved biological nitrogen fixation |
| Genetic improvement and new cell fusion technologies |
| Greater resistance to competing biological systems |
| More efficiency in nutrient uptake and utilization |
| Reduction in losses from nitrification and denitrification |
| Greater resistance to environmental stresses |
| Identification of hormonal systems and mechanisms |

They include identification and control of the mechanisms that regulate and thus could reduce the wasteful processes of both dark and light-induced (photo) respiration. Similar mechanisms are responsible for the redistribution of photosynthates that, in turn, regulate yield and maximize the "harvest index." Other research options include resolution of hormonal systems, identification of the growth regulators and heritable components that control flowering and leaf senescence, improvements in plant anatomy, planting designs, cultural practices for better light reception, and carbon dioxide enrichment of the atmosphere.

Plant-breeding research has not generally been aimed at improving the photosynthetic process. Furthermore, the complex relationship between photosynthesis and crop yield is poorly understood. Photosynthetically positive mutants should be sought after (Nasyrov 1978). Any physiologic-genetic prolongation of the functionally active state of chloroplasts, as well as delay in leaf senescence, would also be important for enhancing photosynthesis.

Much of the basic research on photosynthesis now in progress should involve economically important crops grown under field conditions as well as in the laboratory. As scientific investigation moves from the microscopic level in the laboratory to the macroscopic level of field experiments, the advantages of the highly productive $C_4$ photosynthetic mechanism over the $C_3$ progressively diminish.

BIOLOGICAL NITROGEN FIXATION[17]

Chemically fixed nitrogen is a nonrenewable resource. It is also the single largest and most costly fossil fuel input for agricultural productivity. Up to 35 percent of the total productivity of all crops is now accredited to this single input, and almost one-third of all fossil energy now used in agriculture is used to produce chemical nitrogen fertilizer. The global use of chemically fixed nitrogen fertilizer has grown precipitously. In 1905, 400,000 mt were produced. This increased to 3,500,000 mt in 1950 and to 40,000,000 mt in 1974. The estimate for 1979 exceeds 50,000,000 mt. The United States annually consumes about one-fourth of the world supply, and half of U.S. consumption is for a single crop, maize.

Natural gas is the primary fuel used to produce anhydrous ammonia. It requires 30 ft$^3$ of natural gas to produce 1 lb of nitrogen. In other words, a nitrogen fertilizer factory consumes approximately 1 m$^3$ of natural gas for each kilogram of nitrogen it produces as ammonia. From both an economic and natural resource standpoint this is wasteful and, in the long run, indefensible.

One alternative approach is abiotic nitrogen fixation utilizing renewable energy resouces—solar, wind, or water power (Treharne et al. 1978). Another is enhancement of biologically fixed nitrogen. The inadequacy of current funding levels for research into nitrogen fixation alternatives has been thoroughly documented. Current U.S. expenditures scarcely exceed $5 million annually, and increases in funding for this high-priority research during the past 3 years have hardly kept pace with inflation.

The first objective of this research should be the establishment of rhizobial technology centers. Secondly, there should be research on cropping systems—making more extensive use of legume (green) manure and winter cover crops, forage legumes, and possible intercropping of legumes with nonlegumes. The challenge is to develop systems that are predominantly based on biological nitrogen fixation but are still high-yielding. A third research initiative would be genetic engineering for the improvement of both host plants and microorganisms. Symbiotic relationships now exist for legumes, the actinomycete-nodulated angiosperms, the *Anabaena-Azolla* combinations that enrich rice paddies, and the *Spirillum*-rhizosphere associations in grasses. These relationships need to be optimized.

Biologically fixed nitrogen is slow-release, nonpolluting nitrogen. Losses from nitrification and denitrification, which now approximate 50 to 65 percent of chemical fertilizer, could be reduced by 50 percent. It is imperative that research initiatives discussed above be pursued without delay.

Further research progress in biological nitrogen fixation will be hastened if scientists engaged in basic research are actively linked with those in applied research in the field. Collaborative efforts between scientists in the developed and the less-developed nations should also be encouraged.

The magnitude of biological nitrogen fixation in many crops is already at a high level. The algae-*Azolla* complex (the green scum on the surface of the water in rice paddies) can provide 75 percent of the nitrogen requirement for California rice. Plantings of alfalfa and some clovers can yield up to 500 kg of nitrogen per hectare per year, depending on planting intensities and depth of rooting. Over 50 percent of the nitrogen requirement for wheat in the famous Broadbalk plots at Rothamsted in the United Kingdom since 1943 have come from nitrogen fixation by blue-green algae on the soil surface. And the International Rice Research Institute (IRRI) in the Philippines recently reported that the *Azolla* plant and its *Anabaena* helper can double their mass in 3 to 5 days, and accumulate 30 to 40 kg of nitrogen per hectare in 2 weeks.

*Azolla* is extensively used as a green manure crop in China and Vietnam, but has received little attention in the United States or South Asia even though it is found in abundance. It clearly deserves a research investment.

GENETIC IMPROVEMENT

The genetic resources of the earth are enormous. Botanists have identified approximately 350,000 species of plants. Yet of these, less than 3,000 have been used as food sources, and only about 300 are currently grown. Less than 20 comprise all the major food crops, and a mere 3—rice, wheat, and maize—provide approximately half our food supply. Cereals as a group supply 65 percent of the calories and 50 percent of the protein consumed in the world. Because almost all food comes directly or indirectly from plants, the plant genetic resources now being assembled will profoundly influence future agricultural productivity.

The standard techniques of genetic selection, based on phenotypic expression, controlled hybridization, and, more recently, selection for better nutritional qualities, have given us super strains of rice, wheat, maize, sorghum, millet, some legumes, and many new fruits and vegetables. The selection process is relatively simple for cereal grains, the seed legumes, forages, and many vegetables. Those that are vegetatively propagated (potatoes, sweet potatoes, cassava, fruit trees) pose a special problem, however. Meristems can be frozen in liquid nitrogen to preserve genetic stocks of vegetatively propagated food crops. The challenge is to initiate regrowth, utilizing appropriate metabolites, growth regulators, and culture media.

Equally exciting is research to genetically alter food crops for greater climatic adaptability and to get higher yields from soils that are too acid, toxic, or saline for varieties now in use. No strains of wheat are yet suitable for the lowland tropics, and there are at least 100 million acres not suited for present rice varieties. Thus, vast areas of the earth are either not utilized or under-utilized for economically important food crops. It may well be that production is limited more by the nutritional incompatibility of the plant with its environment than by the inefficiency of the photosynthetic process.[18]

Epstein and Norlyn (1977) report that marketable yields have been obtained with a salt-tolerant barley irrigated with water from the Pacific Ocean. Considerable progress also has been made in producing tomato strains tolerant of salt water. These efforts show that there are significant opportunities to develop plants that can be grown with water of higher salinity. There is also hope that plant breeding will provide an increase in drought resistance.

Genetic research will continue to be utilized for the improvement of the nutritional value of food crops. Progress in genetically raising the levels of protein and amino acids in such cereal grains as rice, wheat, and barley has been outstanding. Both the biological value and the protein level of maize have been enhanced using the opaque-2-recessive gene, and, more recently, in maize of normal background. Similar genetically superior strains of sorghum have been identified. Each of these genetic improvements, however, has thus far been largely in vain. There is still the important issue of food acceptability. Commodities that differ appreciably in color, taste, texture, or general appearance and keeping quality, irrespective of nutritional value, are not accepted quickly. Nevertheless, there is no cheaper, better, or quicker way to solve the protein needs of people in most of the agriculturally developing nations than to improve the cereals they eat. Combining the high productivity of certain "coarse" cereal crops (maize, sorghum, millet) with the superior protein quality of the "noble" grains (wheat, rice) also remains a major challenge for plant geneticists.

GENETIC ENGINEERING: BROADENING THE GENETIC BASE

New techniques of cell culture, protoplast fusion, and plasmid modification and transfer are emerging.[19] (Plasmids are DNA fragments capable of carrying genetic materials.) Significant advances have occurred in defining techniques for isolating protoplasts (plant cells without walls), improving their fusion, and providing cultures (with appropriate growth regulators) for rapid regeneration into new plants. New freeze-storage techniques and the establishment of gene banks for plant cells and meristems have become a means of preserving rare and useful genetic materials. These new cellular approaches to plant breeding, sometimes described as somatic cell genetics, could become a major means for propagating new species with greater yields, resistance to biological and environmental stresses and to toxins, and for improved nutritional quality. Protoplast fusion offers the hope of tapping genetic material not now available because of sterility barriers between genera and species. One recent achievement is a somatic hybrid of the tomato and potato (Melchers 1978). Transformations and regeneration of parasexual hybrids from fixed protoplasts could revolutionize agricultural crop productivity. Our inability to produce material that can be readily introgressed into established plant-breeding programs, however, remains a major challenge. Furthermore, no such hybrids have been produced for any of the cereal grains or legumes, the basic food crops of the earth.

EFFICIENCY IN NUTRIENT UPTAKE[20]

It has been estimated that only 50 percent or less of the nitrogen and less than 35 percent of the phosphorus and potassium applied as fertilizer in the United States are recovered by the crops. Recovery of fertilizer nitrogen in the rice paddies of the tropics is only 25 to 35 percent, and in the corn fields of the American Midwest only 50 percent. The balance is lost to the environment. Denitrification causes loss of nitrogen to the atmosphere, and nitrification encourages losses to the soil from leaching. Agricultural production would be greatly improved if these enormous losses, particularly in the warm soils of the tropics, could be even partially reduced. The single factor responsible for the failure to increase rice yields on Asian farms is the low level of available nitrogen fertilizer.

Denitrification is a process whereby nitrate is reduced to gaseous nitrogen, principally nitrous oxide ($N_2O$) and nitrogen ($N_2$). The process is carried out by diverse bacteria widely distributed in soils. Because $N_2O$ can catalyze the destruction of stratospheric ozone, the amount of $N_2O$ produced during denitrification—as well as nitrification, which pollutes groundwater—can have environmental significance.

A worldwide annual loss of 12 to 15 million tons of nitrogen fertilizer can be ascribed to denitrification alone. Losses from nitrification are equally great. Recent assessments of the fate of nitrogen fertilizer suggest that 25 to 35 percent is lost each by nitrification and denitrification (see Figure 11).

Many variables affect these losses, however, and some can be controlled. Natural and synthetic nitrification inhibitors, applied with ammonia or urea, are effective deterrents to leaching and atmospheric losses of nitrogen. Denitrification inhibitors also will be available soon. We must determine whether a nitrogen-conserving pathway can be designed to out-compete denitrification. The result could be a significant reduction in fertilizer cost and use.

Denitrification occurs only under anaerobic soil conditions. These can be diminished by reducing nitrification and soil compaction, improved drainage, the use of soil-improving crops, and careful attention to irrigation procedures. Research to reduce nitrogen fertilizer losses should be given equal priority with research on nitrogen fixation utilizing renewable resources.

The facilitation of nutrient uptake by microorganisms (fungi) in symbiotic associations with the roots of higher plants is emerging as one of the most exciting frontiers for the enhancement of food crop production.[21] Mycorrhizae, particularly the endomycorrhizae and the subgroup referred to as vesicular-arbuscular, help plant roots to increase substantially their uptake of phosphorus and other poorly mobile nutrients. Vesicular-arbuscular mycorrhizae, in fact, can be viewed as fungal extensions of roots that help them to absorb fertilizer, especially in phosphorus-deficient soils. The mycorrhizal effect comes not only from an increased number of absorbing sites, but also from an increased affinity for nutrient absorption.

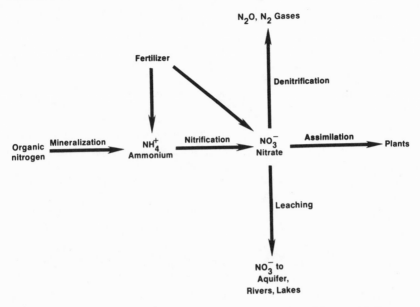

The author is grateful for the assistance of J. M. Tiedje, Professor of Crop and Soil Sciences and Microbiology, Michigan State University.

FIGURE 11  Fates of nitrogen in soils.

Mycorrhizae fungi have been reported to increase significantly the yields of cereal grains and many vegetable crops. The profound effects of these fungi have only recently been appreciated. This discovery opens up new possibilities not only for a substantial increase in conventional crop production while conserving nonrenewable resources, but also for an expansion of the land base so that plants can be grown in hitherto unfavorable areas. The research challenge that remains is to grow mycorrhizal organisms in vitro and then improve them genetically.

Although foliar applications of fertilizer have long been declared the most efficient method of fertilizer placement (Wittwer and Bukovac 1969), an application technology is still lacking. Barriers to increases in yields could be reduced by utilizing the absorptive capacity of leaves as well as roots when applying nutrients at crucial stages of development. Great hope was expressed for foliar sprays following experiments with soybeans in 1975 (Garcia and Hanway 1976), but extensive foliar spraying of nutrients in all major U.S. soybean-producing areas during 1976 and 1977 did not replicate the outstanding results achieved in 1975. Nevertheless, the rising costs of fertilizer and its nonrenewable resource requirement should be a continuing stimulus for further investigation of this technology.

## RESISTANCE TO ENVIRONMENTAL STRESSES

Environmental and climatic stresses, alone or in combination, are the primary factors limiting the production of many, if not all, of the world's food crops. Those that limit crop productivity include drought, cold, heat, salt, toxic ions, and air pollutants. Plants, unlike people, livestock, and other animals, are immobile. Environmental adaptability thus becomes preeminent to survival. Any means of increasing the resistance of plants to high and low temperatures, drought and water stress, adverse soil conditions, and other environmental hazards will enhance agricultural production and dependability of supply. Through the use of short-season, early planted, single-cross hybrids, commercial maize production in the United States has moved 500 miles farther north during the past 50 years.[22] Spring wheat in the USSR has moved 200 miles farther north. The winter wheat zone in the United States could also be moved 200 miles farther north by utilizing wheat strains with a new level of winter hardiness now available genetically. Hybrid sorghum and millets are moving into hot, dry areas not heretofore suitable for cereal grain production. The new synthetic species triticale (a cross of wheat and rye) has resistance to aluminum toxicity. (At present, the USSR is the main producer.) Thus, millions of acres of heretofore nonproductive land can be opened for cropping.

The "green revolution" has produced varieties of rice and wheat that are day-neutral (respond to any length of day) and that produce grain at any latitude. There are also genetic strains of rice, wheat, and barley with greater resistance to both cold and alkalinity. Potato varieties with modest frost resistance and cold hardiness have been identified in the high Andes.[23]

## ATMOSPHERIC STRESSES ON PLANTS

The changing composition of the atmosphere in the industrialized nations may either enhance or detract from agricultural productivity. Atmospheric particulates and gases are absorbed by aerial plant parts (Wittwer and Bukovac 1969). If released through precipitation, these particulates and gases also may be taken up by roots. Acid rainfall is common over all the United States west of the Mississippi River and in localized industrial areas elsewhere.[24] Its full effects on our agricultural productivity have not yet been assessed. Air quality standards thus far have been dominated by concern for human beings, with little attention having been given to agricultural productivity (Williams 1978). Crop losses from the stress of air pollutants may possibly be minimized by genetic selection of resistant cultivars, application of antioxidant chemicals, and modified plant nutrition.

There are currently many warnings about the climatic changes that may occur as a result of the rising level of atmospheric $CO_2$ and the threats to our food supply that might result from climate-induced agricultural dislocations. Much of this apprehension could be alleviated by a reasonable research investment into means of reducing the impact of environmental stresses on crops and livestock. The $CO_2$ in the atmosphere, it must be remembered, is vital for crop production. $CO_2$ concentrations around plant foliage remain the single most important determinant of photosynthesis. No exceptions to increased growth from $CO_2$ enrichment have yet been reported. It works for all the major food crops, and elevated levels also will accelerate the growth of forest trees. It is no longer necessary to design and conduct experiments to establish the efficacy of $CO_2$ enrichment for increasing the yields of commercially grown greenhouse crops. All respond with generally greater production and better quality, especially during early seedling stages. The magnitude of the response is light-dependent, but beneficial effects are derived over a wide spectrum of light intensities, either daylight or artificial. Many experiments have now demonstrated that the optimum concentration of $CO_2$ in the atmosphere ranges from 1,000 to 1,500 ppm. This is three to five times greater than the current level.

A threefold increase (330 to 1,000 ppm) in the levels of atmospheric $CO_2$ would greatly increase photosynthetic productivity and, at the same time, prevent losses from photorespiration (photorespiration would be essentially eliminated). With legumes (soybeans), this would result in almost a sixfold increase in nitrogen fixed per hectare. While these beneficial effects have been recorded, they have been difficult to apply, as yet, on a large scale, other than in commercial greenhouse production. There is a continuing challenge for plant biochemists, geneticists, and physiologists to find ways of increasing photosynthetic efficiency by reducing photorespiration, whether it be through $CO_2$ enrichment, chemicals, or breeding. The translation of increased photosynthates into increased nitrogen fixation in legumes and possibly other plants also needs further exploration. All in all, however, the biological effects of an elevated level of atmospheric $CO_2$ are far better understood than the projected climatic changes.[25]

The most intensive food-producing systems on earth are those where crops are grown in greenhouses or other structures. This method offers the ultimate in stable production at high levels, but it demands maximum capital, management, and resource inputs. Hydroponic culture facilitates control of both plant top and root environments, and water requirements are greatly reduced.[26] Atmospheres enriched by $CO_2$ can be employed; and locating greenhouses near high-population centers, as is done in the USSR, reduces food transportation costs.

## HORMONAL MECHANISMS AND PLANT DEVELOPMENT[27]

There are many chemicals, both endogenous and exogenous, at hormonal levels that permit control of biological processes. The use of chemical inhibitors of plant growth to enhance sugar yields in Hawaii is now standard practice. These inhibitors increase yields by 10 percent, and an equal increase is achieved with gibberellin to promote growth during the "winter" months. Yields of wheat in western Europe have been greatly enhanced by treatment with a chemical now designated as Chloromequat. The latest is Triacontanol (Ries et al. 1977), which in milligram quantities per hectare may significantly increase the yields of several major cereal and vegetable crops. Forty major chemical companies, most of them in the United States, are currently engaged in chemical growth-regulator research.

In the developing countries, however, there has been little effort to focus chemical growth-regulator studies on significant domestic food crop species or on whole plants of local economic importance. Most of their own agricultural research has been on plantation and export crops. But scientists, especially in developing countries, ought to be participating more in field research to help solve food production problems rather than in contributing to the burgeoning growth of scientific journals. Much of the information from growth regulator research in the plant sciences has not been brought to bear on the practical problems of food crop productivity in the Third World. It is likely that a useful role for growth regulators can be found for all crops, for all biological processes heretofore discussed, and for plants in every developmental stage.

## ANIMAL AGRICULTURE IN THE WORLD FOOD SYSTEM

There is a sound basis for efficient animal production in every nation in the world, even if only on a limited scale. Two-thirds of the world's agricultural land is in the form of permanent pasture, range, or meadow. Sixty percent of this land is not suitable for growing cultivated crops. In the United States there are $580 \times 10^6$ hectares of agricultural land, of which $400 \times 10^6$ hectares are used for grazing. The plant species on pasture, range, and meadow, otherwise of little value, are converted into milk and meat by ruminant animals. They are natural protein "factories" and "mobile storehouses" of food. They can also utilize by-products and waste that would otherwise have little value. In 1974, when global grain reserves reached a dangerously low level, the food animals of the world not slaughtered during the year constituted a 40-day reserve food supply. This exceeded available grain stocks, which provided a reserve of only 28 days. The food-animal reserve also was far better distributed than the grain.

Nonetheless, many people see livestock as an inefficient (or immoral) means of supplying food. Meatless days and vegetarian meals have been recommended in many industrialized nations and have been practiced by certain groups in an attempt to cut back food-animal production in favor of grain for human consumption. Yet sales of animal feeds (particularly soybeans and soybean products) and feed grains to developed countries now constitute the largest share of this country's substantial agricultural exports (Josling 1979), which may reach $40 billion in 1979. There is an increasing worldwide demand for meat, milk, and eggs.

Many of the important research issues related to animal agriculture will be explored at a national conference at Boyne Mountain, Michigan, in the spring of 1980. This conference, sponsored by the Michigan State University Agricultural Experiment Station and the College of Veterinary Medicine, four professional societies, the USDA, the EPA, and the American Association for the Advancement of Science, will be patterned after the Conference on Crop Productivity—Research Imperatives that the Michigan Agricultural Experiment Station and the C.F. Kettering Foundation jointly sponsored in 1975, the recommendations of which have since had a major impact on research funding policy in the plant sciences.

Research in animal agriculture thus far has been confined primarily to the enhancement of productivity through genetic improvements, better feeding, disease control, improved management, and control of the environment (Salisbury and Hart 1979). Additional research needs include control of major infectious diseases, minimizing losses from other epidemic diseases, control of endemic diseases, studies of the economic impact of animal diseases, and studies on the biological factors relating to host resistance and parasite infections. Worldwide livestock mortality from disease and parasites annually exceeds 50 million cattle and buffalo, and 100 million sheep and goats. In the United States, losses of about $20 billion occur annually from animal diseases. A reduction of 50 percent of these losses is a possible and realistic goal.

Substantial gains in the utilization of feeds can come from developing genetically superior animals able to subsist on low-quality diets, thus increasing the availability of lignin and cellulose, which are the major feedstuffs in many developing countries and could become increasingly important in the United States. Improved use of nonprotein nitrogen (urea-ammonia) for conversion by ruminants into protein, improved feeding and management at critical times in the life cycle, and eventual development of a rumen bypass for increased protein utilization and appetite stimulation would prove valuable also.

Improved fertility will come from estrus synchronization (control of the reproductive cycle), semen preservation, improved pregnancy detection, multiple births, and superovulation. All of these can help to increase the number of offspring. Low reproductive efficiency now results in 50 percent of the young animals being lost. Twinning in dairy and beef cattle can become a reality through hormone treatment for superovulation, controlled breeding, recovery of fertilized eggs, and nonsurgical embryo transfer to females of lesser breeding value.

Nonsurgical embryo collection is now aided by extremely sensitive microscopic techniques for embryo sexing, freezing, and implantation. These techniques may eventually revolutionize the productivity of dairy cattle. Sexed and frozen embryos soon may be available for cattle breeders to use with either surgical or nonsurgical implantation techniques. This could mean twin males for meat animals and twin females from superior milk producers. These new technologies are moving forward very rapidly.

All of the above should be given equal priority. Little progress in better feed utilization can be achieved without timely research into disease control, genetic improvement, and reproductive efficiency. Similarly, research on disease control will be of little value unless accompanied by better feeding. In fact, improvement of the breeding stock may be impossible in some developing countries until certain diseases are controlled and nutritional disorders are alleviated.

Controlled environments, widely used now for poultry and swine, are being tested for sheep and goats. Programmed lighting (photoperiod) and temperature regulation can have marked effects upon animal health and productivity. The effects of controlled environments on dairy cattle should also be studied more vigorously. A mid-winter photoperiod of 16 hours in Michigan resulted in a 10 percent increase in milk production from high-producing cattle.[28] This was achieved with no additional feed.

Improvements in animal agriculture can be remarkable when modern livestock production technology and improved forage programs are combined with local scientific knowledge in a developing country. In the Punjab and Gujarat states of India, for example, over a million farmers with water buffalo have formed cooperatives to market and distribute the animals' milk to the almost unlimited markets of Bombay, New Delhi, and other large cities. Milk production has been enhanced by genetic improvement through artificial insemination, better feeding utilizing hybrid Napier grass, and disease control. The results are a dependable daily cash income for the farmer, better utilization of wastes and by-products by the animals, improvement of the nutrition of poor rural and urban consumers, and an enterprise that is labor-intensive at the production level.

## IMPROVED FORAGE PRODUCTION

Forages provide feed for approximately 2.5 billion ruminant animals. They are the primary, and often exclusive, feed for livestock in the developing countries. In the United States in 1974 they provided 63 percent of the feed for dairy cattle, 84 percent for beef cattle, and 90 percent for sheep and goats (Hodgson 1978). The percentage varies according to the availability and price of feed grains. Forages also help to reduce soil erosion and enrich the soil, and they are a potential source of biomass production. Their production is an essential part of appropriate long-term land use.

There are many opportunities to enhance the productivity of range and pasture resources. In the United States it is technically and economically feasible to double the carrying capacity of rangelands. A coordinated national program of improved plant species (both legumes and grasses), controlled vegetation, mechanical soil treatments, fertilization, water control, and livestock and wildlife management would add significantly to the food productivity of the nation. Similarly, the land and water resources for forage production in the developing countries are enormous. Those countries contain about 1.5 billion hectares of land that have little utility for cultivated crops and could be used for forages. Livestock grazing in many areas is possible throughout the year, and diverse mixtures of legumes and grains would provide a balance between energy and protein.

Some remarkable genetic improvements in forages have been achieved. Coastal Bermuda grass $F_1$ hybrids in the southeastern United States yield twice as much forage as the common Bermuda grass (Burton 1977). Hybrid Napier grass is highly productive and provides excellent feed for dairy cows in the tropics. Additional scientific effort should be directed toward higher yielding types, increased nutritive values, improved harvesting techniques, and merger of the production and utilization system.

The most important feed constituent in forages is cellulose, the world's most abundant organic compound. Worldwide production of cellulose is estimated at over 100 billion tons (dry weight) per year, which is equivalent to approximately 150 pounds of cellulose produced daily for each of the earth's more than 4 billion inhabitants. Its conversion into food of economic value is accomplished only by ruminants.

## POTENTIALS AND LIMITATIONS OF AQUACULTURE[29]

The current world aquaculture production of 6 million metric tons annually is but a small part of the total world catch of fish and seafood, which amounts to about 70 million tons. Interest in aquaculture, however, is global and growing. Aquaculture provides a significant portion of the total fish consumption of China (40 percent), India (38 percent), Indonesia (22 percent), the Philippines (10 percent), and Japan (6 percent). Interest in fish as a food lags in the United States, where the current focus of aquaculture is on the rearing of luxury fish. Although worldwide aquaculture output has more than doubled since the early 1970s, U.S. production has remained unchanged. One problem in the country is the lack of economic incentive to attract private capital. Another is that a successful and expanded aquaculture requires unpolluted coastal or estuarine areas or supplies of high-quality fresh water, and there are many competitors for these limited resources.

Nevertheless, a reconsideration of the potential value of aquaculture to the United States is in order. More attention should be directed toward efficient energy use in the production of human food, including maximum efficiency in the transfer of energy between food and fish. Under some conditions aquatic animals may be better food converters than poultry and livestock. Fish do not have to maintain a warm body temperature.

Any unpolluted body of water—fresh, salt, or brackish—is a potential site for fish rearing. Although aquaculture is eminently suited to the tropics, it can also be adapted to other climates, and it offers an economical and attractive use of "waste" water. Fresh water simultaneously employed for such other purposes as irrigation, stock watering, or even drinking also can be used for fish culture. Furthermore, aquaculture, unlike agriculture, does not consume water. Wetlands, including swamps and mangroves that are of little agricultural value, can be used for fish rearing with little damage to their recreational value or appearance. There are also opportunities for fish culture at unusual sites, such as the many small prairie ponds in Canada that can be readily stocked with small trout. The introduction of the Coho salmon into the Great Lakes is one of the most significant aquaculture events of the past 15 years.

Research initiatives for aquaculture should include improving reproductive efficiency, genetic improvements, better nutrition through the development of less expensive and nutritionally superior feeds, and disease prevention and control. In the United States the well-established aquaculture industries are oysters, trout, and catfish. Shrimp could also become important. Catfish farming has grown exponentially in Arkansas, Mississippi, Louisiana, Texas, and Alabama in recent decades. More efficient recovery is needed from current harvests. One problem is the lack of machines to separate flesh from bones and skin.

## APPROPRIATE AGRICULTURAL TECHNOLOGY[30]

The concept of "appropriate technology" stems, in part, from the realization that many of the techniques for crop production developed in the industrialized nations may be "inappropriate" for the developing world and may not be appropriate for the future destiny of the developed world. Proponents of the appropriate technology concept criticize the large-scale centralized monoculture of modern U.S. agriculture as damaging to the environment and to human welfare, especially to the welfare of the international poor. The more appropriate direction, they contend, is toward labor-intensive agricultural operations, small farms, polyculture, heterogeneous germ plasm, farming systems, little or no chemical fertilizer, biological control of insects and diseases, and conservation tillage. Appropriate technology emphasizes the nonpolluting decentralized inputs derived from solar energy and is held to have benign environmental and equitable humanistic impacts. According to these criteria, greater photosynthetic efficiency, biological fixation of nitrogen, genetic improvements to build greater resistance to competing biological systems, and efforts to alleviate environmental stresses would all be considered appropriate technologies. Crop rotations, intercropping, cropping systems, and farming systems are emphasized, as is pest management without—or with a minimum of—pesticides. Organic gardening also is a part of the concept. There is emphasis on the construction of storage with local renewable materials for the preservation of indigenous production, which provides production goal incentives, family food security, management of part of the market system, and a means of preserving desirable seed stocks.

### ECO-FARMING AND AGROFORESTRY

Although eco-farming is particularly applicable to the tropics, there are temperate zone applications. The basic objective is to produce a mixture of perennial crops (trees and shrubs) with annual food crops to provide more food, more employment for workers, and better soil conservation. Permanent crops assimilate sunlight for a longer period, take advantage of moisture 12 months of the year, and produce greater output of dry matter per unit of land area per year. Regeneration of soil fertility on eroded hillsides is accomplished by a mixture of local trees, grasses, and food crops, without the aid of commercial fertilizer. A legume ground cover beneath the trees and a 50 percent legume use in the food crop rotation are sufficient to maintain soil fertility. The conventional separation of food crops, pastures, and forests is abandoned, with the three being combined in a parklike landscape.

Agroforestry involves the adaptation of small holdings to prevailing ecological conditions by combining tree crops with cultivated crops, mixed tree crops with food animals, and wood production with food production.[31]

## HOME GARDENS[32]

More than 50 percent of the nation's families are currently involved in home food gardening, the highest percentage since World War II. The reasons include higher food prices, a desire for food of higher quality, and increasing amounts of available time. Home food gardens often involve all family members, old and young, as participants. A home garden can be one or more acres in a rural area, a few hundred square feet next to the home or in a community garden, or several containers in the backyard or on the balcony of a suburban apartment. This "metropolitan agriculture" offers useful employment, utilizes land, water, and solar resources now being wasted, improves the environment and human nutrition, and provides substantial quantities of food. It has been calculated that a well-managed 15 × 20 foot garden can yield up to $500 worth of fresh food in 6 months.

Scientific research into home gardening therefore merits attention. Many new developments in commecial crop production could be adapted to the home garden. These include the use of high-quality, high-yielding, disease-resistant varieties, such as hybrid carrots, squash, tomatoes, and sweet corn; plastic mulches for weed control and early maturity; automatic drip or trickle irrigation; synthetic or natural soil mixes; integrated pest management; and the cycling of wastes and by-products as fertilizer.

The home food garden has many advantages. Production is at the site of use. Energy expenditures from fossil fuels are minimized. (It is likely that, in time, food transportation costs will rise more rapidly than production costs.) Marketing and packaging requirements are essentially eliminated. Dwarf fruit trees can be grown, along with some of the major food crops, such as potatoes, peas, beans, and corn. Pest control is simplified by the use of spray attachments to garden hoses, with simple dilution procedures for the application of pesticides.

Introducing science into home food gardening through the diffusion of information systems already in place (e.g., county agents) is one of the greatest challenges for food production in the United States. Improved technologies should be developed that would result in cropping systems having high-yield potentials and concentrating on the use of renewable resources. The emphasis should be on systems for intensive and stable production at high levels for local consumption. Home food gardening puts food where people are, through a system that is labor-intensive but has low capital, resource, and management needs. The home garden can be a low-input, high-output food resource for people in this nation and throughout the world. If it is coupled with improved storage technology for indigenous production, there is the added advantage of food security, through the protection of seed, food, and surplus stocks. Home gardening is a classic example of appropriate technology.

## POTENTIAL PRODUCTIVITY

Many researchers have made estimates of maximum crop productivity. Buringh et al. (1975) computed potential productivity in grain to be 40 times its present global level. Biological limits have not been reached for the productivity of any of the major food crops. Average, world record, and estimated yields are presented in Table 5 for some of the major food crops in the United States.

The current and potential productivity of nine major crops—maize, sugarcane, sugar beets, rice, wheat, soybeans, peas, potatoes, and cotton—were reviewed by Evans (1975). Current record yields are about one-half the potential estimated maximum yields.

A careful review of the characteristics responsible for the ever-increas-

TABLE 5 Average, Best, and World Record Yields

| Food Crop | Average 1979 (U.S.) Estimate | Best Farmers (U.S.) | World Record | Ratio: Record/Average |
|---|---|---|---|---|
| | (metric tons/hectare) | | | |
| Maize | 6.5 | 14.1 | 22.2 | 3.41 |
| Wheat | 2.4 | 6.7 | 14.5 | 6.04 |
| Soybeans | 2.1 | 3.4 | 5.6 | 2.66 |
| Sorghum | 4.5 | 16.8 | 21.5 | 4.77 |
| Oats | 1.9 | 5.4 | 10.6 | 5.57 |
| Barley | 2.6 | 8.1 | 11.4 | 4.38 |
| Potatoes | 28.7 | 67.3 | 95.0 | 3.31 |
| Sugarcane | 50.0 | 100.0 | 250.0 | 5.00 |
| Sugar Beets | 50.0 | 80.0 | 120.0 | 2.40 |

ing and record yields of corn in the United States could be helpful for the design of future models of crop productivity. Case histories from specific areas are available for analysis. A study of the comparative productivity of various agricultural ecosystems also would be most rewarding. New technologies, resource inputs, and economic incentives will determine future agricultural crop productivity. The combinations that work best will be site-specific.

Maximum yield trials[33] should become a major part of agricultural research. The intent would be for scientists to test constantly the limits of available technology, as well as their ability to put together a systems approach to achieve maximum production. This, after all, is what the farmer is expected to do.

## REMOTE SENSING

Remote sensing is a nondestructive diagnostic tool for detection of plant stresses, crop identification, and yield predictions. The detection and identification systems can be from low- or high-flying aircraft or from satellites. Coupling the aerial signals with ground observations is essential. Use of microwave technology to measure soil moisture levels is a recent development. Large soil moisture reserves in the U.S. Corn Belt in the early spring of 1979, coupled with a cool wet summer, are credited as the most favorable set of environmental factors for optimizing the yield of corn in the north central United States. This was the precise set of climatic circumstances that existed in 1979. It triggered the record corn yields of 106 bushels per acre for the nation.

Satellite sensing for the future should enable accurate prediction of renewable resource productivity. An integrated interagency effort with the U.S. Department of Agriculture, the National Oceanic and Atmospheric Administration, and the National Aeronautics and Space Administration has emerged as *Agricultural and Resources Inventory Survey Through Aerospace Remote Sensing* (AgRISTARS). The information categories to be met by remote sensing include early warning of changes affecting production and quality of renewable resources, commodity production forecasts, renewable resources inventory and assessment, land-use classification and measurement, land-productivity estimates, conservation practices assessment, and pollution detection and impact evaluation. The payoff will come in making early warning crop condition assessments and timely foreign commodity production estimates.

## PRESERVING THE ENVIRONMENT[34]

Future increases in agricultural productivty will come from new combinations of technologies, resource inputs, and economic incentives. The impact on the environment must be minimal. Technological developments that would probably diminish environmental problems and human health hazards are indicated in Table 6. These would include genetic improvements for increased productivity, yield stablity, and greater resistance to competing biological systems and environmental stresses. Greater photosynthetic efficiency and biological nitrogen fixation, as well as solar energy-generating abiotic nitrogen fixation, would also be environmentally neutral. Improved nutrient recovery by crops from the soil generated by reductions in nitrification and denitrification and by microbial (vesicular-arbuscular endomycorrhizae) facilitation would lessen regulatory constraints against fertilizer use, enhance food production, and preserve nonrenewable resources. Greater photosynthetic utilization of atmospheric $CO_2$ would reduce photorespiration, increase yields, and lessen a potential environmental hazard. Integrated pest-management systems can reduce losses from pests, be more environmentally sound, more cost-effective, and help stabilize production at high levels. Greater efficiency in the use of land, water, energy, and atmospheric resources ($CO_2$) should lessen the impact of regulation on agriculture. Classical examples are conservation tillage and drip irrigation. Technologies dependent on solar energy would be dispersed, nonpolluting, add to the earth's resources, and help to preserve nonrenewable energy resources. Technologies for farmers with limited resources and scientific inputs for home gardening would need minimal regulatory constraints.

Certain other technological developments are likely to encounter moderate to severe governmental regulation. These include precipitation augmentation through cloud seeding, the introduction of new toxic chemicals for disease or pest control, chemical or hormonal regulation of biological processes, and increased irrigation by conventional systems.

## CONCLUSION

The nations of the world have an unprecedented opportunity to meet basic human needs for food and fiber. But they must make use of modern means of communication to communicate the results of research to agricutural producers. It took 40 years for hybrid corn to be universally adopted by U.S. farmers. For Iowa farmers, it was only 7 years. The time between the discovery of new technology and its adoption must be shortened. In

TABLE 6 Resource Sparing Technologies that Could Provide a Safe Environment with Sufficient Agricultural Production Output

| Technology | Regulatory Neutral | Regulatory Problematic |
|---|---|---|
| Improved photosynthetic efficiency | x | |
| Improved biological nitrogen fixation | x | |
| Chemical and hormonal regulation of crop growth and metabolism | | x |
| Genetic improvements—tissue culture techniques | | Recombinant DNA |
| Integrated pest management | | On balance fewer regulatory constraints |
| Allelopathy | | Possible toxic plant components |
| Nitrification inhibitors | x | |
| Adaptation of plants to problem soils | x | |
| Microbial enhancement of nutrient uptake by plants | x | |
| New soil and water conservation and management technologies | x | |
| Technologies conserving of resources and useful for small farms | x | |
| Reduced tillage | x except for herbicides | |
| "Blue Revolution"—drip irrigation | x | |
| Cloud seeding—increased snowpack; cumuliform clouds | | x |
| Expansion of irrigated agriculture—total water management systems | | x |
| Genetic adaptation of crops to salt and brackish waters | | x |
| Improved livestock productivity | | |
| • improved production and utilization of feeds | | x |
| • better disease control | | x |
| • genetic improvement | | x |
| Controlled environments for lambs, beef, and dairy cattle | x | |
| Solar energy technologies | | |
| • abiotic nitrogen fixation | x | |
| • greenhouse heating | x | |
| • livestock housing | x | |
| • crop drying | x | |

addition, provision must be made for better communication among scientists, extending from the field researcher to the molecular biologist. The time between a basic research discovery and its first application averages 13 years. The time from introduction of a new technology until its adoption reaches an expected ceiling of 35 years. It now takes 6 to 10 years to train scientists to do research.

We must force the pace of agricultural development. Attention should be directed toward mission-oriented basic research into economically important food crops. The responsiblity of the agricultural scientist no longer ends with a technical report to his professional colleagues in a refereed journal. The future usefulness of the agricultural sciences will depend on how well the results of research relate to the solution of the food production and environmental problems of the 1980s and beyond.

## NOTES

1. The author in the preparation of this paper has drawn heavily from his previous reports. These include "Maximum Production Capacity of Food Crops," BioScience 24:216-224, 1974; "Food Production: Technology and the Resource Base," Science 188:579-584, 1975; Chapter 4, "Increased Crop Yields and Livestock Productivity," *in*: World Food Prospects and Agricultural Potential, Praeger Publishers, N.Y., pp. 66-135, 1977; Chapter 3, "Assessment of Technology in Food Production," *in*: Renewable Resource Management for Forestry and Agriculture, James S. Bethel and Martin A. Massengale, eds., University of Washington Press, Seattle, pp. 35-56, 1978; Chapter 10, "Production Potential of Crop Plants," *in*: Crop Physiology, U.S. Gupta, ed., Oxford and IBH Publishing Co., New Delhi, pp. 334-373, 1978; the concluding chapter "The Shape of Things to Come" *in*: Biology of Crop Productivity, Peter Carlson, ed., Academic Press, N.Y., 1980; Food Production Prospects—Technology and Resource Options, Chicago Council on Foreign Relations, University of Chicago Press, 1979; "Priorities for U.S. Food Research and Management," a position paper prepared for the Presidential Commission on World Hunger, October 1, 1979; the World Food and Nutrition Study, the National Research Council/National Academy of Sciences reports Enhancement of Food Production for the United States, 1975, Potential Contributions of Research, 1977, and Climate and Food, along with the Proceedings of the International Conference on Crop Productivity—Research Imperatives, 1975, Michigan Agricultural Experiment Station and the Charles F. Kettering Foundation, A.W.A. Brown, T.C. Byerly, M. Gibbs, and A. San Pietro, eds., also provided much background information; the report Neither Feast nor Famine, 1978, by S. Enzer, R. Drabrick, and S. Alter, Center for Futures Research, University of Southern California, Lexington Books, D.C. Heath and Co., Lexington, Mass., 185 pp., to which the author contributed, also provided a valuable reference.

2. Crop Productivity—Research Imperatives, Proceedings of an International Conference on Crop Productivity, Michigan Agricultural Experiment Station, East Lansing, Mich., and the C.F. Kettering Foundation, Dayton, Ohio, Boyne Highlands, Mich., October 20-24, 1975.

3. For further development of these concepts see World Food Prospects and Agricultural Potential by Marylin Chou, David P. Harmon, Jr., Herman Kahn, and Sylvan H. Wittwer, Praeger Publishers, N.Y., 1977; Critical Food Issues of the Eighties, Marylin Chou and David P. Harmon, Jr., eds., Pergamon Press, N.Y., 1979; "The Dynamics of Natural Resources and Their Impact on Resource Data," paper presented at the Conference on Systems Aspects of Energy and Mineral Resources, Laxemburg, Austria, August 9-14, 1979, sponsored by IIASA and the Resource System Institute, East-West Center, Honolulu.

4. The information in this section was extracted, in part, from the Coromandel Lecture "Agriculture for the 21st Century," presented by the author, New Delhi, India, September 4, 1979.

5. International Workshop on BioSaline Research, A. San Pietro, ed., National Science Foundation, Washington, D.C., 1977.

6. Significant documents relating hereto include: Landsberg, J.J. and C.V. Cutting, eds., Environmental Effects on Crop Physiology, Academic Press, N.Y., 1977; The National Climate Act of 1978, U.S. Congress; and Agriculture in the New International Development Strategy, FAO/UN, Rome, 1979; The Proceedings of the World Climate Conference, A Conference of Experts on Climate and Mankind, Geneva, Switzerland, February 1979, emphasizes repeatedly the impacts of climate on agriculture, water resources, and food systems.

7. Much progress has been and many recent reports have appeared concerning the potentials of allelopathy in management of weeds. These include: Rice, E.L., Allelopathy, Academic Press, N.Y., 353 pp., 1974; Putnam, A.R. and W.B. Duke, "Allelopathy in Agroecosystems," Ann. Rev. Phyto. Pathol. 16:431-451, 1978; Lockerman, R.H. and A.R. Putnam, "Evaluation of Allelopathic Cucumbers (*Cucumis sativus*) as an Aid in Weed Control," Weed Science 27(1):54-57, 1979; Putnam, A.R. and J. DeFranks, "Use of Allelopathic Cover Crops to Inhibit Weeds," paper presented at the International Congress of Plant Protection, Aug. 8, 1979, Washington, D.C., 1979; Wijewardene, R., Energy Conserving Farming Systems for the Humid Tropics, International Institute of Tropical Agriculture, Ibadan, Nigeria, 1979.

8. The information in this section derived in part from a document prepared by Marvin E. Jensen, entitled "Irrigation Water Management for the Next Decade," presented at the New Zealand Irrigation Conference, Ashburton, April 11-13, 1978; K. Shoji, "Drip Irrigation," Scientific American 237(5):62-68, 1977; and The Nation's Water Resources 1975-2000, Vol. 1, Summary, Second National Water Assessment by the U.S. Water Resources Council, December, 1978.

9. See Water and Water Resources, Consolidated Report of the Texas Agricultural Experiment Station, College Station, Tex., 1978.

10. Derived, in part, from an article prepared by the author in the *Natural History*, 88(9):8, 14, 16, 18, November, 1979.

11. A very comprehensive document has been prepared covering the potentials and problems of weather modification, *The Management of Weather Resources,*

Vol. I, Proposals for a National Policy and Program, report to the Secretary of Commerce from the Weather Modification Advisory Board, June 30, 1978.

12. For further information see Calvin, M., "Petroleum Plantations for Fuel and Materials," *BioScience* 29:333-338, 1979; Hall, D. O., "Solar Energy Use Through Biology—Past, Present, Future," *in*: Future Sources of Organic Raw Materials, Chemrawn Conference, Toronto, 1978; Marzola, D. L. and D. P. Bartholomew, "Photosynthetic Pathway and Biomass Energy Production," *Science* 205:555,559, 1979; Weisz, P. B. and J. F. Marshall, "High-Grade Fuels from Biomass Farming: Potentials and Constraints," *Science* 206:24-29, 1979; Ethanol Production from Biomass with Emphasis on Corn, University of Wisconsin College of Agriculture and Life Sciences, Madison, Sept. 1979; Bassham, J. P., "Increasing Crop Production Through More Controlled Photosynthesis," *Science* 197:630-638, 1977.

13. Background for the Pesticides and Integrated Pest Management sections derived, in part, from Brown, A. W. A., Ecology of Pesticides, John Wiley, N.Y., 1978; Edens, T. C., "Resource Constraints on World Food Production: A System's Perspective," paper presented at the IX International Conference of Plant Protection, Washington, D.C., Aug. 5-11, 1979; Glass, E. H. and H. D. Thurston, "Traditional and Modern Crop Protection in Perspective," *BioScience* 28:109-115; National Academy of Sciences, Contemporary Pest Control Practices and Prospects; Krummel, J., D. Gallan, J. Hough, A. Merrill, I. Schreiner, P. Vittum, F. Koziol, E. Black, D. Yen, and S. Fiance, 1978, "Benefits and Costs of Pesticide Use in U.S. Food Production," *BioScience* 28:772,778-784; Ninth Annual Report of the Council on Environmental Quality, 1978; Integrated Pest Management, A Program of Research for the State Agricultural Experiment Stations and the Colleges of 1890, September 1, 1979; Office of Technology Assessment, Pest Management Strategies in Crop Protection, Vol. I, and Pest Management Strategies, Vol. II, working papers, U.S. Congress, Washington, D.C., 1979.

14. See Ruttan, V. W., "Induced Innovation and Agricultural Development," Food Policy 2(3):196-216, 1977; Hayami, Y. and V. W. Ruttan, "Agricultural Development an International Perspective," Johns Hopkins University Press, Baltimore, Md., 367 pp., 1971.

15. Report of the Jamaica Conference, *in*: Mobilizing Technology for World Development, J. Ramsk and C. Weiss, Jr., eds., pp. 36-37, Overseas Development Council, Washington, D.C., 1979.

16. All major reports of research initiatives for improving agricultural productivity include increased photosynthetic efficiency as a high priority. They are too numerous to list here and are covered under footnotes 3 and 16.

17. An enormous number of reports, books, and magazines have appeared on this topic during the past 5 years. A partial list follows: Ayanaba, A. and P. J. Dart, Biological Nitrogen Fixation in Farming Systems of the Tropics, John Wiley & Sons, Inc., N.Y., 377 pp., 1977; Biological Nitrogen Fixation in Forage-Livestock Systems, American Association of Agronomy Special Publication No. 28, Madison, Wis., 127 pp., 1976; Special Issue: "Future of Biological Nitrogen Fixation" BioScience 28(9) (September Issue); Selecting and Breeding Legumes for Enhanced Nitrogen Fixation, Recommendations for Research and Proceedings of a Workshop, Oct. 23-24, Boyce Thompson Institute at Cornell, 1978; Brill, W. J., "Nitrogen Fixation: Basic to Applied," Amer. Sci. 67(4):458-466; Dobereiner, J.,

R. H. Burris, and Al Hollaender, eds., Limitations and Potentials for Biological Nitrogen Fixation in the Tropics, Plenum Press, N.Y., 398 pp., 1978; Evans, H. J., Enhancing Biological Nitrogen Fixation, Proceedings of a workshop held June 6, 1974, National Science Foundation, 52 pp., 1975; Exploiting the Legume-Rhizobium symbiosis in Tropical Agriculture, Proceedings of Workshop, Aug., 1976, University of Hawaii Niftal Project, United States Agency for International Development, College of Tropical Agriculture Miscellaneous Publication 145, 469 pp., 1977; International Symposium on Biological Applications of Solar Energy, December 1-5, 1978, School of Biological Sciences, Madurai-Kamaraj University, Madurai-625 021 India, 82 pp.; The Legume/Rhizobium Symbiosis in Tropical Agriculture: A Selective Bibliography with Annotations, compiled for the University of Hawaii Niftal Project, United States Agency for International Development by John Bose, II, College of Tropical Agriculture and Human Resources Miscellaneous Publication 161, Department of Agronomy and Soil Science, Hawaii Agricultural Experiment Station, University of Hawaii, 193 pp., 1978; National Science Foundation, Enhancing Biological Production of Ammonia from Atmospheric Nitrogen and Soil Nitrate, University of California, Davis, California, 61 pp., 1978; National Science Foundation, Genetic Engineering for Nitrogen Fixation, Washington, D.C., 122 pp., 1977; Newton, W., J. R. Postgate, and C. Rodriguez-Barrueco, eds., Recent Developments in Nitrogen Fixation, Academic Press, N.Y., 622 pp., 1977; Newton, W. E. and C. J. Nyman, eds., Proceedings of the 1st International Symposium on Nitrogen Fixation, Vols. I and II, 717 pp., 1977; Nitrogen Fixation—An Analysis of Present Research and Implications for the Future, Technical Insights, Inc., 2337 Lemoine Ave., P.O. Box 1304, Fort Lee, N.J. 07024, 198 pp., 1978; Nutman, P.S., ed., Symbiotic Nitrogen Fixation in Plants, Cambridge University Press, Cambridge, 584 pp., 1976; Proceedings of the Steenbock-Kettering International Symposium on Nitrogen Fixation, June 12-16, 1978, University of Wisconsin, Madison, Wis., 87 pp.; Subba Rao, N. S., Soil Microorganisms and Plant Growth, Mohan Primlani, Oxford & IBH Publishing Co., 66 Janpath, New Delhi, India, 289 pp., 1977; Takahashi, H., Nitrogen Fixation and Nitrogen Cycle, Japanese Committee for International Biological Program, Science Council of Japan, University of Tokyo Press, 161 pp., 1975.

18. The potentials in this area were reviewed in a workshop at the National Agricultural Library, Beltsville, Md., Nov. 22-23, 1976, the proceedings of which have been published as *Plant Adaptation to Mineral Stress on Problem Soils*, Office of Agriculture, Technical Assistance Bureau, Agency for International Development, Washington, D.C.; American Society of Agronomy, *Crop Tolerance to Suboptimal Land Conditions*, ASA Special Publication 32, American Society of Agronomy, Madison, Wis., 1978.

19. Genetic Engineering for Nitrogen Fixation, A. Hollaender, ed., Plenum Press, N.Y., 1977.

20. Information for this section derived, in part, from Huber, D. H., H. L. Warren, D. W. Nelson, and C. Y. Tsai, "Nitrification Inhibitors—New Tools for Food Production," *BioScience* 27:523-529, 1977; and from Tiedje, J. M., "Meeting World Food Needs—Problems and Perspectives," paper presented at the Annual Meetings of the American Association for the Advancement of Science Symposium on Biological Transformation of Inorganic Nitrogen, Washington, D.C., 1978;

Hauck, R. D., "Nitrogen Deficits in $^{15}N$ Balance Studies," preliminary analysis for the Denitrification Seminar sponsored by the Fertilizer Institute, San Franciso, Oct. 1977; Tiedje, J. M., J. Sorenson, and Y. Y. L. Chang, "Assimilatory and Dissimilatory Nitrate Reduction: Perspectives and Methodology for Simultaneous Measurement of Several Nitrogen Cycle Processes," presented at International Conference on Terrestrial Nitrogen Cycles—Processes Ecosystem Strategies, and Management Impacts, Osterfarnelo, Sweden, Sept. 16-22, 1979, sponsored by SCOPE/UNEP, to be published in Proceedings Ecol. Res. Comm. (Stockholm); Smith, M. S. and J. M. Tiedje, "The Effect of Roots on Soil Denitrification," Soil Sci. Soc. Amer. Jour. (Sept.-Oct., 1979, in press); Tiedje, J. M., R. B. Firestone, M. K. Betlach, M. S. Smith, and W. H. Cashey, "Methods for the Production and Use of Nitrogen-13 in Studies of Denitrification," Soil Sci. Soc. Amer. Jour. 43(5):709-716, 1979.

21. Principal references are Tansey, M.R., Microbial Facilitation of Plant Nutrition in Microorganisms and Minerals, E. D. Weinberg, ed., Marcel Dekker, pp. 343-385, 1977; G. R. Safir, "Vesicular-Arbuscular Mycorrhizae and Crop Productivity" *in* : Biology and Crop Productivity, Peter Carlson, ed., Academic Press, N.Y. (in press), 1980; and Cress, W. A., G. O. Thronberry, and D. L. Lindsey, "Kinetics of Phosphorus Absorption by Mycorrhizal and Nonmycorrhizal Tomato Roots," Plant Physiol. 64:484-487, 1979; Ruchle, J. L. and D. H. Marx, "Fiber, Food, Fuel and Fungal Symbionts," Science 206:419-422, 1979.

22. See "Interactions of Science and Technology in the Innovative Process: Some Case Studies," final report prepared for the National Science Foundation by Battelle Columbus Laboratories, March 19, 1973.

23. An important volume with contributions from many authors has appeared as an excellent compendium of reports covering resistance of plants to environmental stresses. Mussell, H. and R. C. Staples, eds., Stress Physiology in Crop Plants, Wiley Interscience Publishers, N.Y., 1979.

24. See Mineral Resources and the Environment, pp. 237-240, National Academy of Sciences, Washington, D.C.; Airborne Particles, National Research Council and U.S. Department of Commerce, 554 pp., 1977; Proceedings of the First International Symposium on Acid Precipitation and the Forest Ecosystem, U.S. Forest Service General Technical Report NE-23, 1976; Likens, G. E. and F. H. Bormann, "Acid Rain: A Serious Regional Environmental Problem," Science 184:1176-1179, 1974; Likens, G. E., "Acid Precipitation," Chemical and Engineering News 54, Nov. 1976, pp. 29, 44, 1976; Likens, G. F., R. F. Wright, J. N. Galloway and T. J. Butler, "Acid Rain," Sci. Amer. 241(4):43-51, 1979.

25. There are numerous reports on the carbon dioxide issue—both climatic and biological. Effects on climate are summarized in Energy and Climate, National Academy of Sciences, Washington, D.C., 1977; The Long Term Impact of Atmospheric Carbon Dioxide on Climate, Jason Technical Report JSR-78-07, SRI International Arlington, Va., 1979; Carbon Dioxide Accumulation in the Atmosphere, Synthetic Fuels and Energy Policy, A Symposium, Committee on Government Affairs, U.S. Senate, July 1979; "A report of an Ad Hoc Study Group on Carbon Dioxide and Climate, Woods Hole, Mass., July 23-27, 1979," Climate Research Board, Assembly of Mathematical and Physical Sciences, National Research Council/National Academy of Sciences, Washington, D.C. The biological effects of a rising atmospheric level of $CO_2$ have also been summarized:

Wittwer, S. H. and W. Robb, "Carbon Dioxide Enrichment of Greenhouse Atmospheres for Food Crop Production," Econ. Bot. 18:34-56, 1964; Wittwer, S. H., "Carbon Dioxide Fertilization of Crop Plants," *in*: Crop Physiology, U. S. Gupta, ed., Oxford and IBH Publishing Co., New Delhi, pp. 310-333, 1978; Allen, L. H., "Potentials for Carbon Dioxide Enrichment," *in*: Modification of the Aerial Environment of Crops, B. J. Barfield and J. F. Gerber, eds., Monograph No. 2, American Society of Agricultural Engineers, St. Joseph, Mo., pp. 500-519, 1979; Artica, R. N., B. W. Pooviah, and O. E. Smith, "Changes in Carbon Fixation, Tuberization, and Growth Induced by $CO_2$ Applications to the Root Zone of Potato Plants," Science 205:1279-1280.

26. The latest in hydroponic technology is the nutrient film technique. For further details see D. Rudd-Jones, Root Environmental Control: Nutrient Film Culture, Proceedings of the International Symposium on Controlled Environmental Agriculture, University of Arizona, Tucson, April 7-8, 1977, pp. 216-224; Wittwer, S. H. and S. Honma, Greenhouse Tomatoes, Lettuce and Cucumbers, Michigan State University Press, East Lansing, Mich., 1979; A. J. Cooper, Nutrient Film Technique of Growing Crops, Grower Books, London, 1976.

27. Numerous summaries, reviews, and documentaries have recently been prepared on this topic. These include The proceedings of the first six annual meetings (1973 through 1979) of the Plant Growth Regulator Working Group; the entire issue of Outlook on Agriculture 9(2), 1976; Wittwer, S. H., "Growth Regulants in Agriculture," Outlook on Agriculture 6(5):206-217, 1971; Nickell, L. G., Plant Growth Regulators C and EN, Oct. 9, 1978; Phytohormones and Related Compounds: A Comprehensive Treatise, Vols. I and II,; D. S. Letham, P. B. Goodwin, and T. J. V. Higgins, eds., Elsevier Press, N.Y., 1978; Plant Regulation and World Agriculture, T. K. Scott, ed., Plenum Press, N.Y., 1979.

28. The original disclosure was by Peters, R. R., L. T. Chapin, K. B. Leining, and H. A. Tucke, "Supplemental Lighting Stimulates Growth and Lactation in Cattle," Science 199:911-912, 1978. More recent papers are Tucker, H. A. and W. D. Oxender, "Seasonal Aspects of Reproduction, Growth, and Hormones in Cattle and Horses," presented at the annual meeting of the American Zoological Society, Richmond, Va., February 1979; Tucker, H. A., "Photoperiodic Control of Hormones, Growth, and Lactation in Cattle," Journal Article No. 8842 of the Michigan Agricultural Experiment Station, 1979.

29. The recent literature on aquaculture and fisheries management, both salt and fresh water, is extensive. The author has drawn from the following reports: World Food and Nutrition Study Supporting Papers, Aquatic Food Sources, Vol. 1, pp. 287-318, National Research Council/National Academy of Sciences, Washington, D.C., 1977; Aquaculture in Hawaii, An Assessment by James S. Corbin, Department of Planning and Economic Development, State of Hawaii, 1976; Weatherly, A. H. and B. M. G. Cogger, "Fish Culture: Problems and Prospects," Science 197:427-430, 1977; May, R. M., J. R. Beddington, C. W. Clark, S. J. Holt, and R. M. Laws, "Management of Multispecies Fisheries," Science 205:267-277, 1979; Meyers, S. P., "Marine Fish Farming in Israel," Feedstuffs 49(34):23-25, 1977; Krone, N. "Fish as Food—Present Contribution and Potential," Food Policy 4(4):259-268, 1979.

30. Reports relating to appropriate agricultural technology are numerous. Books have been written, journals now exist, and organizations flourish. Much stems from

E. E. Schumacher's Small is Beautiful, Harper and Row, N.Y., 305 pp., 1973. Many reports relating thereto have come from the Center for the Biology of Natural Systems, Washington University, St. Louis, Mo. Other documents are those of R. J. Congdon, Introduction to Appropriate Technology Toward a Simpler Life Style, Rodale Press, Emmaus, Pa., 1977; Radical Agriculture, Richard Merrill, ed., Harper and Row, N.Y., 459 pp., 1976; "Soft Technologies and Hard Choices," by Colin Norman, Worldwatch Paper No. 21, 48 pp., 1978; "Economic Stability, Natural Resource Conservation, and Pollution Control in U.S. Agriculture," by W. R. Z. Willey, Environmental Defense Fund, 57 page mimeo, 1978; "Energy, Appropriate Technology, and International Interdependence," by D. E. Morrison, Michigan Agricultural Experiment Station Journal Article No. 8818, 60 pp., 1978; "Energy Strategy: The Road Not Taken," by A. Lovins, Foreign Affairs, Fall, 1976; Appropriate Technology—Problems and Promises, N. Jequier, ed., Development Center Studies, Development Center for the Organization for Economic Cooperation, Paris, 1976: Workshop on Appropriate Technology, Final Report and Proceedings, National Science Foundation, January 23-25, 1978; Agriculture Technology for Developing Nations, Farm Mechanization Alternatives for 1-10 Hectare Farms, Proceedings Special International Conference, University of Illinois at Urbana-Champaign, May 23-24, 1978; "Small Farm Research Priorities in the North Central Region," North Central Regional Center for Rural Development, Iowa State University of Science and Technology, Ames, Iowa, 1979.

31. For further information see: Egger, Kurt, "Eco-Farming," report to the German Government on a development project in Rwanda, East Africa, 1976; Plant and Animal Resources for Food Production by Developing Countries in the 1980's, a "state of knowledge" paper prepared for a conference on agricultural production at Bonn, Federal Republic of Germany, October 8-12, 1979.

32. Many recent documents from private and public sources have focused on the science of home gardening. These include Gardening for Food and Fun, Yearbook of Agriculture, U.S. Department of Agriculture, 1977; Mittleider Grow—Box Gardens, International Food Production Methods, Inc., Salt Lake City, Utah; Vegetable Gardening Basics, by D. Bruce Johnstone and Elwood H. Brindle, Burgess Publishing Co., 1976; Successful Home Gardening, by E. Gordon Wells, Jr., 1977; Ortho Book Series—All About Vegetables, Gardening Shortcuts, Weather-Wise Gardening, Chevron Chemical Co., Ortho Division—Garden and Home, 200 Bush Street, San Francisco, Calif., 1973; "Science and the Home Garden," Michigan State University Agricultural Experiment Station, Science in Action No. 28, 1975.

33. These are emphasized by Sterling Wortman and Ralph Cummings, Jr. *in*: To Feed This World, Johns Hopkins University Press, Baltimore, Md., 1978.

34. See Wittwer, S. H., "Future Technological Advances in Agriculture and Their Impact on the Regulatory Environment," BioScience 29(10):603-610.

## REFERENCES

Ackermann, W.C. (1979) Congressional Testimony on Agricultural Productivity and Environmental Quality. Agriculture Committee, Conservation and Credit

Subcommittee, and Science and Technology Committee, Natural Resources and Environment Subcommittee, July 25, 1979, U.S. Congress.

Barlowe, R. (1979) Soils, Plants, and Land Use in the United States. Monograph on Land Use Planning, edited by M.T. Beatty. Madison, Wis.: American Society of Agronomy.

Brown, N.L. and J.W. Howe (1978) Solar energy for village development. Science 199:651-657.

Buringh, P., H.D.J. van Heemst, and G.J. Staring (1975) Computation of the Absolute Maximum Food Production of the World. A contribution to the research project on Problems of Population Doubling and Food Supply, Department of Tropical Soil Science, Agricultural University, Wageningen, The Netherlands.

Burton, G.W. (1977) Pages 71-86, Proceedings of the World Food Conference of 1976. Ames, Iowa: Iowa State University Press.

Correll, D.L. (1978) Estuarine productivity. BioScience 28(10):646-650.

Dalrymple, D.G. (1978) Adoption of high yielding varieties of wheat and rice. Paper presented at a joint meeting of the Agricultural History Society and the American Historical Association, San Francisco, Calif., 1978.

Eckholm, E.P. (1976) Losing Ground. New York: W.W. Norton Co.

Epstein, E. and J.D. Norlyn (1977) Seawater-based crop production: A feasibility study. Science 197:249-251.

Evans, L.T. (1975) Crop Physiology. London: Cambridge University Press.

Evenson, R.E., P.E. Waggoner, and V.W. Ruttan (1979) Economic benefits from research: An example from agriculture. Science 205:1101-1107.

Garcia, L.R. and J.H. Hanway (1976) Foliar fertilization of soybeans during the seed filling period. Agronomy Journal 68:653-657.

Glass, E.H. (1979) Crop protection and integrated pest management. Congressional Testimony on Agricultural Productivity and Environmental Quality. Agriculture Committee, Conservation and Credit Subcommittee, and Science and Technology Committee, Natural Resources and Environment Subcommittee, July 25, 1979, U.S. Congress.

Harlan, J.R. (1977) How green can a revolution be. Pages 105-110, Crop Resources, ed. by D.S. Seigler. New York: Academic Press, Inc.

Hodgson, H.J. (1978) Food from plant products—forage. Presented at a Symposium on the Complementary Role of Plant and Animal Products in the U.S. Food System, November 29-30, 1977, National Academy of Sciences, Washington, D.C.

Josling, T. (1979) International Trade and World Food Production. University of Chicago: Chicago Council on Foreign Relations.

Mayer, A. and J. Mayer (1974) Agriculture, the island empire. Daedalus 103(Summer):83-95.

Melchers, G. (1978) Somatic hybrid plant of potato and tomato regenerated from fused protoplasts. Carlsberg Research Communication 43:203-218.

Nasyrov, Y.S. (1978) Genetic control of photosynthesis and improving of crop productivity. Annual Review of Plant Physiology 29:215-237.

National Research Council (1977) World Food and Nutrition Study, The Potential Contributions of Research. Washington, D.C.: National Academy of Sciences.

Ries, S.K., V. Wert, C.C. Sweeley and R.A. Leavitt (1977) Thiochontonal: A new naturally occurring plant growth regulator. Science 195:1339-1341.

Rosenberg, N.J. (1979) Supply and quality of water for irrigation. Congressional Testimony on Agricultural Productivity and Environmental Quality. Agriculture Committee, Conservation and Credit Subcommittee, and Science and Technology Committee, Natural Resources and Environment Subcommittee, July 25, 1979, U.S. Congress.

Salisbury, G.W. and R.G. Hart (1979) The evaluation and future of American animal agriculture. Perspectives in Biology and Medicine 22(3):394-409.

Schilfgaarde, J. van (1979) Congressional Testimony on Agricultural Productivity and Environmental Quality. Agricultural Committee, Conservation and Credit Subcommittee, and Science and Technology Committee, National Resources and Environment Subcommittee, July 25, 1979, U.S. Congress.

Shalhevet, J., A. Mantell, H. Bielorai, and D. Shimski (1976) Irrigation of Field and Orchard Crops Under Semi-Arid Conditions. International Irrigation Center Publication No. 1, Bet Dagan, Israel.

Treharne, B., M.R. Moles, and C.K. McKibben (1978) A Nitrogen Fertilizer Generator for Farm Use. Technical Note 1. Dayton, Ohio: Charles F. Kettering Foundation.

Triplett, G.B. Jr., and D.M. Van Doren, Jr. (1977) Agriculture without tillage. Scientific American 236(1):28-33.

Vlasin, R.D. (1975) Conservation, use and retention of agricultural lands for all out food production. Pages 35-53, American Society of Agronomy Special Publication 23.

Williams, W.T. (1978) Effects on plants of sulfur pollutants from coal combustion. Report 7866. San Francisco: Citizens for a Better Environment.

Wittwer, S.H. and M.J. Bukovac (1969) The uptake of nutrients through leaf surfaces. Pages 235-261, Handbuch der Pflanzenernahrung und Dungung, edited by K. Scharrer and H. Linser. Berlin: Springer-Verlag.

# DISCUSSANT'S REMARKS ON THE PAPER BY S. H. WITTWER

O. LOUCKS
*The Institute of Ecology*

Six points are mentioned in Dr. Wittwer's paper that should be expanded upon and emphasized for discussion by this task group.

## RESIDUALS OF AGRICULTURAL PRODUCTION

The agro-ecosystem is not a closed system, but is open and dynamic. Manipulations (as an input) are required to maintain outputs sufficient to continue the manipulations, i.e., the farm operator. Thus, a balance is required between the inputs designed to enhance productivity and the residuals or wastes that degrade the system itself, or surrounding resources such as lakes and streams.

One of the important "residuals" is soil, although it is not a conscious input. Soil erosion is currently a serious national problem, compounded now by the high level of related pollutants carried with soil from the agricultural system to the nonagricultural environment. The water quality legislation giving EPA responsibility under Section 208 for control of nonpoint pollution is one approach to limiting residuals from agricultural production.

Control of nonpoint source residuals from agriculture can be achieved in a variety of ways. These include management practices to reduce runoff from cultivated lands, removal and proper storage of animal wastes, protection of streambanks to reduce silt loss, control of drift in the application of fertilizers, herbicides, or pesticides, and control of persistent toxic compounds in sludge applied to cultivated lands.

Prevention of soil loss has both economic and political components. The recent increases in topsoil residuals are of little concern if the economic yield of the crop is high (e.g., as in corn crops). Societal acceptance of programs to control these losses will depend on the extent of perceived benefits, and this varies widely depending on farm ownership. For example, if proposed control programs appear to benefit the nonrural community (less pollution in recreational waters), acceptance is lower than if the benefits are perceived as going primarily to the family farm operator (maintenance of crop productivity for future generations) as a trade-off for higher-cost soil maintenance today.

## NITROGEN LOSS FROM PRESENT AND FUTURE AGRO-ECOSYSTEMS

As the price of chemically based nitrogen fertilizers continues to increase, the amounts of nitrogen used in agricultural systems will change, and the losses to the atmosphere as well as to surface and groundwater will be of greater concern. Quantitative measurements of the extent of nitrogen release to the atmosphere are needed urgently at the present time, as well as assessments designed to assess losses in the future when biologically fixed nitrogen may replace the present chemically fixed nitrogen.

## SLUDGE UTILIZATION ON FARMLAND

The potential exists to increase greatly the use of sludge as a nutrient source on cultivated lands. For some crop systems, municipal sludge could provide all the required nutrient input. The presence of small amounts of toxic compounds (particularly persistent organics and heavy metals) could present serious problems, however, if application of currently available sludges becomes widespread. For example, sludge at up to 10 ppm of PCBs is acceptable for use within current EPA standards. However, when up to 10 tons per acre of fertilizer are applied annually to meet nitrogen requirements, the resulting PCB application is almost a pound per acre, equivalent to past applications of DDT for insect control.

## ANIMAL WASTES

Animal wastes from feedlots and other intensive animal production facilities constitute a serious residual capable of improved utilization. If increasing amounts of these wastes are used as substitutes for chemical fertilizers, the present problem will be reduced, but concerns will shift to issues of pathogen distribution and control.

## FUEL USE

Many agricultural residuals lend themselves to production of methane or alcohol. Within 2 decades, it seems likely that farming units will have to become self-sufficient in energy supply through recycling. Investigations of the advantages and disadvantages of biomass conversion to useable energy sources, and the associated pollutants of this practice, will be needed.

## SIZE OF FARMING UNITS

There is currently a trend toward large and somewhat specialized farm units. Current economic constraints in fertilizer and herbicide costs and in energy availability may possibly exacerbate this farm-size relation, forcing more small units out of intensive management. In addition, the utilization of residuals cited above may shift agricultural practices to more integrated farm systems.

During the discussion we should keep in mind that agricultural practices in the future will have to be practical if they are to be considered seriously by the farming community. The historical reluctance on the part of farmers to accept change will be an important consideration in new technologies and management practices, but the trends seem likely to be in the directions indicated.

# SUMMARY OF THE TASK GROUP

D. PIMENTEL *and* R. LOEHR
*Cornell University*

## INTRODUCTION

Although the potential for future technological developments in agriculture appears to be encouraging, environmental problems associated with agriculture should continue in the future. Several future problem areas were identified. These were not meant to represent all potential problems, but only those that were considered most important to EPA. Many of the changes and environmental problems that are projected depend in part on developments in energy resources, production technology, and use of chemicals, as well as changes in society's priorities for land and water use. Recognizing the interdependency of agriculture with other sectors of society in utilizing similar resources, several future problem areas were identified.

## IDENTIFICATION OF FUTURE PROBLEM AREAS

Ten major problem areas were identified and these are discussed below.

### INTEGRATED PEST MANAGEMENT AND AGRICULTURAL CHEMICAL USE

Current agricultural research is concerned with increasing crop yields, and numerous chemicals play an important role in agricultural productivity. Of particular importance will be the use of pesticides in integrated pest management (IPM) and the use of other chemicals for crop and livestock production. While increased use of IPM should reduce the amount of pesticides applied per acre of cropland, total pesticide use will increase. The total use of all chemicals in agriculture should rise during the next 20 to 50 years. The impact of increased use of chemicals in agriculture should have a growing impact on the environment. This is especially so if the application of pesticides and other chemicals by aircraft continues to rise.

## ANALYTICAL MEASUREMENT AND MONITORING STRATEGIES

Little information exists on the amount of priority pollutants in industrial, municipal, and agricultural discharges and on the removal of such pollutants that takes place through the use of existing pollution control technology, including land application of wastewaters and sludges. The basis for regulation is the ability to: (a) measure what is to be controlled (to know whether something is in the environment in concentrations requiring controls), (b) know the levels that can be achieved with existing or future control technology, and (c) identify whether someone is in compliance. Inadequate measurement and monitoring render regulations worthless or meaningless. Excessive measurement and monitoring is an unnecessary economic burden to the public and industry.

## CONTROL OF SOIL AND CHEMICAL RUNOFF

The United States has a national goal for the maintenance of land and water quality; however, accomplishing this goal while maintaining profitable agricultural production is not possible with current economic incentives. New incentives are needed to encourage farmers to follow established soil and water conservation practices. As competitive demands on land and water increase in society, conservation measures for these resources in the future will become more important.

## LAND DISPOSAL OF WASTE MATERIALS

Land application and storage of waste material (wastewater, sludge, and solid waste) are becoming accepted national practices. The impact of these practices on the future utility of land has not been addressed. Little data currently exist regarding the retention capability of soil, or the transport, transformation, or fate of toxic materials in soil. The quantity of waste material is likely to increase. Thus, the environmental impact of land disposal may be severe and the future agricultural potential of the land may be reduced.

## BIOMASS-ENERGY CONVERSION PROCESSES

Future energy sources might make use of crop and forestry residues and possibly alcohol derived from grains. A major difficulty in using substantial amounts of biomass as an energy source will be the anticipated environmental degradation through soil depletion and pollution. Cropland and forest residues currently help maintain productive soils, alleviate extensive soil erosion and rapid water runoff, reduce the conversion of soil humus to $CO_2$ and serve as a continual source of soil nutrients. The agricultural impact resulting from potential biomass removal could become a serious environmental problem.

## EVALUATION OF NEW AGRICULTURAL CHEMICALS

As the search for new biologically active compounds continues (e.g., plant growth regulators), the current requirement of testing these chemicals by employing one set of procedures needs to be revised. The present practice of classifying plant-growth regulators and similar agricultural chemicals as pesticides could limit the future development of potentially useful agricultural chemicals that under normal use and safety conditions would pose little environmental or health damage.

## AIR EMISSIONS FROM INDUSTRIAL PROCESSES

The impact of air pollutants on plants and agricultural animals will be an increasing problem; of particular concern is their long-range transport and the adverse impact these pollutants and their degradation products may have on agricultural productivity.

## BIOLOGICAL FIXATION OF NITROGEN

Air and water quality trade-offs will become increasingly important with the future rise in the use of nitrogen fertilizer. The extent of nitrogen loss from agricultural lands has not been fully assessed. Substitution of enhanced biologically fixed nitrogen for chemical fertilizers may also be possible in the future. The potential problems and opportunities associated with the use of biologically fixed nitrogen need to be investigated.

## IRRIGATION WATER USE AND EFFICIENCY

Water will continue to be a vital resource for future agricultural development in the United States. If the current trend in over-drawing underground water continues, serious problems will emerge. Runoff from inefficient irrigation could lead to future leaching of chemicals from the soil, result in extensive soil erosion, and further contribute to increased sedimentation in aquatic systems and build-up of salt in agricultural soils.

Remaining water supplies could become more saline as well as contaminated with leached chemicals. Supplemental irrigation is increasing in the Midwest and East, thereby extending such problems to these areas of the nation.

### IMPACTS OF URBANIZATION, TRANSPORTATION SYSTEMS, AND ENERGY RESOURCE DEVELOPMENT SYSTEMS

Because of society's concentration in urban areas and its dependence on increased mobility, increasing demands for energy will affect the quality of available land and water resources for agricultural use. Development of energy-producing facilities and the expansion of cities and transport systems will remove agricultural land from production and degrade land and other resources. This could result in the need to cultivate marginal lands that will require increased demands for agricultural chemicals and other inputs.

### OTHER FUTURE PROBLEMS

In addition to the major areas for potential environmental problems mentioned above, other problems and opportunities may develop. These include:

1. changes in agricultural practices and technology,
2. agricultural plants and animals contributing toward improved environmental quality,
3. economic and legal factors impacting on the distribution and quality of water for agriculture and society,
4. weed control potential employing allelopathic and competetive responses of plants, and
5. use of wastes as livestock feed.

## PRIORITIES OF PROBLEMS

The priorities established for the problem areas outlined above are reflected by the order in which they are presented. It should be pointed out, however, that as new technologies are developed the priorities of these problems will also change. Thus, although integrated pest-management systems and agricultural chemicals, analytical and monitoring strategies, control of soil erosion and chemical runoff, and waste disposal on land are currently considered the top four items demanding investigation, improvements in these problem areas within the next 20 years may justify a shift in priorities as new problems take precedence.

For example, with the development of biological nitrogen fixation, new problems may develop. Also, with the improvement of new pollution-control technologies, adverse effects of industrial emission on agricultural productivity might be reduced. Other problems such as the deteriorating quality of available water supplies, as well as of croplands and rangelands, however, may increase beyond the 20- to 50-year time span if food production technologies do not change while intensity of management grows.

## RECOMMENDATIONS

The Task Group on Agriculture made several research recommendations that, if successful, would help reduce the potential environmental problem areas that were identified. The information and knowledge obtained via the proposed research efforts will provide the basis for development of environmental protection strategies that would help meet the food needs of the nation while protecting environmental quality.

1. Evaluation of the cost effectiveness of pesticide use in IPM and other agricultural chemicals should be made. This should include an assessment of benefits and risks to the environment and society as a whole.

2. Protocols must be developed for adequate sampling and analyses for the presence of chemical pollutants in water, soil and biota. The scientific basis for establishing these protocols must be defined, as well as the frequency, type, and location of sampling. These new monitoring strategies are needed to ensure adequate assessment of future environmental problems.

3. Data are needed on soil erosion and chemical runoff problems to provide a framework within which conservation guidelines can be developed. These studies should include consideration of (a) long-term benefits of soil and water conservation; (b) the costs of conservation structures and their effects on farming operations, energy needs, and pesticide requirements; (c) the impact of these practices on agricultural yield; and (d) incentives to farmers for the control of soil erosion.

4. Research is needed to determine the carrying capacity of land for the retention and conversion of pollutants. Data should be acquired on the fate of toxic materials in soils and the risk of damage

to human health and ecosystems through accumulation of these materials in the soil.

5. The potential of soil and environmental degradation resulting from the removal of biomass should be investigated. Regulatory programs might have to be developed to control soil loss in the event that biomass conversion processes become an important energy resource.

6. Not all chemicals should be classed as pesticides for purposes of toxicological analyses. Growth regulators, for example, should not be tested with the same protocol as a toxic insecticide. This change would improve the availability of essential chemicals for agricultural production while reducing costs. However, the environment should still be protected by the new protocols for less toxic agricultural chemicals.

7. Research is needed to determine projected trends in land use for energy development, urbanization, and transportation systems, and to investigate the society's need for food, water and natural biota. The data generated would assist EPA in establishing regulatory standards for protecting agricultural and forestry lands from degradation effects resulting from other land uses.

8. The impacts of air pollution on agricultural productivity and animal health need to be investigated. Identification of particularly damaging pollutants must be made and data bases established for future policy decisions.

9. Mass balance studies of normal agricultural nitrogen use should be developed to determine the source, amounts, and forms of nitrogen released to the atmosphere as well as surface and groundwaters. Development of systems for biological fixation of nitrogen is needed along with a careful analysis of potential environmental impacts. Models will be needed to assess differences in nitrogen distribution resulting from chemical or biological nitrogen sources.

10. Strategies for more efficient use of water supplies must be developed to ensure adequate sources for future agricultural and societal demands. Research programs should be developed to assess environmental problems and efficiency of various irrigation technologies for agriculture such as flooding, furrow, sprinkle, pivot, high frequency, and drip.

11. Future research efforts should be directed toward identifying opportunities to enhance environmental quality as well as the agricultural enterprise. Agricultural productivity may be improved by appropriate agricultural technology. For example, little is known

about potential benefits as well as harm to plant growth from increased atmospheric concentration of $NO_x$ and $CO_2$ or from nitrification inhibitors and allelopathic systems.

12. Current trends in farm practices and scale of operation provide new opportunities for innovation in environmental enhancement. Research is needed on such topics as rhizosphere production and release of chemicals that promote or inhibit general or specific growth factors, natural herbicides, benefits of crop residues, and the potential to exploit opportunities in soil microbiology.

13. A limited effort has been made, to date, in exploiting natural biological processes to increase agricultural productivity while enhancing the environment. Solutions to future problems may depend on this neglected area of research. Future management strategies in agriculture may depend on a proper balance between biologically and technologically based processes.

14. The need for more agricultural production is obvious. The output per unit land area per unit time must increase. Major opportunities exist to increase this productivity through the effective safe use of fertilizers, pesticides, irrigation, and other inputs in the agricultural system. As the cost of food tends to account for a larger share of citizen income, there will be enhanced small garden and animal husbandry operations. Considerable effort will be needed to monitor both pesticide residues on home-raised foods and residues getting into air and water from the very small operations.

# TASK GROUP ON AGRICULTURE

DAVID PIMENTEL (*Group Chairman*), Cornell University
ROBERT BOXLEY, U.S. Department of Agriculture
RAYMOND LOEHR (*Rapporteur*), Cornell University
ORIE LOUCKS (*Dissussant*), Institute of Ecology
LOUIS NICKELL, Velsicol Chemical Corporation
ARLAND PAULI, Deere & Company
SYLVAN WITTWER (*Paper Author*), Michigan State University
ROBERT YECK, U.S. Department of Agriculture

# 5 Toxic Substances

## FUTURE TRENDS IN THE DEVELOPMENT AND USE OF POTENTIALLY TOXIC SUBSTANCES

J. E. GIBSON
*Chemical Industry Institute of Technology*

### INTRODUCTION

Increased awareness of the potentially adverse effects of chemical use has stimulated the development of methods and procedures to predict the existence of potential hazards and to provide essential knowledge for the control or elimination of risks. Past occurrences (sometimes referred to as catastrophic chemical episodes) involving chlorinated pesticides, vinyl chloride, chlorinated dioxins, cadmium, methyl mercury, polychlorinated biphenyls (PCBs), and polybrominated biphenyls (PBBs) have emphasized the need to prevent similar occurrences in the future. Success will not be achieved easily, however. On the one hand, modern society demands harder, stronger, and longer-lasting materials, more effective pharmaceuticals and pesticides, and new energy sources (e.g., coal liquefaction, shale oil extraction, biomass fermentation), all of which are to be produced at higher speed and lower cost. On the other hand, many substances and materials of the future (like many substances and materials of the past) will possess toxic properties. Under conditions of use some of them will constitute a hazard to workers, consumers, or the ecosystem. Nonetheless, it can be confidently predicted that safe use of these substances and materials can be assured through progress in analytical methods, toxicity testing, quantitative risk/hazard assessments, and pollution-control technology.

One trend influencing the development and use of potentially toxic substances is the present emphasis on predictive models, used prior to widescale production, for determining toxicity or environmental harm. The goal of these activities is to generate quantitative statements concerning the probability of hazards in the manufacture, use, or disposal of chemical substances.

Reliable methods for risk/hazard assessment cannot yet be claimed to exist, however. Even if they did exist, a sufficient number of trained people are not available to carry forward such assessments. A serious gap therefore exists between our desire to conduct conclusive risk/hazard assessments and our ability to do so.

This discussion focuses on trends in toxicology as a predictive science and on the value of toxicology in the risk/hazard assessment process. Trends in the development of control technology at potential sites of toxic emissions are not addressed.

## TRENDS IN ANALYTICAL TECHNIQUES AND PREDICTIVE METHODS

Current advances in analytical techniques are increasing our ability to detect progressively lesser amounts of potentially toxic substances. Sensitive and reliable analytical methods are commonplace and, in some cases, provide measurements of as little as $10^{-14}$ grams of material. These advances are being exploited to provide essential chemical and biological surveillance of the environment. Additionally, these methods are improving our ability to detect unwanted impurities in products of all types and subsequently to improve their purity. The misfortunes of 2,4,5-trichlorophenoxy acetic acid (2,4,5-T) because of dioxin impurities illustrate the desirability of detecting and removing such impurities; but when impurities cannot be feasibly removed, their identification will help to assure proper assessment of their potentially toxic effects. These analytical monitoring advances will greatly improve the opportunity to achieve the goal of reducing the hazards associated with potentially toxic chemicals. A not-inconsequential benefit of these analytical capabilities is that of enabling the researcher in toxicology to identify metabolic pathways, intermediates, and products.

Moreover, reliable and economical predictive methods are being developed for detecting potential toxicity, mutagenicity, carcinogenicity, environmental movement, bioconcentration, and degradability. The development and use of potentially toxic materials will be influenced for many years by methods for predicting their environmental fate or biological effects. Great advances have already occurred. Literally hundreds of scientific papers have appeared describing the utility and shortcomings of various approaches to determining these characteristics. The measurement of mutagenicity has become particularly popular through the use of simple organisms to facilitate the detection of chemicals having potential mutagenic effects. The Ames test, which employs *Salmonella typhimurium* bacteria to detect point mutations induced by base pair substitutions or DNA frame shifts, has received the greatest recognition. When combined with enzyme systems derived from mammalian organisms (usually a post-mitochondrial supernatant of rat liver homogenate), the Ames test permits laboratory "activation" of normally "inactive" compounds into reactive and mutagenic metabolites. This activation is said to mimic the mutagenesis that occurs in living mammals.

Many aspects of the concept are controversial, however, and the lack of normal detoxification enzymes or other protective mechanisms is often cited as a principal disadvantage of the use of bacteria in mutagenic screens. Additionally, bacterial DNA is not compartmentalized like the DNA in mammalian cells, and this important difference casts some doubt on the usefulness of bacteria in screening for mammalian mutagens. Despite these shortcomings, however, bacterial systems can frequently be used to determine the ability of a chemical or mixture of chemicals to induce mutagenic damage. Determinations can be made quickly and at low cost. Extensive use of these systems is foreseen because of these advantages, and when properly used these tests will be valuable in preliminary screening for toxicity.

In the future, however, the use of mammalian cells in vitro or the measurement of cytogenetic injury in whole animals will probably become more important for actual risk/hazard assessment than the use of bacteria. These techniques come closer to demonstrating the actual potential ability of chemicals to inflict genetic injury on higher organisms, particularly mammals, under real-life situations. When the results of these techniques are combined appropriately with information collected through bacterial tests, our ability to predict adverse genetic injury from specific chemicals will become much more reliable.

Unfortunately, however, there has been a tendency to use the results of mutagenicity screening tests as predictions of a chemical agent's potential ability to cause carcinogenicity in man. This misuse of valuable methods may have a negative effect on the development of new technologies, including the development of alternative sources of energy. Further work is needed to establish reliable methods that can be widely used for direct in vitro detection of a chemical's potential ability to induce carcinogenicity. These methods would measure the conversion of normal cells to neoplastic cells by carcinogens, and thus provide a straightforward demonstration of a chemical's potential to induce cancer. In contrast to mutagenicity screens, these methods would avoid the tenuous extrapolation from observations of mutagenicity in bacteria to mammalian carcinogenicity.

Despite the development of in vitro tests for the direct determination of carcinogenic potential, the classic method of long-term animal studies for the detection of carcinogenicity will continue to be used for at least the next decade, along with direct observation of carcinogenicity in human beings. Unfortunately, however, current methodology calls for lifetime exposure of animals to chemical agents and both gross and microscopic examination of tissues to discover induced tumors occurring at greater than spontaneous rates. These time-consuming and costly studies can be greatly improved by methods for determining dose-response relationships as well as determination of other toxic effects. To achieve these goals, as well as to enhance the utility of test data for human risk/hazard assessment, preliminary studies must be conducted to provide a thorough description of the pharmacokinetics and metabolism of the test agent in the species being studied. More basic research is needed in this area to determine how these methods can be used in a cost-effective and timely fashion.

Toxicity testing has shifted from simple determinations of median lethal dose and eye and skin irritation to detailed searches for all manner of toxic effects. These include myelotoxicity, neurotoxicity, immunotoxicity, organ-specific injury, and behavioral toxicity. Other toxic endpoints could be mentioned, but the above suffice to demonstrate the variety of chronic effects that may arise from long-term, low-dose chemical exposure. Methods for the detection and description of these effects are in various stages of development, and as with carcinogenesis and mutagenesis there is incomplete understanding of injury mechanisms. More basic research directed toward an understanding of these mechanisms is needed. In addition to toxicity information, risk/hazard assessment requires better understanding of the conditions of human exposure, including knowledge of the route(s) whereby chemicals enter the body, the frequency of their entrance, and the duration and concentration of the chemicals within the body. To this end it is necessary to know how a potentially toxic substance is released into and is moved through the environment to reach human beings. Much research will be required before we reach a satisfactory understanding of this process, and that research must include the development of screening methods that predict environmental movement, bioconcentration, and biodegradation of chemicals. More attention must be given to the development of model ecosystems.

Meanwhile, growing knowledge of chemical structures and their related biological effects is creating a data base leading to pattern recognition of potentially toxic effects. Eventually these data will be incorporated into computerized information systems that can be used to set testing and research priorities. Measurements of the widest possible spectrum of toxic effects, when correlated with physical properties, chemical structures, dose-response data, and behavior in model ecosystems, will provide highly reliable and inexpensive prediction as to which chemical agents are most likely to be hazardous. These models are not now sufficiently developed to be useful, but eventually they can be expected to play an important role in preventing repetitions of past chemical catastrophes.

## TRENDS IN REGULATION AND POLLUTION-CONTROL STRATEGIES

Federal laws to control the use of chemicals are not new; one of the earliest of such laws was the Food, Drug and Cosmetic Act of 1938. Since 1972, however, Congress has been much more inclined to assert federal control over potentially toxic substances. The most important of recent federal laws enacted to control chemical use include the Water Pollution Control Act Amendments (1972); the Marine Protection, Research, and Sanctuaries Act (1972); the Insecticide, Fungicide, and Rodenticide Act Amendments (1972); the Safe Drinking Water Act (1974); the Toxic Substances Control Act (1976); the Resource Conservation and Recovery Act (1976); the Clean Air Act Amendments (1977); the Clean Water Act (1977); and the Environmental Research, Development, and Demonstration Authorization Act (1977).

Although all these laws have some relation to toxicology, this list also illustrates the nonscientific approach of legislators to scientific problems. Generally speaking, the process consists of a legislator recognizing a specific problem and "doing something about it," namely, persuading fellow legislators to pass a law to deal with the problem. The net result has been a heterogeneous stream of laws and associated enforcement agencies. The potential toxicity of any given chemical is often regulated in a different manner according to the circumstances of public exposure instead of through a single comprehensive risk/hazard assessment process. One may hope that the recent development of the Interagency Regulatory Liaison

Group foreshadows a trend toward more rational and better coordinated regulations based upon scientific judgments of available data.

Such a development would be an improvement over the current situation, in which the implementation of federal laws tends to result in the promulgation of rigid and detailed guidelines for toxicity tests. These rigid guidelines (regulations) are being substituted for the judgments of professional toxicologists in the selection, implementation, and interpretation of toxicity tests. This is not to say that guidelines and minimum testing requirements are unreasonable. A certain amount of testing uniformity and quality assurance is essential. But the publication of detailed "rules" for the conduct of toxicity and environmental tests is bound to be detrimental to scientific progress. Moreover, this approach will not accomplish its stated goals, because each chemical subjected to toxicity testing can alter biological organisms in unexpected ways, depending on such characteristics as species, sex, age, route of exposure, duration of exposure, and dose. In addition, different chemicals have different biological properties and toxic manifestations. Hence, tests for specific chemicals should be designed to take all these factors into account. It is not practicable, necessary, or useful to apply the same battery of tests, conducted in exactly the same way, to every potentially toxic substance. The goal should not be to discover how each chemical behaves in a regimented series of tests, but rather to establish the ability of each chemical to cause harm under intended conditions of use, thereby enabling investigators to make quantitative predictions of the actual risk to a defined population. These quantitative predictions require a data base related to the likely modes of injury.

In short, federal regulations should permit greater flexibility in the rules for testing potentially toxic substances, and greater reliance must be placed on professional judgment in the selection and interpretation of tests. Meaningful results will then be more likely; also it will be possible to test more agents in a shorter period of time and at less cost. Although serious mistakes on the part of a few unwitting toxicologists necessitated rigid rules for quality assurance, quality assurance is different from regimented testing. Quality assurance methods are supported by the scientific community now and will continue to be supported in the future.

Finally, use of the concept of zero risk for carcinogens and other toxic substances is being deemphasized. There is increasing recognition of the impossibility of reducing to zero the exposure to carcinogens, given the thousands of potential carcinogens in the environment. This is not to say that society can or should accept wide distribution of carcinogens, but that society should consider the potential harm of small amounts of carcinogens in relation to other risks and in relation to the potential benefits. If current views about the existence of threshold levels for carcinogens or other toxic substances are accurate, attempts to achieve zero risk will have little social utility. The zero risk concept should be replaced by reliable methods of quantitative risk/hazard assessent. Of course, a great deal of work needs to be done to achieve this end, but continued support of research (preferably greater support) can and will achieve it.

## SOCIETY'S ROLE IN TOXIC SUBSTANCE CONTROL

As scientists continue to contribute better quantitative statements of fact about the degree of risk associated with potentially toxic substances, a continually more sophisticated society is taking firm positions on which risks are to be accepted and which should not. This societal participation is already international and eventually will contribute to the realization of pollution control on a global scale. In discussing risk assessment, Kates (1978) points out that the process involves hazard identification (research, screening, monitoring, and diagnosis), risk estimation (revelation, intuition, and extrapolation), and social evaluation (aversive, balance, benefit-risk, cost-benefit). Risk estimation methods are in the greatest need of improvement. More experience is necessary to make risk estimation an effective part of the risk assessment process. Mathematical models have been devised to predict the incidence of cancer among large numbers of human beings exposed to low doses of carcinogens for long periods of time, but these models presently rely on extrapolations from relatively crude observations of small numbers of animals exposed to very high doses of test agents. The dilemma of inadequate risk estimation has produced a lively research area, but one that is suffering from a lack of actual testing of hypotheses. The predictive value of mathematical models has not been confirmed through high-quality animal experimentation and corresponding human experience. Epidemiological evidence to support or refute predicted response is rare. Some of these much-needed data are presently being collected, however, and there is hope that enough data eventually will be obtained to make the mathematical models accurate for extrapolating from high-dose observations in animals to low-dose exposures in human beings.

Nonetheless, it is likely that discrepancies will continue to exist between the mathematically predicted incidence of toxicity in human beings and that actually observed in studies of animals. Biological explanations for these discrepancies must be discovered, and improved knowledge of the mechanisms of toxic injury, including a better understanding of dose-dependent pharmacokinetics and metabolism, of molecular and tissue-repair mechanisms, and of species-specific responses, may provide the needed explanations.

In the meantime, human experience with toxic substances is improving predictive models in toxicology and environmental science. Relatively precise measurements of chemically induced mortality and morbidity are possible through epidemiological techniques. In combination with actual measurements of exposure and information on the disposition of potentially toxic materials, these techniques are helping to advance the development of predictive models. Parallel human and animal studies for a small number of widely used chemicals also are generating data that will provide a basis for determining the utility of predictive models. By means of these parallel studies, the animal models will be refined to achieve acceptable predictive power.

The efforts of epidemiologists to demonstrate cause and effect relationships between chemicals and morbidity or mortality, however, are complicated by the fact that large numbers of people are being exposed to very small amounts of several chemicals. Increased emphasis, therefore, needs to be placed on identifying human populations whose exposure to one, or no more than a few, chemical agents can be determined in quantitative terms. Such populations exist within the chemical industry and in other specialized occupational groups. Data from studies of these groups are needed to assure the full utilization of toxicology as a predictive science. In other words, the predictive value of any toxicity test or environmental model system must ultimately be determined by comparing the predicted response with that actually observed. For some human functions, such as metabolism and excretion, limited human experimentation may be necessary to fulfill the need for specific knowledge of a substance's behavior.

Data from controlled studies of morbidity and mortality in human beings who have had relatively pure exposure to potentially toxic substances also can be the basis for comparing risks. More often than not, current measurements of the effects on health from exposure to chemicals are the result of exposures that most likely took place before the preventive value of industrial hygiene was appreciated. The hygiene practices of today have generally decreased the risks associated with many occupational settings. Society should be made aware of the degree to which the risks from chemical hazards compare to the risks involved in smoking, automobile operation, mountain climbing, dietary choices, and different lifestyles. Additionally, it should be possible to place all risks into an overall perspective, whether they arise from toxic substances, lifestyles, natural disasters, armed conflicts, or infectious diseases.

The accumulated knowledge of the biological effects of toxic substances on human beings and animals is being assimilated into data bases accessible to all segments of the scientific, industrial, and regulatory communities, as well as the public at large. Except for a small amount of proprietary data, information on all types of chemicals will become more readily available. Although compilation of all these data may seem to be an overwhelming task, these data bases are continually being reviewed and updated. The result will be better perspectives on the actual hazards of chemical substances under varying conditions. These data bases also will contain more information on the relative hazards of chemicals for different groups within society—the young (including the embryo-fetus), the infirm, the aged, the malnourished, and persons with known genetic diseases. Furthermore, the overall data base will help to identify those biological variations typical of all human populations. Biological variation will be given appropriate weight in the risk/hazard equation and will be viewed as an understandable occurrence rather than as an insurmountable problem that can only be solved by reducing the lowest observed no-effect dose by a factor of 1,000 or more.

Another fact that should be recognized is that in the immediate future only a few large international companies will be able to support research and development activities involving new synthetic chemicals. Current stringent and (sometimes) irrational approaches to the regulation of potentially toxic substances are likely to curtail the discovery and use of new chemicals. Higher costs resulting from governmental requirements for more sophisticated and lengthy tests and quality-control requirements are increasing the financial risks that must be taken to develop and market new chemicals. Smaller companies may not be able to meet these requirements in the near term, but this trend may be reversed as better predictive models are developed. When tests can be conducted more efficiently, rapidly, and reliably than at present, greater incentives for the safe development, manufacture, use, and disposal of chemicals will come into existence.

Federal and other regulators should recognize that the industries most likely to have caused pollution problems in the past are now contributing greatly to the solutions of those problems. Disagreements between alleged polluters and regulators on the degree of effort required to minimize pollution will continue to exist as long as numerous scientific questions remain unanswered. Air, water, and ground pollution have begun to decrease as a result of both regulatory pressure and greater awareness of the adverse effects of pollutants. These reductions in pollution have been brought about by, among other things, more efficient motor vehicle engines, increases in the use of public transportation, recycling and reuse of industrial wastes in closed-loop systems, and greater attention to wastewater quality and quantity. Most manufacturing companies have become convinced that there is much to be gained by better pollution control, but they also believe that control should be achieved through an intellectual consensus on the needed degree of control rather than by means of sweeping governmental regulations. Where rapid biodegradation of a chemical occurs with no damage to the ecosystem, it makes little sense to spend large sums of money to deal with the material as a form of pollution. Conversely, there must be a high degree of control over potentially toxic chemical substances that would otherwise persist in the environment.

## BASIC RESEARCH AND EDUCATION IN THE ENVIRONMENTAL SCIENCES, TOXICOLOGY, AND EPIDEMIOLOGY

More and better-quality fundamental research is occurring in toxicology, its ancillary sciences, and epidemiology. The multidisciplinary requirements for the development and safe use of potentially toxic materials demand continuing support for research in all of the relevant physical, biological, and medical sciences. It is still an open question whether the funds needed to pay for the necessary increase in basic knowledge relevant to toxic substances control will be made available. Industry and government alike must maintain their commitment to supporting the essential research required to improve the predictive value of toxicology and epidemiology. This need for basic research should take precedence over the increasing tendency to divert more and more money into rigidly defined toxicity and environmental tests. The state of the art in toxicological testing is relatively primitive, and to continue to spend money on primitive methods is futile. What is needed instead is adequate support for the development of the knowledge required to create adequate predictive models in toxicological and environmental sciences, using these models for making decisions on the development and use of potentially toxic substances.

It must also be recognized that departments of toxicology, environmental sciences, and epidemiology are beginning to assume positions of greater importance in medical schools. Increased scientific understanding and control of most of the serious infectious diseases have led to a shift toward greater attention to the causes and prevention of illness related to environmental factors. The prominence of potentially toxic substances in standard discussions of harmful environmental influences provides a strong justification for a greater interest in toxicology and its ancillary disciplines in schools of medicine and public health. Just as important as the toxic substances themselves, however, are the various interactions that may occur between the toxic substances and other environmental factors. Some of these, notably smoking and dietary habits, are important determinants of toxic effects. Medical schools and the medical profession must play a much larger role in the study of environmental interactions. Indeed, consideration of all aspects of the environment deserves a more prominent position in preventive medicine.

Professional toxicologists possess credentials earned through a detailed knowledge of the fundamental sciences on which toxicology is based and a practical understanding of the proper use of toxicologic testing methods. The modern toxicologist should be expected to maintain accreditation through an active program of continuing education. To meet the need for accreditation and recertification of professionals in environmental sciences and toxicology, professional societies should initiate programs to fulfill certain educational requirements. However, the university community also will need to respond by providing practical uses for new knowledge as part of its continuing education programs. Improved educational opportunity for all scientists in toxicology and related areas will make it more likely that relevant research will be undertaken and brought to fruition. New contributions can be expected from the so-called "testers" as well as the "researchers."

Training programs for toxicologists, environmental scientists, and epidemiologists rely on high-quality training in a number of fundamental scientific disciplines. In addition, practical applications of basic knowledge are being stressed in training programs, and students of higher quality are being attracted to these disciplines because of the increasing importance of these sciences. Rising professional standards, continuing education, accreditation programs, and greater vocational and personal rewards are all improving the profession; a broader scope of training is providing for both professional- and technical-level needs, i.e., doctoral programs and bachelors or masters degree programs, respectively.

## CONCLUSION

Newer chemicals with more desirable properties and greater usefulness are going to be available at lower costs; these goals will be achieved in part through the need to conserve energy and recycle waste products. A more thorough understanding of the potential risks involved in the manufacture, use, and disposal of chemicals is decreasing the likelihood of chemical catastrophes. Although societal pressure to improve our control over pollution and toxic substances may be detrimental to some small industrial firms in the short run, better predictive models will eventually provide smaller companies with new competitive opportunities. Meanwhile, society as a whole will play a larger role in making decisions about the use of potentially toxic substances. In the process, society also will be required to accept a larger degree of responsibility for detrimental consequences, if and when they arise. Such consequences, however, will become less and less likely as the toxicologic, epidemiologic, and environmental sciences continue to advance.

## ACKNOWLEDGMENT

The author is grateful to Mr. Ralph C. Wands and Mr. Robert O. Beauchamp of the Office of Information, Chemical Industry Institute of Toxicology for their assistance in acquiring the background literature used in the preparation of this paper.

## BIBLIOGRAPHY

Albert, R.E. and B. Altshuler (1976) Assessment of environmental carcinogen risks in terms of life shortening. Environ. Health Persp. 13:91-94.

American Chemical Society (1978) Cleaning Our Environment: A Chemical Perspective. A Report by the Committee on Environmental Improvement. Washington, D.C.: American Chemical Society.

Bezelon, D. (1979) Risk and responsibility. Chem. Eng. News 57:5.

Broad, W.J. (1979) News and comment: Jump in funding feeds research on nutrition. Science 204:1060-1064.

Consumer Products Safety Commission et al. (1979) Scientific basis for identification of potential carcinogens and estimation of risks. Fed. Regist. 44:39858-39879.

Cordle, F. and A.C. Kolbye (1979) Food safety and public health: Interaction of science and law in the Federal regulatory process. Cancer 43:2143-2150.

Cornfield, J. (1977) Carcinogenic risk assessment. Science 198:693-699.

Council on Environmental Quality (1979) Toxic Substances Strategy Committee Report to the President. Fed. Regist. 44:48134-48140.

Cramer, G.M. and R.A. Ford (1978) Estimation of toxic hazard—a decision tree approach. Food Cosmet. Toxicol. 16:255-276.

Crow, J.F. (1973) Impact of various types of genetic damage in risk assessment. Environ. Health Persp. 6:1-5.

Doll, R. and A.E.M. McLean, eds. (1979) Long term hazards to man from man-made chemicals in the environment. Proc. R. Soc. Lond., Ser. B: Biol. Sci. 205:1-197.

Eisenbud, M. (1978) Environment, Technology, and Health. Human Ecology in Historical Perspective. New York: New York University Press.

Enslein, K. and P.N. Craig (1979) Status report on development of predictive models of toxicological endpoints. Rochester, N.Y.: Genesee Computer Center, Inc.

Falk, H.L. (1979) Surveillance for future environmental contaminants: Discussion. Ann. N.Y. Acad. Sci. 320:682-683.

Fishbein, L. (1977) Potential Industrial Carcinogens and Mutagens. EPA 560/5-77-005. Washington, D.C.: Government Printing Office.

Hall, R.E. (1978) Benefit/risk assessment today. J. Amer. Oil Chem. Soc. 55:193-197.

Hamburg, D.A. (1979) Disease prevention: A challenge of the future. Amer. J. Pub. Health 69:1026-1033.

Handler, P. (1979) Basic research in the United States. Science 204:474-479.

Henschler, D. (1973) Toxicological problems relating to the changes in the environment. Angewandte Chemie, International Edition in English 12:274-283.

Hoel, D.G., D.W. Gaylor, R.L. Kirschstein, U. Saffiotti, and H.A. Schneiderman (1975) Estimation of risks of irreversible, delayed toxicity. J. Toxicol. Environ. Health 1:133-151.

Howard, P.H. et al. (1978) Determining the fate of chemicals. Environ. Sci. Technol. 12:398-407.

Kates, R.W., ed. (1978) Risk Assessment of Environmental Hazard (Scope 8). New York: John Wiley & Sons.

Kone, E.H. and H.J. Jordan, eds. (1974) The Greatest Adventure (Basic Research that Shapes our Lives). New York: The Rockefeller University Press.

Lawless, E.W. (1977) Technology and Social Shock. New Brunswick, N.J.: Rutgers University Press.

Ligon, J.R. and W.V. Ligon, Jr. (1979) Molecular analysis by mass spectrometry. Science 205:151-157.

Mantel, N. (1978) Letter to the editor. Cancer Res. 38:1835-1838.

Maugh, T.H. (1979) Toxic waste disposal a growing problem. Science 204:819-823.

Menkart, J. (1978) Hair coloring—a case study in risk assessment. Cutis 22:670-693, 724.

Moeller, D.W. et al. (1979) Trends in university environmental health research and training. Amer. J. Pub. Health 69:125-129.

Monarch, M.R. et al. (1978) Priorities for New Source Performance Standards under the Clean Air Act Amendments of 1977. EPA-450/3-78-019. Washington, D.C.: Government Printing Office.

Murray, C. (1979) Chemical waste disposal a costly problem. Chem. Eng. News 57:12-16.

Public Law 94-469 (1976) An act to regulate commerce and protect human health and the environment by requiring testing and necessary use restrictions on certain chemical substances, and for other purposes. 90 Stat. 2003-2051.

Rall, D.P. and P.E. Schambra (1979) Environmental health research and regulation. Environ. Health Persp. 30:9-11.

Ramsey, J.C. et al. (1978) Carcinogenic risk assessment: ethylene dibromide. Toxicol. Appl. Pharmacol. 47:411-414.

Report of a Task Group (1978) Air pollution cancer: Risk assessment methodology and epidemiological evidence. Environ. Health Persp. 22:1-12.

Smith, R.J. (1979) News and comment: Toxic substances—EPA and OSHA are reluctant regulators. Science 203:28-32.

Smyth, H.F., Jr. (1979) Current confidence in occupational health. Amer. Indus. Hyg. Assoc. J. 40:659-665.

Stevenson, D.E. (1979) Current problems in the choice of animals for toxicity testing. J. Toxicol. Environ. Health 5:9-15.

U.K. Department of Health and Social Security (1979) A Consultative Document on Guidelines for the Testing of Chemicals for Carcinogenicity. Committee on Carcinogenicity of Chemicals and Food Consumer Products in the Environment. London, England.

U.K. Department of Health and Social Security (1979) A Consultative Document on Guidelines for the Testing of Chemicals for Mutagenicity. Committee on Mutagenicity of Chemicals in Food Consumer Products in the Environment. London, England.

U.S. Congress (1979) A bill to provide for a federal mechanism within the Office of Science and Technology Policy for assessing the comparative risks involved in actions in scientific, technological and related fields. H.R. 4939 96th Congress, 1st Session.

U.S. Department of Health, Education and Welfare (1970) Man's Health and the Environment—Some Research Needs. Report of the Task Force on Research Planning and Environmental Health Science. Washington, D.C.: Government Printing Office.

U.S. Department of Health, Education and Welfare (1977) Basic Concepts of Environmental Health. DHEW Publication No. (NIH) 77-1254. Washington, D.C.: Government Printing Office.

U.S. Environmental Protection Agency (1976) Health, Environmental Effects, and Control Technology of Energy Use. EPA 600/7-76-002. Washington, D.C.: Government Printing Office

U.S. Environmental Protection Agency (1978) Social Decision-Making for High Consequence, Low Probability Occurrences. EPA-600/5-78-121. Washington, D.C.: Government Printing Office

U.S. Environmental Protection Agency (1978) Research Outlook 1978. EPA 600/9 789-001. Washington, D.C.: Government Printing Office

U.S. Environmental Protection Agency (1978) Research Highlights 1978. EPA 600/9-78-040. Washington, D.C.: Government Printing Office

U.S. Environmental Protection Agency (1979) Research Outlook 1979. EPA 600/9-79-005. Washington, D.C.: Government Printing Office

U.S. Office of Technology Assessment (1977) Cancer Testing Technology and Saccharin. Stock No. 052-003-004712. Washington, D.C.: Government Printing Office.

Van Noordwyk, H. J. and M. A. Santoro (1978) Minnesota Mining and Manufacturing Company's hazardous waste program. Environ. Health Persp. 27:245-249.

Woods, J.S. (1979) Epidemiological considerations in the design of toxicologic studies: An approach to risk assessment in humans. Fed. Proc. 38:1891-1996.

Worldwatch Institute (1978) The Global Environment and Basic Human Needs. No. 252-444/6169. Washington, D.C.: Government Printing Office.

Young, V.R. and N.S. Scrimshaw (1979) Genetic and biological variability and human nutrient requirements. Amer. J. Clin. Nutr. 32:486-500.

# DISCUSSANT'S REMARKS ON THE PAPER BY J. E. GIBSON

S. GUSMAN
*Conservation Foundation*

The emphasis in Dr. Gibson's well-written paper is on current trends. The 25- to 50-year future, extending into the early part of the twenty-first century, is likely to depend more upon problems only now emerging or hardly identified. Hence, in these remarks, I will place less emphasis than Dr. Gibson did on current trends and controversies, and indeed believe that he has over-emphasized, from a long-term point of view, the significance of some current controversies. I propose that the following 10 issues, some of which are covered in Dr. Gibson's paper, merit special attention.

## TOXICOLOGY

Toxicology, as a science, is in an early descriptive phase. Greater regularity can be expected to emerge in the future based on theoretical relationships and/or generally accepted decision rules. Scientific research is needed, and is of course under way, to establish toxicology as a science with a theoretical base; but much more is needed in order to create the predictive capabilities that will ultimately establish broadly useful relationships between chemical structure and biological activity. Research is also needed to make explicit the decision rules used in the practice of toxicology, much as there now is interest in the decision rules used by the physician in developing and using information to diagnose disease.

Current emphasis in toxicology is on carcinogenicity, mutagenicity, and teratogenicity. With better methods and increased understanding of these effects over the next few years, emphasis will likely shift to other important effects, e.g., immunotoxicology and behavioral toxicology.

As structure-activity relations are established on a firmer scientific basis, assessment of the toxicology of chemicals in categories will likely become more generally useful and acceptable, perhaps in categories based upon physical chemical characteristics of substances as well as categories directly related to chemical structure.

Finally, ecotoxicity even today is receiving more attention than it is given in Dr. Gibson's paper, and this is likely to increase.

## EXTRAPOLATION FROM ANIMAL STUDIES TO MAN

Laboratory studies are, for good reason, usually performed under controlled conditions. In most toxicological tests, animals have common genetic history and are kept in controlled environments.

In contrast, humans are genetically heterogeneous in health and other aspects of their life condition and resistance to stress. Hence, in addition to the general problem of extrapolating from animal studies to man, there are the special problems of understanding the relationships between laboratory information, developed under controlled (homogeneous) conditions, as compared with responses by a very heterogeneous human population comprised of individuals and groups that differ in their sensitivities to risk. The concepts of thresholds, no-effect levels, and safety factors are likely to become increasingly tenuous as applied to the protection of people who are heterogeneous in their sensitivity to risk. The identification of specially sensitive human populations is in its infancy.

## SYNERGISMS AND ANTAGONISMS

Toxicology traditionally evaluates chemicals one at a time, while people are exposed simultaneously to many. There is the need to explore toxicological practice as it may be changed and made more completely relevant to the reality of the human condition. This implies much greater emphasis on the study of synergisms and antagonisms in total environments comprised of many chemicals, with diverse test subjects.

## EXPOSURE AND DOSAGE

Risk depends upon inherent toxicological characteristics and exposure. Exposure assessment is an even more embryonic science than toxicology. (In some respects it is a sub-discipline of toxicology.) Much more research is needed to define and characterize exposure that occurs through usage of products by consumers, and in occupational settings (the social environment), as well as during and after distribution of chemicals in the natural environment. Dosage to an organism cannot be assumed to correlate with exposure, i.e., the level of a chemical in the environment surrounding the organism. Since the risk depends upon dosage, better understanding is needed of the relationships between dosage and exposure.

## RISK-TO-WHOM

With a heterogeneous population, the risk to a few members of sensitive populations may be much greater than the risk to the overall population.

Levels of protection that are essentially "zero risk" for most people may cause substantial risk for some. There is the need for more explicit public acknowledgment that (almost) any level of (most) toxic chemicals will injure some sensitive people, and, consequently, that there is a need to develop methodologies for articulating levels of injury that are acceptable to the public (some of whom receive benefits from the use of these chemicals).

## UNCERTAINTY OF RISK

For many reasons, there are uncertainties about the relevance to the human condition of laboratory toxicological tests. We need much more explicit attention to the development of public policy based on imperfect and incomplete data. Even data that meet the best current state-of-the-art standards of "scientific acceptability" are frequently uncertain in their relevance to man. Data of even lesser certainty will frequently be all that is available for reasons of economics, time, priorities, etc. From a public policy point of view, it would be beneficial to create an analytical framework that defines "valid" decision making based on uncertain (or incomplete) information, i.e., valid to a degree that would be supportable even under court challenge.

## ACCEPTABILITY OF RISK

Risk assessment may be an objective exercise, but assessment of the *acceptability* or *reasonableness* of risk is inherently subjective and value laden. Expressing risks and benefits quantitatively does not eliminate the subjectivity of balancing them against each other, and the expression of noncommensurate risks and benefits in terms of one measuring stick (conventionally dollars) merely shifts the value laden decision to the selection of conversion factors for expressing all units in dollar terms. More explicit expression of each of the noncommensurate factors (lives, dollars, quality of life, etc.) that are weighed in public policy decisions would permit more relevant public debate. This would require much research over an extended period of time.

## VOLUNTARY RISK

In order for a risk to be voluntarily assumed, the risk must be (a) known, (b) disclosed to the person at risk, and (c) understood by the person at risk. Disclosure of information does not assure that it will be understood. This is the subject of research in marketing and advertising and some of these findings may be applicable to hazard communication, although much more research directly on communicating fear-inducing hazard warning information will undoubtedly be needed in this highly empirical area. Communications can also have the goal of changing behavior, e.g., to encourage behavior that avoids risks. (This raises ethical issues regarding intentional behavior modification.) Hence, if public policy moves in the direction of favoring the conversion of involuntary risks to voluntary risks by disclosure and communication of risk, more study will be needed of the ways in which hazard warning information can be communicated effectively (and, if desired, be made to influence behavior).

## REGULATION

In principle, risks and benefits to health, the environment, the economy, innovation, and society are balanced by a decision maker in arriving at a public policy for control of a chemical hazard. These decisions can be made much more explicit, if not objective, thus fostering better understanding of the manner in which factors were balanced in arriving at decisions. In so doing it will likely become evident that decision makers in government may also value factors that affect their own situations, for example, administrative simplicity, how costly the chosen course will be to the departmental budgets, etc. Retrospective auditing of decisions can be a valuable research tool for examining the decision making process and, in the long run, improving it.

## ALTERNATIVES TO ADVERSARY PROCEEDINGS

Adversary proceedings may not lead to "best" outcomes, most "efficient" in time, resources, or public acceptability. Various attempts have been made, and are being made, to use alternative procedures of a more consensual type. Further exploratory use of these procedures in appropriate cases may lead to identification of the circumstances in which they are useful and work best.

# SUMMARY OF THE TASK GROUP

J. DOULL, *University of Kansas Medical Center*
A. K. MALONE, *National Research Council*

## INTRODUCTION

This Task Group saw its charge as including a longer time-frame than that encompassed in the paper by J. E. Gibson. He focused on current trends and the Task Group basically endorses Gibson's assessment of these trends. However, the Task Group felt that the charge also should include:

1. a discussion of the shift in environmenal problems that might be expected during the next 20 to 50 years,

2. a prediction of future scenarios for this period, and

3. recommendations for health and environmental research directions to meet future regulatory needs.

Four major topics were considered by the Task Group: trends in the manufacture of potentially toxic substances by U.S. chemical industries, including future scenarios regarding the development and use of such substances, and the resulting mix of chemicals in the environment; hazardous waste disposal; science base for hazard evaluation, which includes methodology/tools for assessment of human health and ecosystem effects, mixtures of chemicals, synergisms and antagonisms, exposure, dose, risk assessment, and monitoring; public policy, including acceptability of voluntary and involuntary risk, regulatory distortions, and alternative modes of decision making.

The discussion focused on manufactured chemicals and their use, and subsequent impacts on the environment including environmental and human toxic effects. Concern for end-users of products in the home setting was emphasized as an area that had thus far not received enough attention in regulatory decision making. Topics that were not specifically addressed included biologically toxic substances, pesticides to any great extent, pollutants from energy production, and global aspects of the toxic substances problems.

# IDENTIFICATION OF FUTURE PROBLEM AREAS

## MANUFACTURING TRENDS

Over the next 20 to 50 years, the factors or constraints that would exert a major influence on U.S. industries manufacturing toxic chemicals, and on the resultant mix of chemicals in the environment, were identified as economic, health-related, and regulatory. The cost of metals, for example, was predicted to increase, resulting in a shift away from use of toxic metals in new products. In general, the availability of resources was predicted to decrease with a resultant rise in recycling and conservation of materials by manufacturers and consumers. It was suggested that as recycling increased this could in turn produce a trend toward purer end-products. On the other hand, some participants suggested that as resource availability decreases, an increase in synthetic organic chemicals could result, thus overshadowing the impact of recycling and conservation efforts. Economic factors also are expected to decrease the number of small chemical producers.

In the next 20 to 50 years toxic substances currently identified as posing health problems, (e.g., asbestos and cadmium) would be controlled more tightly, resulting in major changes in product composition. It was agreed that current regulatory trends are producing a decrease in rate of new chemicals introductions. Regulatory trends are also promoting better-quality texts for detecting hazardous effects. These trends are viewed as positive; however, a more efficient testing and decision process would increase innovation in new chemical development. The threat of new regulations also are viewed as detrimental to new chemical development. Finally, regulations are expected to have an impact on the market place via disclosure of information to consumers.

## HAZARDOUS WASTE DISPOSAL

Waste disposal is an immediate and immense problem that cannot be solved over the next 5 to 10 years. In the long-term future (20 to 50 years) the problem is expected to decrease as industry develops the required disposal technologies. Because development of sufficient numbers of safe disposal sites is difficult, the industrial response may be to reduce the amount of toxic substances in new products. Economic factors also are expected to force a decrease in the number of small chemical producers.

Another immediate problem involves the state of the art for analytical techniques and hazard assessment techniques. Because analytical chemistry is much more sophisticated than toxicological evaluations, current decision making is based on analytical capability rather than an assessment of toxic effects. The result is a "tail wagging the dog" situation.

## SCIENCE BASE FOR HAZARD EVALUATION

Toxicity testing using animals is the major tool whereby toxic hazards for humans are currently evaluated. Although animal toxicology is still in its infancy, it has a good record for accurate prediction regarding the safety of specific chemicals being tested. Other methods used to determine levels of chemical toxicity for humans, such as epidemiology or short-term toxicity tests, either lack sufficient data for hazard evaluation or are even less developed than animal toxicology and, therefore, are less reliable independently.

Two major problems currently exist: (1) there is an overwhelming number of chemical agents that need to be tested, and (2) current techniques are inadequate to provide reliable and predictive data on the toxicity of chemical mixtures. The science of toxicology has not developed rapidly enough to cope with these problems. The assessment of current trends and problems related to toxicological testing presented by Gibson is generally endorsed by the Task Group.

More specific problem areas that relate to the lack of adequate hazard evaluation approaches follow:

1. Approaches to studying ecosystem or multi-species effects are inadequate.

2. Exposure as a result of end-product use (e.g., in the home) is not being adequately assessed.

3. Dosage (uptake resulting from exposure) is often assumed to be related to or the same as exposure, but this is not a sound assumption. The kinetics of uptake are often unknown.

4. Factors influencing bioavailability of toxic chemicals in the environment are often unknown.

5. Models used to predict the low-dose effects in humans based upon high-dose data from animals (e.g., the models used by EPA's Carcinogen Assessment Group) are inadequate.

6. The regulatory process and the concommitant effort to expand and evaluate the scientific data base have focused on cancer so that inadequate attention is given to other human health and environmental effects.

## PUBLIC POLICY

The major problems related to public policy are identified as the inconsistency between how different risks are perceived by different individuals and public groups and by decision makers, as well as the inadequate understanding of public behavior in response to risk. The group noted that risk is valued by different sectors of the public in different ways, and that when decisions are made, the resulting risk to individuals and society is not always consistent with that from other decisions.

The problem is summarized in an excerpt from *An Issue Report: Determining Unreasonable Risk Under the Toxic Substances Control Act* (Davies et al. 1979):

Decision makers frequently argue that each regulatory decision poses a unique set of problems and involves consideration of a unique data base. To some degree, this is unquestionably true. Given the large universe of disparate factors that can bear on chemical regulation, the permutations and combinations are almost infinite. It is also undeniable that regulators act as if each decision were novel. In the absence of a systematic framework, it is hard to see how they could act otherwise.

There are, however, major disadvantages to considering each decision as unique. The decision maker may exaggerate the importance of some factors and overlook other significant areas. His thinking may be excessively influenced by short-term considerations such as the morning newspaper coverage or a telephone call from a congressional staff person. In any case, the decision is likely to appear "political" to outside observers. Institutional memory within the agency is minimized, so that the lessons learned in making one decision are not transferred to the next. With so little carry-over, the regulated parties find it impossible to predict what the agency considers important or how it really defines unreasonable risk, thus complicating efforts of voluntary compliance.

Generally, the participants in this Task Group held an optimistic long-term view. The number of chemicals in the environment will be decreasing; the 20- to 50-year trend could be toward fewer hazardous chemicals entering the environment, toward less complex mixtures, and toward lower human exposures to hazardous substances. This prediction is based on the belief that current health problems will be resolved, while in the longer term the emergence of new problems will be reduced because of economic and regulatory efforts leading toward better testing methodology, improved manufacturing technologies and recycling processes, and increased consumer awareness of potential hazards. Control of pollutant dispersal can be expected because of the release of fewer chemicals, as well as improved inventories of the movement of these chemicals.

A minority view is not as optimistic and takes the position that resource problems could force the development of a multitude of new, potentially toxic substances; economic and regulatory constraints on domestic manufacturers could promote increased importation of chemicals into the United States. Both would result in an increase in the distribution of hazardous substances.

During the final plenary session, a definite split of opinion was evident on whether or not the hazard from chemicals in the environment would increase in the long-range future. Toxicologists seemed to be most optimistic about the ability of improved testing techniques to screen out hazardous chemicals before they enter widespread use and about industrial trends toward releasing fewer potentially hazardous chemicals into the environment, resulting in a smaller problem for the future. Workshop participants from other disciplines hold the more pessimistic view.

## PROBLEM PRIORITIES

The problems identified and discussed above can be divided into immediate and long-term categories. The hazardous waste disposal problem is seen as the most pressing immediate problem. In the long run, however, this problem is expected to decrease because it is currently so well identified and because major efforts to solve it are under way. The major long-term problems, the group felt, involved improving the science base for hazard evaluation and increasing consistency in the evaluation of risk and the understanding of public behavior regarding risk. In particular, the lack of short-term tools for testing the vast volume of chemicals and mixtures were viewed as especially high-priority problems.

## RECOMMENDATIONS

The priority order in which the recommended research should be undertaken will depend to a large extent on what research is already under way. The Task Group feels that research toward alleviating the long-term problems should be undertaken immediately and given high priority, despite the crisis aura that tends to push research on immediate problems to the front.

1. Research should be conducted into the effects on industry and other sectors of agency regulatory actions and related activity (e.g., the threat or perceived threat of regulation) to determine how agency actions can influence the mix of chemicals entering the environment. Some of this research would be retrospective, examining the real-world effects of past regulatory actions (or threat of action).

2. Research should be conducted on the effects of market forces and effective communication techniques to assist EPA in moving to a more enlightened approach to influencing public health and ecosystem toxicity issues.

3. Retrospective analyses should be conducted on the response of industry to incentives for reducing the waste problem. How do different industrial structures respond to economic or regulatory

incentives? Industrial response should be examined regarding approaches to product disposal and modifications in waste generation.

4. The feasibility of including a degradation mandate in new product packages should be examined.

5. Research should be continued on disposal methods such as incineration, chemical breakdown, and bacterial (or other biological) methods.

6. There is a pressing need to develop new hazard assessment methods that are quicker than the traditional toxicological animal bioassay systems. These new methods should be predictive, useful in complex environments or in testing complex mixtures, and should be reliable enough to justify their use in public policy decision making. In addition to optimizing existing short-term testing approaches for mutagenesis, other areas to explore include: (a) new short-term biological tests for immunological, behavioral, target-organ focus, and ecotoxicity tests (e.g., fish embryo larval testing and multi-species systems); (b) new capability to estimate no-effect exposures using short-term dose response data; (c) nonbiological models and computer systems using data such as the structure-activity relationship information with a sophisticated self-learning data base.

7. In order to use short-term tests more efficiently, the feasibility of applying risk-benefit analysis to the acceptability of risk data should be explored. There is often more uncertainty associated with short-term test data than 2-year animal bioassay data, however, the trade-offs in terms of time might tip the risk-benefit balance of using short-term test results. This possibility should be examined and, if real, demonstrated so that the use of short-term tests in decision making can be legally defended.

8. Research into methods for studying ecosystem toxicity effects has been neglected too long. There is a pressing need for the development of *multi-species* tests systems: (a) microcosms and (b) communities (microbial, sewage bacteria, phytoplankton, or estuarine larval communities).

9. Research should be continued to improve the efficiency of current toxicological testing and evaluation methods (e.g., research into the mechanisms of carcinogenesis).

10. The human data base needs to be improved and expanded. For example, the feasibility of obtaining field data on humans by allowing experimental use-permits and collecting data from the resultant limited exposure situations should be explored. This step should be ethically acceptable, because in effect it adds a level of testing between animal experiments and uncontrolled market exposure.

11. The problem of evaluating hazards from mixtures of chemicals in the environment is of great importance. The entire approach for analyzing and assessing anticipated effects of chemical mixtures—including effects of synergizers, antagonizers, promoters—is in its infancy and needs emphasis. Research should be conducted on modeling techniques and testing approaches. One direction that should be explored is the use of a dimensionless analysis model for predicting the activity coefficients of mixtures and the environmental distribution of each component. This approach has been used successfully, for example, to develop a method for predicting the equilibrium between liquid and vapor phases of mixtures (Fredenslund et al. 1975).

12. A data base for exposure assessment has been established for the workplace environment and in various pollution situations, e.g., air pollution and spills. However, data and approaches to evaluating exposure as the result of the end-use of products and receptor dosage is not being satisfactorily addressed. Research should be conducted to develop *target(receptor)-oriented* models for estimating exposure.

13. "Cradle-to-grave" bookkeeping is needed for toxic chemicals, including distribution, environmental fate, degradation, and toxicokinetics (absorption, distribution in the end target, excretion).

14. Research is needed on factors influencing uptake in end-receptors (e.g., bioavailability) and on toxicokinetics to improve prediction of toxic effects in organisms and ecosystems.

15. Receptor-oriented, as opposed to the current ambient level-oriented, monitoring should be developed. Methods for collecting and the actual collection of exposed data at the final receptor site are needed.

16. Zero risk is being deemphasized in regulatory actions; the concept of thresholds, in general, does not adequately recognize the tremendous heterogeneity among individuals in a population. Research directions that might be pursued in this area include (a) more attention to Baysian analytical techniques, (b) methods for making the risk-benefit assessment behind decisions more explicit, and (c) new approaches to predicting risk to humans other than current cancer extrapolation models.

17. It is recommended that the scientific data base for risk assessment be expanded and evaluated to encompass a variety of health end-points other than cancer.

18. The difficulties arising from diverse evaluation of risk—among different sections of the public, among decision makers, and from decision to decision—could be ameliorated if an attempt were made

to put decision analysis on a more systematic and predictable basis. Research should be conducted to identify and define the values and risk factors considered in decision making. These values and factors should be made explicit for each decision.

19. Research is needed to acquire a better understanding of why people behave in different ways when faced with apparently comparable risk. Such research would be useful in understanding how to elicit the intended response to a decision.

20. Research should be conducted to determine how to communicate risk ("fearful") information to the public effectively. Such research might focus, for example, on the most effective use of label information in regulatory decisions.

## REFERENCES

Davies, J.C., S. Gusman, and F. Irwin (1979) An Issue Report: Determining Unreasonable Risk Under the Toxic Substance Control Act. Washington, D.C.: The Conservation Foundation.

Fredenslund, A., R.L. Jones, and J.M. Prausnips (1975) Group contribution estimation of activity coefficients in nonideal liquid mixtures. Amer. Indus. Chem. J. 21(6):1086.

# TASK GROUP ON TOXIC SUBSTANCES

JOHN DOULL, M.D. (*Group Chairman*), University of Kansas Medical Center
DEAN BRANSON, Dow Chemical Company
THOMAS CROCKER, University of Wyoming
JAMES GIBSON (*Paper author*), Chemical Industry Institute of Toxicology
LESTER GRANT, U.S. Environmental Protection Agency
SAM GUSMAN (*Discussant*), Conservation Foundation
JOSEPH T. LING, 3M Company
ADELE KING MALONE (*Rapporteur*), National Research Council
IAN C. T. NISBET, Massachusetts Audubon Society
BERNARD SCHWETZ, Dow Chemical Company
W. LEIGH SHORT, Environmental Research and Technology
P. SHELLY WILLIAMSON, U.S. Environmental Protection Agency

# 6 Hazardous Facilities

## SITING OF INDUSTRIAL FACILITIES—A LOOK INTO THE FUTURE[1]

D. W. STEVER, JR.
*U.S. Department of Justice*

### INTRODUCTION

The dreams of many mid-century planners were filled with visions of vast, shiny clusters of smoothly humming factories on the outskirts of busy industrial cities. Powered by electricity from nuclear-generating plants, these factories would produce a myriad of goods for a constantly growing society. Foremost in the minds of these planners were such considerations as access to the labor market, availability of raw materials, access to transportation facilities, and access to the relevant product market. Often, they had to recognize specific additional needs, such as the availability of very large amounts of water and energy for processing purposes.

The realization of those dreams produced the patterns of land use that exist in the United States today. We live in an environment shaped largely by the industrial visionaries of the era between 1940 and 1965. It is that era that created what might be called—for want of a better term—dangerous

145

facilities: nuclear power plants and enormous increases in the size of organic chemical and petrochemical manufacturing plants.

In addition to the considerations mentioned above, the decisions of mid-century industrial planners were based on a number of other assumptions, some conscious and some unconscious: (1) that there would be no shortage of energy, (2) that the disposal of industrial waste was not a significant political or economic problem, and, in all events, was somebody else's problem, (3) that public "risk" did not enter into the siting calculus, and (4) that there would be no scarcity of industrial sites.

As is now known, these were false assumptions that can be accounted for, at least in part, by the fact that certain technologies had developed to the point of being able to produce the intended product (e.g., nuclear-generated electricity, 2,4,5-T), but not to neutralize or manage all of the production by-products (e.g., radioactive waste, dioxins). The scientific community's ability to perceive the risks associated with a given production cycle lagged substantially behind the implementation of the cycle. Tetrachlorodibenzo dioxin (TCDD) is formed during the production of phenoxy compounds, of which 2,4,5-T is the best-known example. The amount of the dioxin produced is related to the temperature at which a chemical reaction occurs during production. The identification of TCDD as a toxic waste product of 2,4,5-T production, for example, came many years after commercial production of the chemical began, and then only because of technological advances allowing the detection of minute quantities of contaminants in organic compounds.

Industrial siting and, hence, land-use patterns for the next 20 to 50 years are still being determined by corporate decision makers today. If one assumes, not unreasonably, that major industrial facilities require a 10-year planning and construction period that is followed by a useful life of 40 years, it is easy to see how relatively straightforward corporate decisions have long-term ramifications, some of which may not become apparent until those who made the decisions have long since retired.

But in recent years the assumptions underlying industrial siting decisions have changed radically. Energy is now perceived as a scarce resource, and its cost has become a significant cost of production. Waste management is becoming a cost of production, and the problems of waste disposal may become a significant siting constraint for dangerous facilities because of the risk of harm to the public. Furthermore, industrial siting decisions are increasingly being influenced by the various levels of government and by citizen groups.[2] Will these changes produce significant changes in industrial siting? If so, what will they be? Can we objectively assess the risks involved in the siting of dangerous facilities? Who should be the final assessor of risk?

Superimposed on all these issues is the overall question of the ability of industrial site planners to anticipate and meet socioeconomic goals while protecting the complex natural ecosystems and microenvironments where new facilities are placed. There are hopeful signs. Computer technology has brought predictive models to a level of sophistication that makes them functional for land-use planning purposes, and land-use suitability models (still used primarily by academics) are beginning to attract industry planners.[3] State-of-the-art modeling techniques can produce sufficient data to enable planners to identify which sites are clearly unsuitable for a particular industrial use.[4]

Regardless of the sophistication of such analytical tools, however, their impact on siting decisions will depend to a large extent upon the regulatory or other decision-making framework within which they are employed. Moreover, they are useful only at a site-specific level and do not come into play within a regulatory context until a choice of region and locality has already been made. Without some control over industrial siting at a higher level of government than the municipality, at least some industrial siting decisions are likely to be made without public input. Prior to any discussion of the desirability of state and federal industrial siting laws, however, it is important to set out some of the indirect governmental policies and other factors that will affect the siting of industrial facilities over the next 20 years or so.

## INDIRECT GOVERNMENT AND OTHER INFLUENCES ON INDUSTRIAL SITING

Regulatory laws that are not site-related can affect industrial siting decisions, as can general governmental policies on such matters as taxes and energy use. Technological advances can eliminate siting constraints or impose new ones, and so can public attitudes. The following paragraphs briefly discuss a few of the more important factors likely to have an impact on siting in the foreseeable future.

### HAZARDOUS WASTE REGULATION

The U.S. Environmental Protection Agency (EPA) is currently considering final regulations by which it will implement the Resource Conservation and Recovery Act of 1976 (RCRA).[5] It is also reasonable to assume that future amendments to this law will place further curbs on the generation of hazardous wastes. At present, industries that produce such wastes are able to pass on responsibility for their disposal to third parties. Thus, chemical production facilities need not be placed on sites designed to store or

148 D. W. STEVER, JR.

dispose of toxic chemicals. But if the law were changed to make generators responsible for the toxic wastes they generate and they were prohibited from transporting such wastes away from the site, chemical industry siting practices would be profoundly affected.

ENERGY POLICY

Industrial siting will be closely interrelated with energy policy choices in the next 20 to 50 years. The scarcity and increasing cost of gasoline will undoubtedly result in at least a partial reversal of the urban sprawl that characterized the 1950s and 1960s. Other changes are harder to predict.

A crude oil allocation program that limited the petrochemical industry's access to crude oil feedstocks might induce much of that industry to shift to carbohydrate (as opposed to hydrocarbon) feedstocks. The present concentration of the industry's facilities in industrial areas close to seaports might then shift to areas of new sugar production.

Similarly, a requirement that future nuclear-generating stations be built in remote multi-unit energy parks would provide a substantial incentive for heavy industrial users to move their factories closer to the energy parks, particularly if transmission line costs are not cut drastically by technological innovation. The effects of such relocations on rural land use would be significant.

Finally, the extent to which coal and oil shale development is pursued in the mountain states will drastically affect the amount of industrial concentration in that region.

ENVIRONMENTAL REGULATIONS

Air and water pollution regulations can have a significant impact on land-use decisions. EPA, for example, is now beginning to promulgate regulations for the pretreatment of toxic materials under Section 307 of the Clean Water Act, a statute that prohibits the introduction of substances into public sewer systems that are incompatible with the system's waste treatment process. Industrial manufacturers will be required to remove from their waste discharges any materials that would either go through a publicly owned treatment plant untreated or interfere with the treatment of other wastes. Some treatment plants accommodate a wider range of waste substances than others, and thus the cost of removing certain substances before waste materials enter public sewers will vary from one municipality to another. For some manufacturers the additional costs may be high enough to affect siting decisions.[6]

Regulations promulgated under the Clean Air Act will also affect the location of new industrial facilities. The act states that "clean air" areas will not be allowed to deteriorate significantly and that the construction of new facilities that would add to air pollution in "dirty air" areas will not be allowed unless there is a corresponding reduction in the amount of pollutants from other sources in the area. Industrial growth in "clean air" areas within a state will be allowed only up to a given increment over a specified baseline level of contamination. Thus, limits on air pollution are becoming a powerful land-use control mechanism.

### TRANSPORTATION

Changes in transportation may also have an impact on industrial siting. Significant increases in commuter costs may result either in the recentralization of industry and housing in older cities or the demise of those cities because of the emergence of new towns where industrial, commercial, and residential areas are better integrated.

### TECHNOLOGICAL DEVELOPMENTS

Technological developments are hard to predict, but the impact they may have on land use can be illustrated by a hypothetical example. Let us assume that production of a useful chemical compound results in a toxic by-product that is long-lived in the environment. Both public pressure and regulatory constraints would require the factory producing the compound to be located at a remote and geologically stable site so that the by-product could be disposed of without contaminating the groundwater. If a way were found to eliminate the by-product from the production process, these constraints would be removed.

## DIRECT GOVERNMENT CONTROL OF INDUSTRIAL FACILITY SITING

One of the major political issues of the 1980s will probably be the extent to which governments will exert control over industrial siting. Before discussing possible scenarios for increased public control, a brief look at the recent past is useful.

Except in the siting of nuclear power plants, which have been subjected to federal regulation since the inception of the Atomic Energy Act, industrial planners have not been much constrained by government. Most regulation has been at the local level and has been restricted to zoning or land-use planning ordinances that do little more than segregate industrial areas from residential and commercial areas. A few states have enacted statutes requiring industrial or utility companies to obtain a license or permit from a state board before constructing a power plant[7] or petroleum refining facility.[8] In 1970, both Maine and Vermont enacted statutes requiring landowners to obtain a state land-use permit for any "large-scale" industrial or commercial development. Generally, these laws allow industrial developers to pick their own site and then attempt to justify their selection to a state agency that can say "no" if it finds that the site or the facility cannot meet some general land-use standard because it will have "unreasonable" environmental impact or impose an undue burden on the local infrastructure.

By and large, however, industrial siting has not been closely regulated. Local zoning administrators generally have not asked whether hazardous wastes would be stored at the site or hauled to the town dump, or what kinds of substances would be emitted from roof vents. Since most organic compounds were not subject to air or water pollution emission limitations until recently (and many are still not), human exposure to such substances has been determined primarily by site selection.

Federal and state environmental and other regulatory legislation has begun to induce private industrial planners to work more closely with government officials. The major question for the future is whether industrial planners will be permitted to try to fit together the pieces of the economic and regulatory jigsaw puzzle in hopes of finding a site that satisfies both private and public demands, or whether public officials will plan an even larger role in private industrial siting decisions.

There is evidence from the nuclear power industry that subjecting private site selection to regulatory veto has not worked well in the past. Attempts to accommodate competing private and regulatory requirements within the context of a broad licensing system like the one managed by the U.S. Nuclear Regulatory Commission (NRC) have simply not produced rational results. Consider, for example, population density as a function of nuclear power plant siting. The NRC's predecessor, the Atomic Energy Commission (AEC), established national criteria[9] intended to ensure that nuclear power plants would be remote from large population centers.[10] That is, the criteria were designed to maintain sparsely populated distances between nuclear plants and population centers of more than 25,000 people. In practice, however, the criteria have not produced anything approaching a uniform site-to-population ratio.

Table 7, extracted from an International Atomic Energy Agency (IAEA) publication, lists nuclear power plants granted AEC construction permits prior to 1970. Several conclusions can be drawn from the data in

TABLE 7   Nuclear Reactor Sites Licensed Before 1970 and Surrounding Population Distribution

| Station | Licensed Station Capacity MWe Net | Exclusion Distance (miles) | Population Center Distance (miles) | Population 0 to 5 Miles | Population 0 to 10 Miles |
|---|---|---|---|---|---|
| Turkey Point Units No. 3, 4 | 1,302 | 0.85 | 20 | 0 | 42,000 |
| Palisades | 700 | 0.44 | 16 | 4,500 | 15,000 |
| Browns Ferry Units No. 1, 2 | 2,130 | 0.76 | 10 | 2,800 | 30,600 |
| Peach Bottom Units No. 1, 2, 3 | 2,170 | 0.48 | 21 | 6,145 | 23,550 |
| Point Beach Units No. 1, 2 | 910 | 0.7 | 13 | 1,241 | 20,845 |
| Diablo Canyon | 1,060 | 0.5 | 10 | 10 | |
| Monticello | 471 | 0.3 | 22 | 3,942 | |
| Oconee Units No. 1, 2 | 1,678 | 1.0 | 21 | 2,163 | 36,334 |
| H. B. Robinson Unit No. 2 | 663 | 0.26 | 56 | 10,800 | |
| Burlington | 993 | 0.23 | 11 | 119,370 | 17 mi.-Phil.[1] |
| Fort St. Vrain | 330 | 0.40 | 14 | 1,951 | 8,420 |
| Vermont Yankee | 514 | 0.17 | 25 | 7,400 | 29,200 |
| Quad-Cities Units No. 1, 2 | 1,430 | 0.23 | 5 | 5,369 | |
| Indian Point Units No. 1, 2 | 1,128 | 0.32 | 1 | 53,040 | 155,510 |
| Dresden Units No. 1, 2, 3 | 1,630 | 0.5 | 14 | 2,500 | 23,000 |
| Connecticut Yankee | 462 | 0.32 | 9 | 10,000 | 49,500 |
| Oyster Creek | 515 | 0.25 | 25 | 38,500 | 106,500 |
| Nine Mile Point | 500 | 0.75 | 6 | 1,900 | 30,900 |
| Millstone Point | 549 | 0.4 | 3 | 60,000 | 96,000 |
| R. E. Ginna | 412 | 0.29 | 12 | 1,500 | 8,000 |
| Malibu | 462 | 0.20 | 10 | 6,000 | 11,900 |
| La Crosse | 50 | 0.21 | 15 | 1,000 | 7,500 |
| San Onoire | 430 | 2.0 | 10 | 8,800 | 22,000 |
| Shippingport | 90 | 0.4 | 7 | 20,000 | 22 mi.-Pitts.[1] |
| Yankee | 175 | 0.5 | 21 | 2,000 | 30,000 |
| Big Rock Point | 72.8 | 0.5 | 135 | 5,000 | 9,000 |
| Elk River | 23 | 0.23 | 20 | 8,000 | 30 mi.-Minn.[1] |
| Carolinas-Virginia | 17 | 0.5 | 25 | 2,000 | 8,000 |
| Enrico Fermi | 60.9 | 0.75 | 7 | 9,000 | 61,000 |
| Humboldt Bay Unit No. 3 | 70 | 0.25 | 3 | 35,000 | 40,000 |
| Piqua | 11.4 | 0.14 | 27 | 21,000 | 42,000 |
| Pathfinder | 58.5 | 0.5 | 3 | | |

[1] Distance from the nearest major city.

this table. One is that plant sites are unrelated to the surrounding population distribution or the distance to the nearest population center. Moreover, population center distance is a relatively meaningless concept. The Burlington nuclear plant, for example, is 11 miles away from the nearest population center of 25,000 people, but 119,370 people live within 5 miles of the facility. One analysis concluded that the population at risk from the Zion, Illinois, nuclear plant was a thousand times larger than that from the Maine-Yankee facility in Wiscasset, Maine, even though the two plants were similar and the calculations postulated identical accident conditions.[11]

The purpose here is not to criticize the AEC/NRC but to underscore the point that federal regulatory standards have not ensured uniform site selection. The site suitability criteria have failed because the agency refused to establish a uniform standard, on the grounds that to have done so would have meant substituting its own judgment for that of corporate planners. Instead, the AEC developed a vague guideline and left determination of compliance with the guideline to specific regulatory proceedings held to license nuclear plants at sites already chosen by private utilities. As a result, different licensing boards over the years have approved different sites with varying degrees of compliance with the guideline.

The conclusion to be drawn from this state of affairs is that attempts will be made to change the governmental role in siting decisions. As an alternative to public regulation of private site selection, we may eventually see some kind of public site selection. The selection of industrial sites is increasingly being seen as a primary rather than a secondary determinant of planning. Any given site carries with it a number of costs and benefits, and a site whose characteristics make it acceptable for a particular use in one region may not be acceptable for that use in another region. Assume, for example, the existence in state $X$ of two sites that, from a marketing and resource availability standpoint, would both be acceptable to a corporate planner as the location of a pulp mill. One site is located in a "clean air" area that could accommodate a new pulp mill's emissions but in so doing would reach the maximum air pollution level allowable under EPA regulations. The other site has no such impediment. Although either site would be acceptable to both the corporate planner and federal regulators, the state may wish to have the mill located in the unencumbered area, favoring development of a larger number of smaller sources of pollution in the clean air area for economic reasons.

Regulatory schemes are not good mechanisms for imposing this kind of public decision on private industry. Typically, such constraints only come to light after the company has invested substantial amounts of money in land options and ordinary licensing costs. It is unreasonable for a state to impose its preference in the guise of a regulatory requirement. Were the state to act as site planner, however, imposing such restrictions at the outset, the inequity would not arise.

CITIZEN GROUP PARTICIPATION AND DISPUTE RESOLUTION

Historically, organized public opposition to industrial siting proposals has focused on nuclear power plants and on industrial facilities in those few states having industrial facility siting laws. (In the case of nuclear plants, federal law provides for public hearings.) Local opposition to manufacturing or waste disposal facilities has necessarily been confined to narrow regulatory actions, such as the issuance of water or air pollution permits. Since these permits are designed simply to assure compliance with an established limit or standard, opponents of the facilities can achieve no more than rigid adherence to the standard. Except in unusual circumstances, a change in site is unlikely. Although opponents can, of course, seek redress through the political process, such as legislation to change a site's zoning classification,[12] the political process is often both inefficient and unpredictable.

Any increased governmental role in industrial siting seems likely to bring with it greater opposition to site development. This is because the government must provide due process of law to citizens affected by its actions. Thus, whenever the government enters a new field of activity, it must provide citizens with an opportunity to be heard.

When the government regulates private site selection, disputes are resolved differently than they would be if government itself chose the sites. One important difference is that in the former case the dispute is between opposing private interests, with the government acting as mediator. In the latter case, however, the government is an affirmative agent receiving input from competing interests. These are not semantic differences, for the legal requirements for providing due process are different for the two roles.[13] Moreover, regulatory decision making is complicated by the fact that a specific proposal in which both of the opposing parties may have opposed economic stakes must be accepted or rejected. As the level of acrimony in a regulatory proceeding increases, so does the possibility that the decision will be based on factors not material to the issue at hand.

Given realities like these, it seems possible that future industrial siting decisions may become part of an integrated system of local, state, and federal land-use planning. If industrial sites are seen as public resources rather than simply as real estate, it necessarily follows that they must be managed as public resources. Resource management requires a continuing governmental presence and accountability to the public that is not achieved either by *laissez-faire* economics or by site-regulating methods like those employed by the NRC.

Public ownership of industrial sites[14] also would provide certain side benefits. It would simplify the problems of accountability that now arise in many situations involving contamination by hazardous wastes. Many of the sites where hazardous chemicals have been produced, stored, or buried have had several owners. The sale of production facilities, corporate mergers, and other commercial transactions have tended to obscure the identity of the generators of specific wastes and raised doubts as to the liability of present owners for public health problems stemming from a previous owner's activities. Proprietary control of industrial sites by the government would not only eliminate this problem but would also provide far greater control over industrial sites than that which can be achieved through regulation alone.

JUDGING THE ACCEPTABILITY OF A RISK

The most troublesome aspect of major industrial facility siting is the risk posed by facilities that in certain circumstances could become potentially lethal to large numbers of people. Nuclear power plants and some chemical manufacturing facilities fall within this category. The risk can range from instant death from catastrophic accidents to long-term exposure to minute amounts of toxic substances.

Risk assessment has not been a traditional component of site determination, but it is likely to become of greater importance as the risks posed by industrial facilities become better understood. Judging the acceptability of risk is not a question that can be answered solely in scientific terms. It is also a political question that must be resolved in an appropriate political forum. The choice of an appropriate forum is an issue of fundamental importance that is complicated by the problem of how to present the issue fairly, clearly, and accurately to the decision maker(s), and by the fact that any decision will be influenced as much by emotion as by reason.

The decision makers range from residents in the immediate vicinity of a proposed facility to state legislatures and Congress. Who decides the issue will determine both the relative importance assigned to various types of information and the standard by which acceptability is judged. Local decision making, for example, is likely to involve a "purer" evaluation of a proposed industrial site, because local residents are likely to have a clearer perception of the potential risks and their judgments are less likely to be clouded by notions of a trade-off between benefits and risks. Yet the transiency of many local populations raises questions as to who is deciding the fate of whom. At any rate, risk assessment is clearly a function that the government, either as site regulator or site owner, cannot confidently take upon itself alone. It is both site- and facility-specific.

## SITING BY POPULAR VOTE

In order for a plebiscite on siting to work successfully, voters would have to be given a clear, unbiased, and sophisticated understanding of the choices facing them. Only then could the popular decision be considered valid. What would be required, in other words, would be (1) an impartial presentation of the facts by the scientific community, and (2) assurance that no viewpoint had at its command greater financial or other resources, and hence, greater potential influence on the voters. First Amendment rights probably relegate the second requirement to the status of a pipe dream. The U.S. Supreme Court recently struck down a voter initiative law containing such a requirement.[15] Moreover, clear definition of the potential risks to public health is often impossible, at least in terms that do not require personal judgment about unknown factors. Abstract statistical analysis phrased in such terms as "X persons will get cancer who otherwise would not," or "there would be a Y percent chance of an accident, which would result in a Z number of cancers and a B number of birth defects," are of little use to the voter, who must try to judge the issue within his or her own existential framework.

Congress has wrestled with the problem of risk assessment in the past. The Food, Drug and Cosmetic Act, for example, contains food additive standards based on a very stringent concept of risk acceptability.[16] It might even be argued that the present civilian nuclear power program represents a general form of risk assessment undertaken by the NRC for society at large.

Who it is that evaluates a risk will determine, at least in part, the methodology by which standards of acceptability are established. It is impossible to construct an empirical standard for use in a public referendum, because each voter's estimate of the potential risk will necessarily be subjective. It makes no difference to voters whether the risk is "reasonable" or that the postulated number of deaths from an accident is "insignificant." The voters will react to what they perceive as the risk to them, and they will decide whether to accept the risk not on the basis of abstract notions of acceptability but on the basis of emotion alone, or at best on the basis of emotion slightly tempered by rational considerations.

If acceptability of risk is decided in a legislative forum, however, outcome of the decision-making process will be a standard or guide. This may take one of two forms—the establishment of rigid acceptability criteria based on some generally accepted level of risk or the enactment of more general standards to be applied by a regulatory agency to specific sites. One example of the former approach was a proposed regulatory guide developed by the NRC staff in 1972 that would have discouraged the siting of nuclear plants in areas having a population density in excess of 500 people per square mile over any radial distance up to 30 miles.[17]

The adoption of a standard or guide requires prior use of yet another standard, namely, one which permits the legislative body to determine for itself the acceptable degree of risk. One published study on risk assessment[18] specifies the following as possible guides in determining acceptability: reasonableness, custom, prevailing professional practice, best-available control, highest practicable protection or lowest practicable exposure, degree of necessity or benefit, zero risk, no detectable adverse effect, toxicologically insignificant levels, and the threshold principle. All of these standards except custom and professional practice are available to legislative assessors of risk. Each will produce a different level of acceptable risk.

Reasonableness is a nonstandard and usually results in a risk-benefit approach to decision making, as do the highest practicable and lowest practicable approaches. The danger of these approaches is that where the benefits are concrete and easily quantified and the risks theoretical and in the future (as in the case of a nuclear power plant), a risk-benefit comparison is methodologically unworkable.

Zero risk or insignificant level of risk would in all probability eliminate all but a very few very remote sites, thereby destroying the entire nuclear power industry and much of the chemical industry. We are left, therefore, with the threshold principle—asking the legislators, in essence, to decide how many hypothetical deaths would be "acceptable." The remaining standards have been applied by regulatory agencies from time to time. Each has its own particular drawbacks that affect its usefulness. Unfortunately, a detailed discussion of them is beyond the scope of this paper.

I am not confident that the potential dangers posed by an industrial facility or a nuclear power plant can ever be accounted for in a sufficiently rational manner to permit them to be factored into a logically constructed site-suitability equation. At the same time, I am convinced that the potential dangers must somehow be accounted for.

In view of the difficulties inherent in site-specific risk assessment, the "remote location" concept that originally formed the basis of the AEC's site-suitability criteria may be the only solution for siting potentially dangerous facilities in the future. The concept's principal virtues are its simplicity of application and its ability to substantially reduce the weight assigned to public safety in individual site-selection decisions.

## LOCAL, STATE, OR NATIONAL SITE SELECTION

This discussion of risk assessment suggests one final issue that must be resolved: How will the local, state, and national interests in siting decisions be accommodated to each other? It has already been noted that industrial siting has traditionally been a local responsibility but that under certain circumstances the logical concerns of state governments should dominate the process by which sites and facilities are matched together. There are, in addition, national interests and standards that should predominate in some cases. Nuclear power plants, for example, obviously demand a significant degree of uniform control over site selection as well as construction and operation. Such controls can only be exerted effectively by the federal government. The same argument can be made with respect to other dangerous facilities, particularly chemical manufacturing facilities that produce toxic by-products or wastes. One need not be very imaginative to see similarities between the disastrous accident at a hexachloraphene manufacturing plant in Seveso, Italy, in 1975, which resulted in widespread dioxin contamination of the surrounding countryside, and the Three Mile Island nuclear mishap. The Seveso incident was worse, since it resulted in actual illness and substantial property loss.[19]

Because the risks posed by dangerous facilities are so great, decisions on their location and the necessary environmental impact and risk assessment that precedes such decision making should be undertaken at the highest level of government, pursuant to a generous commitment of analytical resources. Many states lack resources for even the beginnings of an adequate site evaluation program for such facilities, and I therefore look with disfavor on proposals to streamline nuclear site verdicts by delegating a larger decision-making role to the states. Indeed, it may well be in the public interest not to expedite the siting of dangerous facilities but to require their promoters to satisy federal, state, and local demands, so that final siting decisions are the result of an excruciatingly rigorous, multilayered pattern of review.

We do not now have a rationally structured system for locating large industrial facilities on sites that are suitable from the standpoint of the public good. We should begin to devise such a system now. In order for it to work successfully, government will have to perform well both in roles that are new to it and in roles in which it heretofore failed. Industry will have to become accustomed to a closer relationship with public sector planners. Our children will see whether either is able to rise to the occasion.

## NOTES

1. Portions of this paper are taken from *Seabrook and the Nuclear Regulatory Commission* to be published by the University Press of New England in 1980.

2. For a review of recent legislative attempts to coordinate industrial and government planning, see Bosselman et al., *The Permit Explosion*, Urban Land Institute (1977). A more theoretical discussion is contained in Barum et al., *Environmental Law and the Siting of Facilities*, Ballinger Publishing Co.

3. See, e.g., R. Keeney and K. Nair, *Nuclear Siting Using Decision Analysis*, 5 Energy Policy 223 (12/77).

4. See M. C. Roberts et al., *A Land Suitability Model for the Evaluation of Land-Use Change*, Environmental Management, Vol. 3, No. 4, at 339(July, 1979) and references cited therein.

5. 15 U.S.C. Sec. 7,000 et seq.

6. In comments filed with EPA, the electroplating and metal finishing industry complained that the agency's electroplating subcategory pretreatment standards would impose significant costs on some segments of the industry.

7. See, e.g., Art. 66 C, Anno. Code Md. Sec. 763-768 (Ch. 31).

8. See, e.g., New Hampshire Rev. Stat. Ann. Chapter 162-H.

9. 10 C.F.R. Part 100.

10. 27 Federal Register 3509 (1962).

11. Article by Y. Yellin, 7 Bell Journal of Economics, No. 1, at 317 (1975).

12. This tactic was employed successfully in Durham, New Hampshire, in 1975 to block construction of an oil refinery.

13. Compare, for example, the provisions of the federal administration procedure act (5 U.S.C. Sec. 501 et seq.) governing "adjudications," (Secs. 554 and 556) with those governing "rule making" proceedings (e.g., Sec. 553).

14. I assume, for the purpose of this discussion, that the sites would be leased to industry.

15. *First National Bank of Boston* v. *Bellotti*, 435 U.S. 765 (1978).

16. W. Lowrance, *Of Acceptable Risk: Science and the Determination of Safety*, William Kaufmann Co., Los Altos, Calif., 1976.

17. See, Regulatory Guide 4.7 (Revision 1), U.S. NRC (1975).

18. Lowrance, note 16 above.

19. See Whiteside (1978), *The Pendulum and the Toxic Cloud*, Harper & Row (1978).

## DISCUSSANT'S REMARKS ON THE PAPER BY D. W. STEVER, JR.

R. R. RIDKER
*Resources for the Future*

While I agree that the future geographic distribution of population and economic activities will be influenced by rising energy costs, the need to dispose of increasing quantities of hazardous materials in safe places, and a steadily increasing role played by government and citizen groups, one should be cautious about overstating the role that these factors play relative to availability of labor, access to markets and raw materials, and similar factors that industrial planners have traditionally taken into account.

Consider energy prices, for example. There are at least three reasons for believing that their effects will be—or at least can be made to be—relatively small. First, to the extent that energy price increases are emanating from abroad, the effect will be relatively uniform throughout the country. While energy costs are lower in some parts of the country than others, they will rise everywhere. Second, during the next 20 or more years, I believe we can look forward to a near revolution in communications technology. Future changes should reduce transportation requirements and the necessity for workers who deal primarily with paper and communications to live relatively near their offices. Third, I am impressed with the point made in the energy paper (Chapter 3, Ayres et al.) that toxic wastes can be minimized or eliminated through process design. Perhaps in the long run it is more important to find ways to induce such process changes; only to the extent that we are unsuccessful in doing so will problems associated with the disposal of toxic wastes seriously influence geographic distribution.

One should, of course, expect some shift from energy-consuming to energy-producing areas, and from areas where more energy is needed to those where less is required; and there are a few indications that such shifts are occurring. My colleague, Erving Hoch, has found that in 1972 residential consumption of energy cost for residents of Massachusetts was $100 per capita more than residents of California (partly because of higher prices and partly because of greater consumption) and that by 1978 this difference had increased by $40 per capita. While this is a large percentage increase over that time period, it remains a small percent of per capita incomes. Thus, while increased energy prices have made California a bit more attractive than Massachusetts, the change has so far not been so overwhelming or massive as to make us expect any dramatic acceleration or alteration in trends that have been present for some time.

The second point I would like to make about Stever's paper pertains to his suggestions for more systematic land-use planning by government bodies. At the outset of his paper, Stevers describes the dream that industrial planners had in the 1950s. As I was reading the rest of his paper and began reflecting on the problems with the regulatory approach that he so ably presents, an alternative image—indeed a nightmarish vision—of the 1980s began to form in my mind. In this scenario of the 1980s, federal, state, and local regulations, combined with local opposition to the siting of dangerous and dirty facilities in one's backyard, result in the choking off of national economic growth. The only people getting rich will be the lawyers.

What can be done about this emerging problem? Stever suggests land-use planning by bodies at the state or federal level, and he is optimistic about the use of modeling and other techniques to predict and select sites, or at least to separate out unsuitable sites. There are, if I understand the situation correctly, two principal arguments in favor of this approach. First, it should be able to take into account more national goals as well as the local characteristics of microenvironments. Second, it should be able to reduce opposition by employing site banking and by securing an agreement to share burdens before difficult individual decisions must be made.

However, it is extremely hard to anticipate requirements. In the early 1950s, the government projected that there would be nearly 1,000 nuclear power plants by the year 2000; today it predicts that the number will be more like 150. But the demand for electricity is relatively easy to project in comparison to the demand for the output of chemical plants: What is the future demand for chemicals that have not yet been invented? It is also very difficult to project the characteristics of facilities. The suitability of a site depends on these characteristics. Suppose, for example, that nuclear plants were located underground; in that event, the sites selected might have to be far different from those that would be set aside if the plants were located above ground.

I do not want to make too much of this point, because I agree fundamentally with Stever, but it is important to point out that planning is no panacea. There are too many open questions that will still have to be answered through the use of regulations. We must try, but at the same time we must not expect that planning will solve many problems.

Are there any alternatives or complementary procedures that might mitigate the problems? I can think of at least three that are worthy of discussion. The first involves the development of a new institution that has the authority to say "yes" as well as "no." All private planners and regulatory bodies would have to appeal to this overriding authority. Every agency would make some input, but the new institution could be given overarching authority to make positive decisions as well as negative ones. The proposed Energy Mobilization Board is a rather drastic form of such an authority. More serious thought should be given to representative bodies that can accomplish this goal.

Second, perhaps more use can be made of existing sites than has been done in the past. It should, for example, be easier to concentrate new nuclear plants on existing sites that have the capacity to expand and that have been found to be acceptable on other grounds, and then to feed the national grid from them. While transmission costs would be somewhat higher, this approach would prevent each new plant from becoming a new siting battle. Furthermore, economies of scale are likely to exist in the areas of safety, skill, emergency procedures, etc. This type of growth may reduce social friction. It cannot quite be called long-term planning, but is perhaps a practical second-best. I gather that siting practices have in fact been moving in this direction, and it is not a bad idea.

Third, more serious thought should be given to the possibility of using incentives, compensation payments, and effluent charges. It should be possible to develop incentives that encourage process change and to evolve markets for waste products so as to reduce the quantities of residual matter that must be disposed of or stored. It should also be possible to develop procedures for encouraging people to move out of, and not into, areas that are to be set aside as waste-disposal facilities. A good deal of consideration has been given to effluent charges as a means of encouraging pollution control. Has a similar incentive scheme yet been applied to improving or speeding up decisions about siting? It would provide a good deal of scope for the exercise of creative imagination.

## SUMMARY OF THE TASK GROUP

R. D'ARGE, *University of Wyoming*
S. W. PIRAGES, *National Research Council*

### INTRODUCTION

Problems associated with siting decisions for potentially hazardous facilities stem from the environmental impacts identified by the previous three task groups. In addition to the specific environmental problems of an industry (waste residual flows and stocks, process types) that must be considered when assessing risk to human health and ecosystems, there are social, political, and economic issues and conflicts that must be resolved. If current practices of governmental agencies continue, consideration of siting issues may be protracted because of insufficient advance analysis and discussion.

This Task Group identified four main issues within this topic area: identification of facilities that would have future problems associated with siting, the geographical implications of industrial siting, the siting decision process, and siting within the broader context of technological hazard management.

## IDENTIFICATION OF FUTURE PROBLEM AREAS

Nine categories of industrial activities were identified as being potentially hazardous in the future, and for each the scope of the environmental problem was outlined.

### CHEMICAL-PROCESSING INDUSTRIES

The term chemical process is used here in the broadest sense to include a wide spectrum of industrial facilities. The siting problems encountered will range from the need to locate new chemical-producing facilities, to the turnover of existing facilities, and to establishment of suitable waste disposal sites. The latter set of problems will involve current waste build-up that could be expected to continue as an important issue in a long-range environmental outlook. The location of new facilties will receive greater public pressure for choice of sites that do not result in chronic exposure of humans or ecosystems to hazardous pollutants and that will provide some protection against acute or accidental exposure. Questions of whether to use existing industrial sites for new facilities or decide on new locations will need to be addressed by weighing benefits, costs, and risks involved.

### NUCLEAR FUEL CYCLES

Important future environmental problems can be expected to arise from inadequate disposal of mining, milling, and reprocessing wastes, emissions from power-generating plants, and reactor accidents. Environmental problems also may arise with regard to the spatial configuration of nuclear sites (for example, dispersed versus consolidated; underground versus above ground).

## FOSSIL FUEL POWER PLANTS

For the next 20 or 30 years, the energy future of the United States is likely to include a significant increase in coal-fired power-generating plants; traditional and new environmental problems can be expected as siting decisions for these facilities are made. The problems will emerge from attempts to control air emissions and the consequent build-up of solid and liquid waste material. Environmental problems associated with disposal of scrubber sludge, aggregated effects of several plants, and chronic low-level emissions of $SO_x$, $NO_x$, and $CO_2$ will undoubtedly have an influence on locating plants and disposal sites. Long-distance dispersion of these pollutants (e.g., in acid precipitation) will not be greatly ameliorated by site selection in small geographic regions by substituting fossil fuel with nuclear power plants.

## ALTERNATIVE ENERGY SOURCES

Alternative energy systems (e.g., solar, photovoltaic, wind, ocean wave, tidal, thermal, and biomass) will constitute a noticeable fraction of energy production within the next 50 years. Environmental impacts will be quite different from those of traditional energy production processes and must be considered in the siting decision process. Current knowledge on the extent of the impacts is inadequate. Some environmental disturbances will be localized if the system is consolidated to a few sites, while locations in urban or rural areas may pose specific problems. The increased use of exotic materials may generate siting problems far removed from the energy conversion site themselves.

## COGENERATION

The economic constraints of transporting heat over long distances require that cogeneration plants be sited near the end consumer. This proximity may enhance the environmental impacts of this energy source. The major problems associated with cogeneration will be excessive noise, $NO_x$ and pollutant emissions, and these will be aggravated by the nearby high-density populations. Public opposition to selected sites could become a serious problem.

## SYNTHETIC FUEL FACILITIES

Synthetic fuel technology includes development of gas and liquid derivitives of coal, and oil from shale rock and tar sands. The hazards associated with these technologies have some general components that must be considered when assessing suitable sites: direct pollution or contamination of water, air, or soil; aggregate pollution problems of the synthetic fuel facility and traditional energy-production industries; constraints on conflict mitigation because of the perceived need for rapid development of synthetic fuels; and the potential of locking industry and government into first-generation technologies without investigating the possibilities of second- and third-generation approaches with fewer environmental problems. The question of whether to site these plants near the fossil fuel deposits or elsewhere will further complicate the issue.

TRANSPORTATION FACILITIES

In the next 50 years the transportation of a richer array of materials and energy over long distances will become more commonplace, with a consequent increase in nonsite-specific risks. A variety of methods will be used: pipelines, electrical transmission lines, microwave transmissions, barges, ships, railroads, and highways. These activities will involve a large number of potential conflicts that must be considered in selecting the rights of way and in expanding depots, ports, and receivers. For example, impacts such as accidents involving spillage and burning of energy materials, release of toxic materials, radiation impacts, and resource or land-use demands may have priority consideration over benefits that can be derived from the site (e.g., land-use options in coastal areas, water use needs in semi-arid and arid regions).

BIOMEDICAL AND PHARMACEUTICAL FACILITIES

Just as this era has produced rapid advances in biological research (DNA processing), the next 20 to 50 years will likely involve rapid expansion in commercial and industrial applications of these research techniques. Thus, increasing numbers of renewable, biological resources will be produced in factory settings. Potentially hazardous or obnoxious gaseous, liquid or solid wastes, as well as potentially infectious microorganisms or recombinant DNA, will be generated. Although it is difficult to predict how these facilities will alter siting issues as contrasted to current biological research, testing and production facilities, the increase in number of sites and public concern over risks could create difficulties for identifying suitable locations.

## FACILITY RELOCATION

The need to replace existing facilities depends on the age and useful economic life span; the latter is often influenced by a variety of factors: new technological developments; competition among states and municipalities for attracting industry, safety, health, tax, and environmental legislation; and changes in product demand, price or both. It is anticipated that many facilities, such as steel mills and copper smelters, will require replacement in 10 to 30 years. The need to identify and develop new sites poses both problems and opportunities with respect to environmental concerns and land-use planning.

## GEOGRAPHICAL IMPLICATIONS OF INDUSTRIAL SITING ISSUES

Several factors impose limitations on the site-selection process, and these will create more serious problems in the future. Environmental regulation by local, state, and federal agencies, individually or in combination, specify certain geographical regions as off-limits for particular industries. Thus, as unembargoed areas become scarce, suitable industrial sites will become more difficult to locate. Other factors, such as population concentrations, resource and energy availability, or existing standards for air and water quality, will put additional constraints on selection of industrial sites. Public opinion will be a particularly strong determinant for potentially very hazardous facilities. As energy scarcities emerge over the next 50 years, shifts in population locations will influence future industrial siting. It will be necessary to anticipate these shifts in order to determine future risks and environmental impacts of alternative sites.

## THE DECISION PROCESS OF INDUSTRIAL FACILITY SITING

A lesson has emerged from recent experiences in attempts to site hazardous facilities, e.g., technical expertise in assessing potential sites is important but not sufficient to address the range of issues involved in siting decisions. The social, political, and economic considerations of site selection are as important as questions of technical feasibility. If future siting of hazardous facilities is to be more fully understood and determined, it will be necessary to develop new institut and siting methodologies that consider all issues.

Governmental institutions are ill-equipped to deal

siting problems noted in the above sections. Siting processes exist for some of these facilities, but the institutional arrangements are inadequate to make effective decisions. The institutional considerations do not seem to match the scale of problems or risks posed. Possible institutional approaches are illustrated in Figure 12.

Most siting methodologies currently in use do not consider (1) the aggregate effects (environmental and health) of several facillities, (2) public opposition, and (3) the range of trade-offs that are inherent in any siting decision. The emphasis in site decisions generally is on the identification of one technically feasible location with inadequate assessment of alternative sites. The decision process would be improved if analytical methodologies were matched to specific problems and institutional arrangements.

### SITING DECISIONS WITHIN A TECHNOLOGICAL HAZARD MANAGEMENT SCHEME

Site selection is only one of many options in hazard facility management strategy, and it is important to consider siting issues in this larger context, illustrated in Figure 13. As this figure indicates, the hazards associated with any particular facility can be eliminated through the use of several management options: using alternative technology, removing the hazardous substance, blocking the release, or through careful selection of the facility location. The possibility of eliminating siting problems exists when alternative actions are taken elsewhere in the management scheme.

### PRIORITIES OF PROBLEM AREAS

The Task Group was reluctant to set priorities for the problems listed in industrial categories. However, it was emphasized that the decision process for site selection must be improved if any future problem is to be effectively resolved. Thus, priority attention should be given to development of siting assessment methodologies including methods for assessing risk and the relative efficacy of various institutional organizations. At the least, attempts should be made to match institutional arrangements with the scope of siting problems.

### RECOMMENDATIONS

The following range of research recommendations is made by the Task Group. However, these do not necessarily reflect a consensus of the group.

1. For specific problem areas more research will be needed garding specific environmental impacts and the information incor-

**Traditional Siting Scenario** (excluding nuclear facilities)

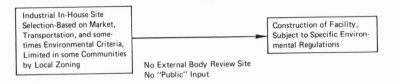

**Siting Under Typical State Site Evaluation Law of the 1970s**

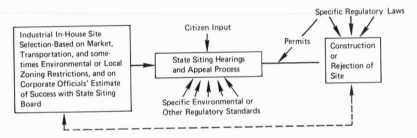

**Alternative "Public" Site Selection Scenario for Major Industrial Facilities**

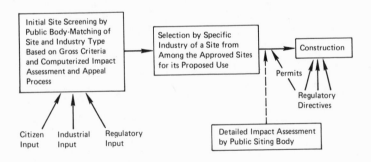

SOURCE: D. Stever, U.S. Department of Justice, Washington, D.C.

FIGURE 12 Three institutional approaches to site selection decisions.

168

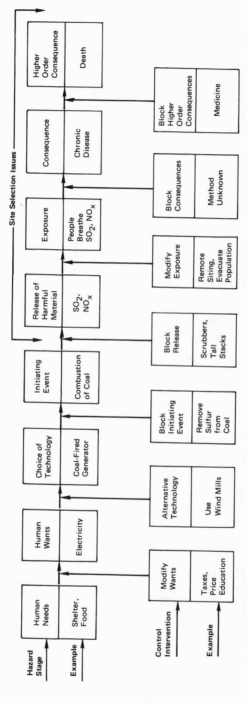

SOURCE: C. Hohenemser, Clark University, Worcester, Mass.

FIGURE 13  Technical hazard management scheme, illustrated for coal-fired electrical generating plant. The hazard stages and logical structure of control intervention are generic in nature. The examples indicated for each step are not meant to be comprehensive.

porated into the site-selection process. The number of potential sites needed should be considered and questions of dispersed versus concentrated and above ground versus below ground addressed wherever appropriate.

2. Re-use or recycling of industrial waste material should be encouraged to minimize waste disposal problems.

3. Full deployment of new technologies should be phased such that our understanding of the impacts will make future site choices more acceptable.

4. It was emphasized that for each area or industry a menu of alternative sites, rather than only one or two, should be required and that selection of one be made on the basis of an analysis of the important trade-offs: cost and risks to health or environment. Current decision making appears to be too single-minded (i.e., a specific plant and a specific location).

5. In many siting circumstances, regional or national cumulative effects will be of importance in the future, and retrospective studies of choosing one or more potential sites should improve the quality of the decision-making process.

6. Long-range research related to siting problems will have to anticipate in so far as possible such variables as demographic changes, technological advances, life-style changes, resource discovery as well as depletion and the policy or regulatory issues that will directly or indirectly affect these variables.

7. It will be necessary to establish criteria and general principles that receive wide public acceptance and are consistently employed in making decisions on plant sites. The ad hoc manner currently in use will not work as the number and complexity of these decisions increase. Such principles must be all-encompassing to adequately consider efficiency, equity, and compensation of those adversely affected by choice of site.

8. Single-purpose regulatory agencies will not be adequate for meeting future problems; either governmental agencies must become more comprehensive in scope or stronger coordinating of mechanisms among agencies must be developed.

9. In developing adequate methodology for choosing appropriate sites, three types of data will be needed: data on material flow into and out of facilities and sites; information concerning the probabilities of system failures and the anticipated damage resulting from such failures; and data on acceptance attitude and social priorities for relevant citizen groups. Future conflicts could be prevented or more easily resolved if these data were available.

10. Alternatives to regulatory action should be investigated; in particular, studies should be initiated on the potential utility of specific types of incentives and compensatory payment schemes. These have been studied for pollution abatement but not in the context of siting decisions.

11. Siting problems could be reduced if veiwed in the larger strategy of hazard management. Siting decisions are only one option for hazard control; others include alternative technologies and processes, control of emissions, and detoxification of wastes. The development of a strategy for hazard management that includes plant siting in the options and sound site-selection criteria may reduce public opposition and distrust regarding future hazard location choices.

# TASK GROUP ON HAZARDOUS FACILITIES

RALPH D'ARGE (*Group Chairman*), University of Wyoming
PAUL ARBESMAN, New Jersey Department of Environmental Protection
JARED COHON, Johns Hopkins University
JAMES FAY, Massachusetts Institute of Technology
CHRISTOPH HOHENEMSER, Clark University
JOHN D. KOUTSANDREAS, U.S. Environmental Protection Agency
JAMES MONAGHAN, Office of the Governor of Colorado
SUELLEN PIRAGES (*Rapporteur*), National Research Council
RONALD RIDKER (*Discussant*), Resources for the Future
LEONARD SLOSKEY, Office of the Governor of Colorado
DONALD STEVER (*Paper Author*), U.S. Department of Justice

171

# 7 Long-Range Environmental Problems: A Review of Previous National Academy of Sciences Reports

S. W. PIRAGES
*National Research Council*

## INTRODUCTION

As part of the preparation for the Workshop on a Long-Range Environmental Outlook, a request was made to review previous National Academy of Sciences (NAS) reports, summarizing Academy recommendations on anticipated environmental problems or recommendations for new research activities that would provide tools for identifying problems at an early stage. NAS publications of the last 10 years that have dealt with environmental issues were surveyed to determine their relevance to a long-range outlook. The conclusions and recommendations of pertinent reports are presented in this chapter.

The main focus for this paper corresponds to the four general topics chosen for the workshop: future trends in energy, agriculture, toxic materials, and hazardous facility siting, including waste management. However, the initial review was not limited to these areas, as a wide range of reports was included (see "NAS Reports" at the end of this chapter). All conclusions and recommendations dealing with future environmental problems are summarized below. It should be emphasized that not all recommendations presented in any one report are included here, only those that relate to development of a long-range environmental outlook.

Most NAS studies concentrate primarily on assessments of past or current environmental problems. Many offer recommendations for future research needs, but these are often stated in very general terms (e.g., that more data are needed to understand a process, that EPA should monitor environmental quality, or that EPA should develop anticipatory research programs).

## ENERGY SOURCES/POLLUTION-CONTROL TECHNOLOGY

The development and efficient use of major energy resources have been the subject of reports prepared by several sections of the Academy. The major resources investigated include coal, geothermal sources, nuclear power, and natural gas. Future national needs for the use of these resources are often discussed, but the impact of various energy-producing processes on the environment receives relatively little attention. The study committees do acknowledge, however, the need to consider environmental consequences of energy resource development.

The Proceedings of the Academy Forum, *Coal as an Energy Resource: Conflict and Consensus* (1977), discusses several aspects of coal development for meeting future energy needs. The paper by S. Rezneck, presented in the Proceedings, describes some of the potential environmental impacts, including destruction of ecosystems and aesthetically pleasing environments because of increased surface mining activities and environmental contamination by sulfur through increased use of high-sulfur coal. Dr. Rezneck emphasizes that these problems would be difficult to prevent and the resulting damage difficult to correct. Full restoration of destroyed ecosystems might not be possible, as such efforts would be constrained by climatic factors, variable water supplies, and condition of the disturbed soil.

The paper emphasizes that increased use of coal and new coal-transformation processes (i.e., synthetic fuel production) will result in greater releases of air pollutants, unless stringent and effective control measures are developed and implemented. The health problems associated with exposure to these pollutants will differ from those associated with petroleum refining, because emissions from coal processing can be expected to contain greater concentrations of carcinogens. Dr. Rezneck stresses that if future environmental and health hazards resulting from increased coal use are to be "held in check," research on prevention and control of these hazards must be conducted in conjunction with the development of new energy technologies.

Among the recommendations found in the above-mentioned proceedings are the following:

1. Processes designed to clean coal for conventional or advanced combustion uses and technologies for coal gasification or liquefaction produce residuals or by-products having unknown or unquantified

environmental consequences. Research will be needed to characterize the chemicals found in emissions and effluents and to determine their environmental transport, transformation, and fate, as well as ecological effects of representative classes of these compounds.

2. In some areas, the existing air quality standards are exceeded already by "natural" conditions; while in others, the available margin for additional degradation is sufficiently small to preclude installation of new power-generating plants that use present technologies. New research programs should include reassessing the need for stringent air quality standards, assessing the desirability of regional rather than national standards, and developing more effective and efficient emission control technologies.

3. The amount of water available for energy-related uses in the West is a matter of considerable controversy. Any over-appropriation of available water supplies for energy purposes, especially in drought years, could have severe consequences for many sectors of the economy as well as the environment. More efficient techniques for water storage need developing. In addition, the hydrologic and groundwater quality consequences of coal mining must be assessed.

4. Even if clean combustion of coal can be achieved, leaching and water runoff from the sites where coal wastes are stored will create another set of environmental problems. Development of the capability to regenerate these mineral wastes and an economic assessment of the use of recycled products are required.

5. Most, if not all, phases of coal-producing and coal-using cycles release trace elements and heavy metals causing increased stress to ecosystems. The effects of these contaminants on specific organisms are either well-known or can be obtained relatively easily. However, research is needed to develop the ability for extrapolation of acute or chronic effects from single species to changes in ecosystem structure, function, or diversity, and to develop methods of predicting ecosystem resiliency once the stress has been removed.

6. Continued research on trace element contamination in specific air basins also is urged, as the chemical compositions of air basins can and often do vary. The chemical form of trace elements in air should be identified because their effects on an organism depend on the form of the element at the time of exposure.

7. Reclamation efforts are important to maintain the environment. Research efforts should be directed towards the development of reclamation techniques that will ensure biological productivity of land after initial land-maintenance efforts (e.g., irrigation and fertilization) have ceased. Techniques for limiting off-site (e.g., stream pollution)

effects of strip mining both during mining and after abandonment should be investigated.

The report entitled *Rehabilitation Potential of Western Coal Lands* (1974) dealt with the consequences of increased coal use. It recommends that rehabilitation plans be designed to minimize adverse impacts on the environment and take into account regional air and water pollution regulations. The report urged that effective monitoring of environmental conditions is required to determine the impact of surface mining. Establishment of a comprehensive nonindustrially managed monitoring program is recommended. As stated in the report, it is necessary

. . . to monitor and evaluate the rehabilitation of all current and future coal surface mining operations. Through such experience, performance standards for rehabilitation can be based on technical knowledge. The evidence must include a complete baseline inventory of the existing ecology, geology, and hydrology prior to granting a permit and the establishment of a set of continuing observations to monitor the on-site and off-site effects of mining and rehabilitation. Such studies must also include the determination of the chemical properties of the soils and overburden and the hydrologic effects of surface mining on groundwater, surface drainage and water quality as affected both on-site and off-site. These data will be a necessary measure of what has been accomplished and serve as an essential guide for ongoing and future operations. The observations should be verified by agencies independent of the mining operation, because many years of objective observations are required and organizational continuity is essential.

In discussing the importance of adequate water resources for planning future development of coal resources in the western United States, the report continues:

. . . enough water is available for mining and rehabilitation at most sites, not enough water exists for large-scale conversion of coal to other energy forms (e.g., gasification or steam electric power). The potential environmental and social impacts of the use of this water for large scale energy conversion projects would exceed by far the anticipated impact of mining alone . . . that alternate locations be considered for energy conversion facilities, and that adequate evaluations be made of the options (including rehabilitation) for the various local uses of the available water.

The report further emphasizes that

. . . plans for rehabilitating surface mined land in the West must begin with an assessment of public goals. These goals will strongly influence the selection of sites toward those where surface mining would be of least total impact to identified sets of perceived values and will exercise positive control over the mining methods that give shape to the end product. The goals would also influence rehabilitation plans by formulating standards for eventual land use.

A major problem discussed in this report concerns the potential competition for water resource needs among agricultural, recreational, wildlife and industrial sectors.

Until recently, it has been tacitly assumed that the unappropriated water in the coal region would be used for some combination of irrigation, wildlife management, and municipal and industrial purposes including perhaps lumber mills, paper and pulp plants, mineral or other processing plants, and assembly plants. In 1972-73 the use of this water became, as far as government reports are concerned, more importantly directed toward energy conversion: cooling of steam plants, gasification, synthetic crude oil production, and other aspects of coal development. Such a sharp reversal in government policy came about with little or no public awareness.

The recommendation is made that national and regional goals and priorities be established to resolve the issue. In addition, alternatives to large-scale transport of water for use in energy conversion have not been pursued adequately.

Options do exist for the transport of fuel, water, and power, and in choices among uses of water for energy conversion and transport. The potential differences in impacts among options in water use, including the option of non-development, and in the location of generating plants in the western states could be profound. Present provisions for analysis of alternatives for land use planning at all levels of government do not appear to be commensurate with the public stake in the outcome.

In 1972, a report was released entitled *Engineering for Resolution of the Energy-Environment Dilemma: A Summary*. The report stated that a crisis does exist in the nation's ability to supply sufficient electrical power and that this contributes to the developing conflict between energy needs and environmental protection. Among the recommendations for improved application of engineering "know-how" to supplying electrical power is an acknowledgement that environmental impacts must be minimized:

The power plant siting process must involve comprehensive engineering. Such engineering must take into account not only the possibilities of more advanced technology, but also constraints based upon the best available information about possible environmental effects. Engineering, which includes a consideration of economic factors, must also be integrated in decision-making with the processes of law and public participation. A primary responsibility of the engineer is to synthesize viable solutions to the problems of producing new electric power capacity without unacceptable environmental impacts.

To assist engineers with meeting this responsibility, it is suggested that a national bank of information on environmental standards, identified impacts, and management strategies might be established.

This report stressed that an urgent need existed for research on the impacts from nuclear-powered generating plants. The range of issues include studies of the breeder reactors, investigations of temperature tolerances for aquatic organisms related to the disposal of millions of gallons of warm water per minute into the ocean, lakes, or rivers, and the need for restricting the escape of radioactive elements into the environment. The range in costs is also large (e.g., $300 million/year for breeder reactor development and $30 thousand/year for biological research). More data are needed to better understand ecosystem resilience and response to environmental stress. The type of data needed include

1. the heat tolerance of different ecosystems,
2. effects of thermal plumes on fish, plankton, and other marine organisms,
3. the potential impact of the thermal, chemical, and biocide properties of cooling tower blowdown,
4. life-cycle changes and migration patterns of estuarine and off-shore fauna in response to thermal and chemical loadings in coastal water,
5. the significance of daily and seasonal fluctuations in temperature and dissolved oxygen in aquatic systems.

Other future research needs presented in this report include investigating the role of vegetation in recycling elements and as temporary sinks for pollutants (i.e., plant susceptibility to industrial emissions, genetic changes resulting from repeated exposure), surveying major bodies of water to determine species composition, disposition and species-specific behavioral responses, and developing engineering technology and plant design to minimize environmental perturbations.

A recent report, *Geothermal Resources and Technology in the United States* (1979), states that while environmental problems do exist in geothermal energy operations (i.e., concerning issues of aesthetics, acoustics, wildlife, recreation, odorous emissions, disposal of waste water, thermal pollution, subsidence, seismicity, and worker health and safety), effective resolution of these problems is possible. The environmental and health problems are not considered trivial, but they are small relative to many more common industrial operations. Because the effects of geothermal energy production are local in nature, it may be possible to assess, control, and monitor these effects more easily.

In *Energy and Climate* (1977), the potential environmental impact and climatic consequences of future sources of energy are discussed. The report concludes that direct generation of heat through the production and use of fossil fuel will result in only small increases in average global air temperatures, although the local increase might be large. The uncertainties surrounding the interdependence of climate and the global carbon cycles, however, might be the primary factor limiting fossil fuel energy production.

This report recommends the establishment of comprehensive research programs and the development of new institutional mechanisms that will integrate scientific expertise with federal government needs in dealing with climate-related problems. Long-range research efforts are required to increase our basic understanding of the carbon cycle, climate, future population shifts, energy demands, and the environmental consequences resulting from interactions of these factors.

The report also discusses some of the anticipated consequences of increased global temperatures. Warming of the upper layers in oceans could result in a decrease of sea ice, an increase in sea level, additional movement of $CO_2$ from the ocean to the atmosphere, a decrease in vertical stirring of ocean water, and poleward movements or shifts in marine ecosystems. In polar regions of the globe a potential increase in snowfall because of climatic changes might result in increased ice thickness, thus causing horizontal stress in the ice cap. This phenomenon could lead to ice slides that might destroy the ice cap and ultimately contribute to a rise in sea level. The report emphasizes that alternative strategies for responding to these possible scenarios need to be developed.

*Energy Consumption Measurements: Data Needs for Public Policy* (1977) points out the need to develop technology for recycling industrial-process waste heat. In addition, it is suggested that in order to meet future energy demands effective planning will require gaining an understanding of current energy consumption, developing models for predicting changes in short- and long-term patterns of energy use, and assessing potential effects (social, economic, and environmental) of changes in energy policy. The environmental consequences resulting from changing energy resource use might include potential perturbations of atmospheric $CO_2$ levels, shifts in agricultural productivity through direct effects from changes in energy supply and indirect effects from climatic changes induced by new energy-use patterns, and increased acid precipitation leading to adverse effects on marine, freshwater, and terrestrial ecosystems.

A report entitled *Implications of Environmental Regulations for Energy Production and Consumption* (1977) suggests that the available data bases for evaluating environmental impacts of particular types of energy and for assessing the effect of environmental regulations on energy development are quite poor. The recommendation is made to increase efforts to establish data-gathering capabilities and to develop methods for improving the quality of those data.

*Mineral Resources and the Environment* (1975) presents recommendations regarding natural resource use. Perhaps the most significant is that assessments of environmental impacts related to resource use (e.g., energy or mineral development) should make use of a systems approach to materials cycles. The report further suggests that intensive studies be conducted to determine the effects of waste heat and energy-related pollutants on ecosystems and climate. Data must be collected that will permit an assessment of energy and pollution-related consequences of recovering valuable minerals from waste ores and that will assist in creating institutional capabilities for long-range forcasting of mineral-related issues. Policies of conservation of materials, energy, and environmental resources need to be developed. Recommendations for improving available pollution control technology include developing information banks on general designs for pollution control systems, developing basic control technology for specific pollutants emitted from combustion processes, developing technological uses for recycling waste materials, determining the effects of pollutants on biological systems, and developing instrumentation necessary for detecting these effects.

## AGRICULTURAL TECHNOLOGY AND MANAGEMENT PRACTICES

Although many NAS reports that are concerned with agricultural management policies and technologies have been prepared, most do not address the future environmental implications of proposed technologies or management practices. Those that do, mainly reports on pest-management strategies and on the relationship between climate and food production, are discussed below.

A report mentioned in the above section, *Energy and Climate* (1977), presents the implications of climatic changes for agricultural productivity. It is stressed that additional data are needed to determine the effect of climatic change on the biosphere and, in particular, on agriculture. Future projections in agricultural trends require knowledge on certain issues, including a better understanding of

1. the effects of increased atmospheric $CO_2$ levels on plant metabolism, photosynthesis, and respiration;
2. the effects of increased average temperatures on plant yield;
3. the potential spatial shifts in agricultural regions; and
4. the effects of changes in annual climate on plant productivity, (e.g., changes in precipitation or amount of available sunlight).

If future adverse environmental, social, and economic consequences are to be forestalled, it will be necessary to predict shifts in semiarid and arid regions. Methods for social and economic adjustments to these shifts must be developed and implemented. Policy options should be formulated in anticipation of both short- and long-term consequences of changes in regional agricultural productivity.

*Pest Control: An Assessment of Present and Alternative Technologies, Vol. I* (1975), emphasizes that future development of new pest-control strategies will depend on improved understanding of the basic scientific principles relevant to pest management, and that basic (as opposed to applied) research programs will have to be implemented. The report's discussion of future trends in pest control is based on three main assumptions:

1. Agricultural commodities will be used increasingly as trade to meet the international balance of payments.

2. Fuel shortages will be chronic, thus seriously affecting the development of technologies or products that depend on fossil fuels, (e.g., production and supply of petroleum based fertilizer will lag fertilizer demand).

3. In the United States the exchange of labor-intensive practices for capital-intensive techniques will be unlikely.

Using these assumptions, the report predicts continued and probably increasing pressures to expand agricultural production in the United States. As the need for this expansion develops, demands for more effective pest-control technology will emerge. It is suggested (a) that changes could be expected in the type of crops grown on a global scale (e.g., small grains and high yield commodities), (b) that decreasing fertilizer supplies will result in the increased production of crops with low nitrogen demands, and (c) that technical breakthroughs might permit a restructure of pest-control strategies, (e.g., genetic manipulation of plants to develop insect-resistant crops).

However, if practices such as use of single-crop farming or monoculture development were to increase, the result might be a greater dependence on pesticides. Because current environmental regulations limit the type of chemicals available for pest-control use and because supplies of petroleum-based products are limited, the diversity of pest-control options as well as the supply of pesticides might be adversely affected in the future.

The report suggests that future agricultural demands can lead to an increase in pesticide use per acre of cultivated land, and thus result in a greater potential for environmental degradation. Monocultural practices and the demand for greater agricultural productivity can result in the increased use of marginal lands. Unless sound land-use strategies are developed, a probable result will be depletion of soil nutrient levels and increased requirements for nitrogen and phosphate fertilizers, the latter also resulting in greater environmental contamination. The report emphasizes the need to develop research programs for exploring new or alternative agricultural strategies, thus reducing agricultural dependence on chemical applications.

Future pest-control strategies will not be limited to agricultural areas. The report indicates that as demands for wood increase pest-control problems in forestry also may become a future high-priority issue.

In discussing integrated pest-control strategies and requirements the report indicates that successful integrative management depends on an adequate understanding of the population dynamics of known and potential pests, of the ecology and economics of cropping systems, and of the possible harmful effects of these crop systems and management practices on the general environment. Future agricultural demands and chemical regulations might necessitate that maximum reliance be placed on combinations of natural pest controls that might include pest-specific diseases, resistant crop varieties, autolethal techniques, biological pest attractants, augmentation of pest parasites or predators, and chemical pesticides. Each of these strategies can initiate new environmental issues that will require research for determining potential impacts (e.g., target species resistance to control strategies, spillover/drift of pesticides beyond the application area, and build-up of residues in soil, water, and foods).

The report suggests some future alternative strategies in pest control that might prove successful. These include developing third-generation chemicals (hormones or pheromones) and insect or pest pathogens. Research would be needed to determine the effectiveness of each option, as well as the human and animal susceptibility to potential pest pathogens. Pilot programs in autolethal techniques also are suggested along with investigations of other strategies using genetic-control techniques. The report emphasizes that future research efforts also should be directed toward developing chemical application technology to reduce widespread environmental contamination (e.g., technology to reduce compound particle size, thus decreasing pesticide drift, and to increase the efficiency of application machinery).

In *Pesticide Decision Making* (1978) the need for adequate scientific data to be used in formulating policy and making decisions on pesticide registrations is emphasized. This need can be met in part by creating carefully designed data acquisition systems, by requiring more research on human and environmental impacts, and by adopting (or developing) procedures for effective benefit-risk analyses. Monitoring programs are suggested as a means for providing continuous long-term information on environmental conditions.

The report *Climate and Food* (1976) emphasizes that by the year 2000 the world population will exceed 6 billion. Although the developed countries have doubled their food production over the past 10 years, the less developed countries have increased their production by only 15 percent. In order to meet future food production demands, this report suggests a number of research efforts. These include

    1. intensify efforts to improve long-range climatic forecasts;

    2. develop water management strategies for more efficient use of available water;

    3. develop soil conservation practices in response to potential use of marginal agricultural lands;

    4. develop crops with increased tolerance for climatic stresses through biological and genetic research; and

    5. improve techniques to reduce soil erosion and deterioration.

The *World Food and Nutrition Study* (1977) identifies priority areas for increased research in the four areas of nutrition, food production, food marketing, and institutional arrangements. Some of the topics discussed are directly relevant to assessments of a long-range environmental outlook. Research support is needed, for example, in three aspects of plant breeding and genetic manipulation: classical genetics to develop economically useful plants, cellular biology to produce preconceived plant traits, and plant stocks development. The fact that nitrogen fixation is critical to plant protein formulation and growth is recognized in the report. Thus, the recommendation is made that biological alternatives to petroleum-based fertilizers should be developed, leading to benefits of increased agricultural productivity with reduced environmental contamination. Promising areas for accelerated research include identifying and improving the symbiotic associations between leguminous plants and microorganisms, developing a similar association between microorganisms and cereal grains, and transferring the genetic capability for nitrogen fixation directly from bacteria to plants. It is suggested that the fertilizers can be designed for efficient use in the tropics, that use of rock phosphates and larger percentages of phosphate ores can be expanded, and that slow-release fertilizers can be developed.

Research on methods of increasing photosynthetic potential is recommended also, along with investigating ways to improve crop resistance to environmental stress. Development of integrated and improved pest-management systems receives high priority as an important future concern. Also, the need to preserve diversity of plant species and to protect soil resources for long-term agricultural production is emphasized in the report.

## TOXIC SUBSTANCES

The Academy has been asked on several occasions to make assessments of the distribution of toxic elements and their effects on human health and environmental stability. Reports have been prepared for such pollutants as heavy metals, nitrates, kepone, asbestos, sulfates, and ozone and are part of two NAS publication series, *Scientific and Technical Assessments of Environmental Pollutants* (1978) and the *Medical and Biological Effects of Environmental Pollutants Series* (1971-1979). For all of these elements, future recommended activities follow the same general tone.

1. For a better understanding of the impact of toxic elements on environmental stability, basic scientific research on components of terrestrial, freshwater, and marine ecosystems is needed. An understanding of the principles governing ecosystem composition, structural relationships, and functional qualities must be developed.

2. An improved system of environmental monitoring will be essential to assess a long-range outlook on environmental stability.

3. Increased knowledge of the mechanisms involved in the transport of toxic materials through the environment is needed to better predict location of ultimate sinks and immobile reservoirs. These mechanisms include physical as well as biological transformation in air, land, water, and sediment.

4. The role of toxic materials in environmental degradation processes (e.g., eutrophication of freshwater systems, nutrient loss in soils) requires careful investigation.

5. Much more information is needed regarding the availability of toxic materials to biota and the transport of these materials through trophic levels.

6. More research is needed to fully understand the interactions among materials in the environment and the consequences of physical processes on transformation and transport of mixtures.

In an early report, *The Atmospheric Sciences and Man's Needs: Priorities for the Future* (1971), it is stressed that air-resource management programs must be designed to recognize the finite capacity of the atmosphere in dispersing or storing waste materials. The report lists several research goals relating to urban and global air pollution problems. These include

1. reliable methods for assessing alternative urban pollution control technology, including development of simulation models of sources and atmospheric systems and measurements to determine the fate of pollutants emitted from urban areas;
2. an effective system for global monitoring of atmospheric contaminants; and
3. an understanding of the processes contributing to regional air pollution levels and the chemical composition of wet and dry precipitation.

The report *Effects of a Polluted Environment* (1977) suggests that the emphasis in research must shift from analysis of each individual substance to include investigations of mixtures of material and the effects on biota and environmental deterioration. The panel stresses that multidisciplinary assessments are needed to develop effective analysis of national strategies. Another recommendation in the report is that long-term research priorities must include the determination of toxic material effects on critical ecosystem functions, such as energy flow and nutrient cycling. Pollutant-induced changes in climate are suggested as having the most far-reaching consequences. Simple models for estimating the limits of potential change are needed to make crucial decisions. Important issues for future analysis include

1. the consequences of increased atmospheric $CO_2$,
2. the climatic and biotic impacts of changes in ozone concentrations,
3. the effect of sulfur oxide emissions on climate, local weather, and biota, and
4. the implications of remedial actions at the international level.

In addition, it is emphasized that answers to basic science questions will help reduce the uncertainties surrounding future decisions. Thus it will be necessary to understand the subtle changes resulting from exposure to toxic materials. The chemical, physical, and biological mechanisms inducing these changes must be documented.

Further research efforts must be directed toward understanding the potential effects of chemical pollutants on biogeochemical cycles, with the results of this research included in assessments of the long-term environmental impact.

The importance of understanding both the anthropogenic impact on ecosystems and potential for the ecosystem recovery from these impacts is also recognized in *Effects of a Polluted Environment*:

Spatial heterogeneity, the mobility of organisms, dormant structures, and other mechanisms give most ecosystems a capacity to recover from many kinds of perturbations, even those that have severe immediate impacts. Some environmental impacts, however, might produce long-lasting or irreversible detrimental ecological changes. It is therefore important to know not only the kinds of effects that may occur, but also the ability of the system to recover from those impacts it may absorb.

Finally the suggestion is made that integrative models be developed as tools for effective decision making:

If simulations of the spatial and temporal distribution of toxic agents in an ecosystem could be integrated with models identifying the locations and time scales of critical structural or functional properties of the system, the result would be a "map" that could point to particularly vulnerable, as well as especially resilient, elements of the system. Such predictions would need to be verified by field measurements, but models could assist that effort immensely by indicating what, where, and when to measure.

In *Sources of Residuals and Techniques for Their Control* (1977) an important caution is made and should be re-emphasized here.

The characteristics of anticipating problems are shaped by existing institutions, and any attempt to improve matters that ignores this fact will probably come to very little. No amount of monitoring, or science advising, or projection modeling is going to improve our record if the relevant problem-recognition system, the approaches to mitigate the problems, and the incentive systems to provide alternatives remain unchanged. The key here is to ask if a system can be devised that gives some person, board, or group the incentive to keep up with the relevant predictions, to sift through them, to make recommendations for action where that seems warranted, and to provide funds for current study if there is reason to doubt the wisdom of any action.

Recommendations for developing the capability to anticipate future problems include

1. extension and expansion of those activities that assist in identifying and measuring potentially hazardous materials;
2. development and application of modeling techniques to predict changes in environmental quality;
3. investigation and documentation of "environmental surprises" as they occur, assessing in an historical context the predictive indicators and the impact of regulatory actions.

In *Drinking Water and Health* (1977) the recommendation is made that major toxicological and epidemiological efforts are needed to characterize and identify those pollutants contributing to chronic, irreversible and progressive diseases. Estimates of risk for large populations with variable susceptibilities and that are exposed to small quantities of toxic materials are needed. Future research efforts should be directed toward understanding the mechanisms that produce toxic effects in an organism, such as pharmaco-kinetic processes, detoxification-toxification mechanisms, biochemical, and pathological actions. Future development of techniques to control the quality of drinking water also will be required.

Most of the NAS reports on environmental pollutants stress that any anticipatory research program must include a well-developed monitoring capability. *Environmental Monitoring* (1977) addresses the current difficulties in EPA's monitoring program. Most of the past effort has been developed in response to legislative and enforcement requirements, and has not been based on scientific principles following clear objectives, priorities, or criteria related to an effective and extensive national monitoring program.

The current use of monitoring data is to check the effectiveness of pollution control technology and not to use monitoring as a tool for anticipating problems. To forestall the practice of continually responding to "crisis" situations, it is sugested that EPA use monitoring data to detect early changes in pollutant accumulation or distribution, thus allowing early application of control mechanisms. Future programs must be designed to provide the quality of data needed in understanding causes of pollution, in measuring trends in levels of residuals, and in detecting responses of ecosystems to changes in environmental quality.

Data obtained through monitoring programs should permit progress evaluations of pollution control programs, should alert officials to changes in ambient environmental quality, and should be used to determine the diversity of relationships among sources of pollution, ambient quality, and the impact on human health and the environment.

Monitoring programs have been fragmentary with little coordination of data collection or integration of data results in planning for the future. For example, the concentration of a pollutant often is measured in water but not in air or soil. Although the concentration values are given, no indication of the flow rate for the system is specified, and thus no estimate of the potential distribution is possible. There has been no coordination of spatial or temporal sampling and apparently little standardization of collection methods or analytical techniques.

The report then suggests certain short-term activities that might have long-term benefits. For example, an inventory of pollutant sources and material composition could be compiled, including estimates of discharge rates; this information can be used to identify critical stress points or be used in predictive models. In this way scientifically sound monitoring programs can be designed and implemented in a national network for detecting trends in environmental deterioration. These efforts must include collection of those data most useful for future assessments of environmental problems.

## HAZARDOUS FACILITY SITING/WASTE MANAGEMENT

To date, only a few studies have dealt with hazardous facility siting. *Engineering for Resolution of the Energy-Environment Dilemma: A Summary* (1972) emphasizes the need for environmental impact assessment of facility siting but does not present specific criteria for the assessment process. In *Resource Recovery from Municipal Solid Wastes: Mineral Resources and the Environment Supplimentary Report* (1975) it is stated that some resource recovery processes do contribute to environmental problems. Even the most efficient recovery process residue is present in the waste material and therefore the waste must be contained to prevent environmental contamination.

*Wastes Management Concepts for the Coastal Zone* (1970) recommends establishing quantitative guidelines for the design of waste treatment and disposal facilities in coastal areas. Such facilities should be "tailored to preserve and enhance the specific receiving-water values of concern." Monitoring programs are suggested as a means of early identification of emerging environmental contamination. The report emphasizes the need to understand biological, chemical, and physical processes in coastal zone ecosystems and to use these data in developing a quantitative predictive model of waste constituent distribution.

*Disposal in the Marine Environment: An Oceanographic Assessment* (1976) emphasizes the need to reduce scientific uncertainties associated with ocean disposal of waste materials. New analytical techniques must be developed and verified to assist in identifying known or suspected entry of pollutions into the oceans. Studies on the fate, effects, and bioaccumulation of disposed materials are needed. It is stressed in this report that criteria for establishing ocean disposal and monitoring systems cannot assume that the environmental impacts will always be reversible and not catastrophic. A recommendation in this report states that waste management strategies must attempt to (a) confine the material to be disposed, (b) exclude wastes of unknown toxicity, (c) avoid an irreversible dependence on the ocean as a disposal site, (d) exclude wastes that are known to bioconcentrate in food chains, (e) control the rate of disposal to prevent overloading the site capacity, (f) continually reevaluate effectiveness of the management strategies, and (g) develop new knowledge as necessary.

On the issue of site selection the report states:

Timely baseline and monitoring studies of current and proposed ocean disposal sites are essential. No disposal site should be abandoned in favor of a new site until field data evaluation demonstrates that the new site would be less objectionable from an environmental standpoint than the old site. Such evaluation might adequately describe seasonal variation that would usually require data gathered for at least a year. Chemical changes resulting from ocean disposal should be the primary considerations for disposal site selection. The composition of the material being dumped would be of initial interest only. The crucial issue for site selection should be the transient, steady-state, and long-term chemical changes brought about on the site and its surroundings and biological effects of these changes. To evaluate this ultimate question, a description of the waste should determine whether dispersal or containment in the enviroment would be most desirable. With this goal in mind, the characteristics of potential sites might then be evaluated through predictive analyses of dispersion and biological effects. The prediction of potential biological impact has often been attempted by qualitative analogy with previous discharges and their effects. The prediction of dispersion might be largely determined by models of nearshore physical oceanographic processes.

The report also continues with the following warning:

Data supporting the deep sea as a site for waste disposal are lacking; therefore, extreme caution must be applied to any but the most innocuous use of the area.

Another waste management study, *Multimedium Management of Municipal Sludge* (1978), assesses land-based waste management practices. The report emphasizes the need to develop policies that will optimize environmental benefits rather than simply improve water quality.

Criteria for site selection, as for other management options, depend upon whether the sludge is to be considered a resource or a waste material. Where recovery of the nutrient values for land or sea is the intention, the site should be selected with a view to enhancing the environmental impacts; where sludge is to be disposed of, the site should be selected to reduce impacts. Provision for positive impacts and reduction of negative impacts depend upon thorough investigation of the sites before selection and use.

One way of reducing impact is containment, as by landfilling. Dispersal by discharge into the ocean or atmosphere is less easily controlled, but should also minimize alteration of the existing environment. Whether intended for dispersal or containment, the properties of the site should be the basis for determining its potential usefulness.

Regarding monitoring of disposal systems, "carefully-designed and continuing monitoring programs to identify and evaluate environmental impacts of sludge disposal or reuse should be an integral part of operation of the total municipal wastewater management system." It is suggested that future monitoring programs must establish baseline data against which environmental changes can be assessed, identify effects that might endanger human health or ecosystems, identify and provide information for evaluating changes in the disposal medium and inter-medium movements of sludge constituents, assess the potential effects of these changes, and continue long enough to account for both natural and human-induced variations. To this effect, it is further recommended that EPA should issue guidelines for waste management and monitoring strategies for each disposal medium.

Future research needs are discussed in this report including the following:

1. research on all movement of sludge constituents known to be harmful to humans (accumulation in marine organisms present in seawater, or sea spray near sludge disposal sites) for evaluating the potential health risk of ocean disposal compared with disposal in other media;

2. research on specific disposal operations to quantify the environmental impact of sewage sludge disposal on coastal ocean waters in the context of other waste disposal operations or other uses of the same waters;

3. systematic synthesis of current research results to assess the overall risks to human health, agricultural productivity and environmental stability from harmful sludge constituents; and

4. research on scrubbers or other means of capturing metallic compounds, with actual measurements of amounts of hazardous metals discharged by typical thermal oxidation processes.

Other NAS reports have discussed appropriate waste management techniques for specific materials such as coal—*Underground Disposal of Coal Mine Wastes* (1975)—and nuclear waste material—*The Shallow Land Burial of Low-Level Radioactively Contaminated Solid Wastes* (1976), *The Disposal of Radioactive Waste on Land* (1978), and *Geologic Aspects of Radioactive Waste Disposal* (1978). These studies consider the economic or technological feasibility of particular disposal methods. General criteria for hazardous waste disposal and site selection have yet to receive attention.

## APPLICATION OF SCIENCE IN POLICY FORMATION

In addition to the four areas addressed above, NAS reports have discussed future trends and needs in applying scientific information to processes of policy formation. The report *Research and Development in the Environmental Protection Agency* (1977) suggests future EPA activities that will lead to anticipatory capabilities. These include

1. establishment of a coordinated program of economic and social research related to environmental issues, with cost-benefit assessments of policy alternatives, technologies, and methods for multidisciplinary analyses;

2. standardization of measurement technology;
3. development of a range of alternative control technologies;
4. designing effective and scientifically sound monitoring systems;
5. characterization of pollutants and waste discharges;
6. analyses of trends in environmental quality;
7. determination of the fate of known or suspected pollutants;
8. analysis of long-term anthropogenic impacts;
9. elucidation of the physical, chemical and biological processes affecting environmental stability and/or deterioration;
10. development of predictive models of environmental impacts on ecosystem structure and function; and
11. development of alternative strategies for environmental management.

This report stresses the need for EPA to develop anticipatory research programs to permit a shift in agency policy from a response-to-crisis manner of operation to becoming an agency that plans for the future.

## SUMMARY

### ENERGY

If energy development is not carefully controlled, adverse environmental consequences can be expected. Examples of anticipated problems include destruction of land surfaces, reducing the potential use of the land, increases in levels of air pollutants, reduction of the quality of water supplies, increased competition for the use of water, increases in concentrations of trace elements and heavy metals, and changes in global temperatures through continued production and use of fossil fuels.

### AGRICULTURE

As energy use practices affect regional temperatures, changes in agricultural productivity can be expected. With continuing demands for increased food production, methods for controlling plant diseases and pests must be improved and if marginal agricultural lands are used in meeting these demands then depletion of soil conditions and consequent further decline in productivity could be expected. A possible greater dependence on agricultural chemicals may emerge.

### TOXIC SUBSTANCES

...e monitoring programs are needed to provide early warning of ...emical accumulation. Problems of environmental contamination ... be resolved after an understanding of ecosystem structure and function has been gained. The build-up of current toxic waste materials will create public health and environmental problems in the future unless proper disposal mechanisms are developed.

## HAZARDOUS FACILITY SITING

Future problems will include the need to identify appropriate and self-contained water disposal sites that will optimize environmental benefits. General criteria on choosing sites, either for waste disposal or for new industrial facilities, need to be developed that will include all aspects of site selection policies (e.g., environmental problems and benefits, social and economic disruptions).

It must be recognized that approaches to identifying and solving anticipated environmental problems will depend on the existing institutional arrangements. Therefore, it will be necessary to assess the effectiveness of current systems in monitoring environmental conditions, in predicting future trends, and in providing incentives to address problems at an early stage. Waste disposal problems exist now, and the emergence of critical sites can be expected. Resolution of these problems will require an understanding of basic scientific principles governing material movement through ecosystems.

## NAS REPORTS REVIEWED IN CHAPTER 7

*Climate and Food* (1976) ISBN No. 0-309-02522-2.

*Coal as an Energy Resource* (1977) ISBN No. 0-309-02728-4.

*Disposal in the Marine Environment* (1976) ISBN No. 0-309-02446-3.

*Drinking Water and Health* (1977) ISBN No. 0-309-02619-9.

*Effects of a Polluted Environment* (1977) Environmental Research Assessment Committee, Commission on Natural Resources.

*Energy and Climate* (1977) ISBN No. 0-309-02636-9.

*Energy Consumption Measurement: Data Needs for Public Policy* (1979) ISBN No. 0-309-02624-5.

*Engineering for Resolution of the Energy-Environment Dilemma* (1972) ISBN No. 0-309-01943-5.

*Environmental Monitoring* (1977) ISBN No. 0-309-02639-3.

*Geologic Aspects of Radioactive Waste Disposal* (1978) Commission on Natural Resources.

*Geothermal Resources and Technology in the United States* (1979) ISBN No. 0-309-02874.

*Implications of Environmental Regulations for Energy Production and Consumption* (1977) ISBN No. 0-309-20632-6.

*Medical and Biological Effects of Environmental Pollutants Series* (1971-1979) Division of Medical Sciences, Assembly of Life Sciences.

*Mineral Resources and the Environment* (1975) ISBN No. 0-309-02343-2.

*Multimedium Management of Municipal Sludge* (1978) ISBN No. 0-309-02733-0.

*Pest Control: An Assessment of Present and Alternative Technologies, Vol. 1* (1975) ISBN No. 0-309-02410-2.

*Pesticide Decision Making* (1978) ISBN No. 0-309-02734-9.

*Rehabilitation Potential of Western Coal Lands* (1974) ISBN No. -88410-331-5.

*Research and Development in the Environmental Protection Agency* (1977) ISBN No. 0-309-02617-2.

*Resource Recovery from Municipal Solid Wastes: Mineral Resources and the Environment Supplementary Report* (1975) ISBN No. 0-309-02422-6.

*Scientific and Technical Assessments of Environmental Pollutants Series* (1978) Environmental Studies Board, Commission on Natural Resources.

*Sources of Residuals and Techniques for Their Control* (1977) Environmental Research Assessment Committee, Commission on Natural Resources.

*The Atmospheric Sciences and Man's Needs: Priorities for the Future* (1971) ISBN No. 0-309-01912-5.

*The Disposal of Radioactive Waste on Land* (1978) Commission on Natural Resources.

*The Shallow Land Burial of Low-Level Radioactively Contaminated Solid Wastes* (1976) ISBN No. 0-309-02535-4.

*Underground Disposal of Coal Mine Wastes* (1975) Commission on Natural Resources.

*Waste Management Concepts for the Coastal Zone* (1970) ISBN No. 0-309-01855-2.

*World Food and Nutrition Study* (1977) ISBN No. 0-309-02628-8.

The following NAS reports also were reviewed. However, these reports did not address specific future issues; general recommendations were made for more scientific research, more data to understand a process, monitoring environmental quality, and development of anticipatory research programs.

*Agricultural Production Efficiency* (1975) ISBN No. 0-309-02310-6.

*Alternatives in Water Management* (1966) ISBN No. 0-309-01408-5.

*An Evaluation of the Concept of Storing Radioactive Wastes in Bedrock Below the Savannah River Plant Site* (1972) ISBN No. 0-309-02035-2.

*A Review of Short Haul Passenger Transportation* (1976) ISBN No. 0-309-02445-5.

*Asbestos: The Need for and Feasibility of Air Pollution Controls* (1971) ISBN No. 0-309-01927-3.

*Assessing Potential Ocean Pollutants* (1975) ISBN No. 0-309-02325-4.

*A Strategic Approach to Urban Research and Development: Social and Behavioral Science Considerations* (1969) ISBN No. 0-309-01728-9.

*Beneficial Modifications of the Marine Environment* (1972) ISBN No. 0-309-02034-4.

*Climate, Climatic Change, and Water Supply* (1977) ISBN No. 0-309-02625-3.

*Controlled Nuclear Fusion: Current Research and Potential Progress* (1978) ISBN No. 0-309-02863-9.

*Critical Issues in Coal Transportation Systems* (1979) ISBN No. 0-309-02869-8.

*Decision Making for Regulating Chemicals in the Environment* (1975) ISBN No. 0-309-02401-3.

*Degradation of Synthetic Organic Molecules in the Biosphere* (1972) ISBN No. 0-309-02046-8.

*Enhancement of Food Production for the United States: World Food and Nutrition Study* (1975) ISBN No. 0-309-02435-8.

*Environmental Quality and Social Behavior: Strategies for Research* (1973) ISBN No. 0-309-02048-4.

*Estuaries, Geophysics, and the Environment* (1977) ISBN No. 0-309-02629-6.

*Eutrophication: Causes, Consequences, Correctives* (1969) ISBN No. 0-309-01700-9.

*Geochemistry and the Environment: The Relation of Selected Trace Elements to Health and Disease* (1974) ISBN No. 0-309-02223-1.

*Geographical Perspectives and Urban Problems* (1973) ISBN No. 0-309-02106-5.

*Global Earthquake Monitoring: Its Uses, Potentials, and Support Requirements* (1977) ISBN No. 0-309-02608-3.

*Interim Storage of Solidified High-Level Radioactive Wastes* (1975) ISBN No. 0-309-02400-S.

*Jamaica Bay and Kennedy Airport: A Multidisciplinary Environmental Study. Volumes I and II* (1971) ISBN No. 0-309-01871-4.

*Land Use and Wildlife Resources* (1970) ISBN No. 0-309-01729-7.

*Long-Range Planning for Urban Research and Development (1969) ISBN No. 0-309-01729-7.*

*Manpower for Environmental Pollution Control* (1977) ISBN No. 0-309-02634-2.

*Materials Technology in the Near-Term Energy Program* (1974) ISBN No. 0-309-02322-X.

*Mineral Resources and the Environment* (1975) ISBN No. 0-309-02343-2.

*Noise Abatement: Policy Alternatives for Transportation* (1977) ISBN No. 0-309-02648-2.

*OCS Oil and Gas: An Assessment of the Department of the Interior Environmental Studies Program* (1978) ISBN No. 0-309-02739-X.

*Ozone and Other Photochemical Oxidants* (1977) ISBN No. 0-309-02531-1.

*Perspectives on Technical Information for Environmental Protection* (1977) ISBN No. 0-309-02623-7.

*Pest Control and Public Health* (1976) ISBN No. 0-309-02414-5.

*Pest Control: Strategies for the Future* (1972) ISBN No. 0-309-01945-1.

*Principles and Procedures for Evaluating the Toxicity of Household Substances* (1977) ISBN No. 0-309-02644-X.

*Principles for Evaluating Chemicals in the Environment* (1975) ISBN No. 0-309-02248-7.

*Productivity of World Ecosystems* (1975) ISBN No. 0-309-02317-3.

*Renewable Resources for Industrial Materials* (1976) ISBN No. 0-309-02528-1.

*Science: An American Bicentennial View* (1977) ISBN No. 0-309-02630-X.

*Science Development: An Evaluation Study* (1975) ISBN No. 0-309-02329-7.

*Specifications and Criteria for Biochemical Compounds, Third Edition* (1977) ISBN No. 0-309-02601-6.

*Technological Innovation and Forces for Change in the Mineral Industry* (1978) ISBN No. 0-309-02768-3.

*The Future of Animals, Cells, Models and Systems in Research, Development, Education, and Testing* (1977) ISBN No. 0-309-02603-2.

*The Impact of Science and Technology on Regional Economic Development* (1969) ISBN No. 0-309-01731-9.

*Trends and Opportunities in Seismology* (1977) ISBN No. 0-309-02612-1.

*Urban Growth and Land Development: The Land Conversion Process* (1972) ISBN No. 0-309-02044-1.

*U.S. Energy Prospects: An Engineering Viewpoint* (1974) ISBN No. 0-309-02237-1.

*Waste Management and Control* (1966) ISBN No. 0-309-01400-X.

# Workshop
# Participants

PAUL ARBESMAN, Assistant Commissioner, New Jersey Department of Environmental Protection, P.O. Box 1390, Trenton, New Jersey 08625

STANLEY AUERBACH, Director, Environmental Sciences Division, Oak Ridge National Laboratory, P.O. Box X, Oak Ridge, Tennessee 37830

ROBERT AYRES, Department of Engineering and Public Policy, Carnegie Mellon University, Pittsburgh, Pennsylvania 15213

ROBERT BOXLEY, Agricultural Land Studies, U.S. Department of Agriculture, 722 Jackson Place, N.W., Room 5020, Washington, D.C. 20006

DEAN BRANSON, Health and Environmental Research, Dow Chemical Company, Midland, Michigan 48640

JOHN CANTLON, Vice President for Research and Graduate Studies, Michigan State University, East Lansing, Michigan 48824

JARED COHON, Department of Geography and Environmental Engineering, Johns Hopkins University, Baltimore, Maryland 21218

THOMAS CROCKER, Department of Economic, University of Wyoming, Laramie, Wyoming 92071

RALPH D'ARGE, Professor of Economics, University of Wyoming, Laramie, Wyoming 92071

JOEL DARMSTADTER, Resources for the Future, Inc., 1755 Massachusetts Ave., N.W., Washington, D.C. 20036

JOHN DOULL, M.D., Department of Pharmacology, University of Kansas Medical Center, Kansas City, Kansas 66103

195

HARRY ETTINGER, Group Leader, Industrial Hygiene, Los Alamos Scientific Laboratory, P.O. Box 1663, Mailstop 486 Los Alamos, New Mexico 87545

JAMES ALAN FAY, Massachusetts Institute of Technology, Department of Engineering, Cambridge, Massachusetts 02139

JAMES E. GIBSON, Vice President and Director of Research, Chemical Industry Institute of Toxicology, P.O. Box 12137, Research Triangle Park, North Carolina 27709

DAN GOLOMB, Office of Environmental Processes and Effects Research, U.S. Environmental Protection Agency, 401 M St., S.W., RD 682, Washington, D.C. 20460

LESTER GRANT, Environmental Criteria and Assessment Officer, U.S. Environmental Protection Agency, MD-52, Research Triangle Park, North Carolina 27711

SAM GUSMAN, The Conservation Foundation, 1717 Massachusetts Avenue, N.W., Washington, D.C. 20036

CHRISTOPH HOHENEMSER, Department of Physics, Clark University, Worcester, Massachusetts 01610

JANIS HORWITZ, Environmental Studies Board, National Research Council, 2101 Constitution Ave., Washington, D.C. 20418

HERMAN KOENIG, Director, Center for Environmental Quality, Michigan State University, East Lansing, Michigan 48824

JAY KOPELMAN, Policy Planning Office, Electric Power Research Institute, 3412 Hillview Ave., P.O. Box 10412, Palo Alto, California 94303

JOHN D. KOUTSANDREAS, Office of Research and Development, U.S. Environmental Protection Agency, 401 M St., S.W., RD 681, Washington, D.C. 20460

DON LEWIS, Office of Environmental Engineering & Technology, U.S. Environmental Protection Agency, 401 M St., S.W., RD 681, Washington, D.C. 20460

JOSEPH T. LING, Vice President, Environmental Engineering & Pollution Control, 3M Company, 900 Bush Avenue, Box 33331, St. Paul, Minnesota 55133

RAYMOND LOEHR, Director, Environmental Studies Program, Riley-Robb Hall, Cornell University, Ithaca, New York 14853

ORIE LOUCKS, Science Director, Institute of Ecology, Indianapolis, Indiana 46208

ADELE KING MALONE, Environmental Studies Board, National Research Council, 2101 Constitution Avenue, Washington, D.C. 20418

PERRY MCCARTY, Professor Environmental Engineering, Stanford University, Stanford, California 94305

JAMES MONAGHAN, Executive Director, Intergovernmental Relations Department, Colorado State Government, 136 State Capital Boulevard, Denver, Colorado 80203

LOUIS NICKELL, Vice President for Research & Development, Vilsicol Chemical Corporation, 341 E. Ohio St., Chicago, illinois 60611

IAN C.T. NISBET, Director of Scientific Staff, Massachusetts Audubon Society, Lincoln, Massachusetts 01773

ARLAND PAULI, Manager, Research Planning & Coordination, Deere and Co. Technical Section, 3300 River Dr., Moline, Illinois 61265

DAVID PIMENTEL, Department of Entomology, Cornell University, Ithaca, New York 14850

SUELLEN PIRAGES, Environmental Studies Board, National Research Council, 2101 Constitution Ave., Washington, D.C. 20418

KENT REED, Argonne National Laboratories, Argonne, Illinois 60439

PAOLO RICCI, Project Manager, Energy Risk Assessment and Large-Scale Mathematical Modeling, Electric Power Research Institute, 3412 Hillview Ave., P.O. Box 10412, Palo Alto, California 94303

JOHN RICHARDSON, Environmental Studies Board, National Research Council, 2101 Constitution Ave., Washington, D.C. 20418

RONALD RIDKER, Resources for the Future, Inc., 1755 Massachusetts Ave., N.W., Washington, D.C. 20036

BERNARD SCHWETZ, Health and Environmental Research, Dow Chemical Company, Midland, Michigan 48640

W. LEIGH SHORT, Manager, Engineering Division, Environmental Research & Technology, 6630 Harwin Dr., Suite 175, Houston, Texas 77036

LEONARD SLOSKEY, Intergovernmental Relations Department, Colorado State Government, 136 State Capital Boulevard, Denver, Colorado 80203

LOWELL SMITH, Office of Environmental Engineering and Technology, U.S. Environmental Protection Agency, 401 M St., S.W., RD 681, Washington, D.C. 20460

GUS SPETH, Chairman, Council on Environmental Quality, 722 Jackson Place, N.W., Washington, D.C. 20006

DONALD STEVER, Room 2625, Land and Natural Resources Division, U.S. Department of Justice, 10th and Pennsylvania Ave., N.W., Washington, D.C. 20530

DENNIS TIRPAK, Office of Anticipatory Research, U.S. Environmental Protection Agency, 401 M St., S.W., RD 681, Washington, D.C. 20460

IRWIN L. WHITE, Strategic Analysis Group, U.S. Environmental Protection Agency, 401 M St., S.W., RD 681, Washington, D.C. 20460

HAVEN WHITESIDE, Strategic Analysis Group, U.S. Environmental Protection Agency, 401 M St., S.W., RD 681, Washington, D.C. 20460

P. SHELLY WILLIAMSON, Office of Health Research, U.S. Environmental Protection Agency, 401 M St., S.W., RD 681, Washington, D.C. 20460

SYLVAN WITTWER, Director, Agricultural Experiment Station, Michigan State University, East Lansing, Michigan 48824

ROBERT YECK, Staff Scientist, SEA-AR, U.S. Dept. of Agriculture, Room 201, Building 005, BARC-W, Beltsville, Maryland 20705